Race and Ethnicity in the United States

NINTH EDITION

Richard T. Schaefer
DePaul University

Pearson

330 Hudson Street, NY, NY 10013

Editor: Jeff Marshall
Development Editor: Steven Rigolosi
Marketing Manager: Brad Parkins
Program Manager: Erin Bosco
Project Coordination, Text Design, and Electronic Page Makeup: Integra-Chicago
Cover Designer: Jennifer Hart Design
Cover Photo: John Lund/Blend Images/Getty Images
Manufacturing Buyer: Carol Melville
Printer/Binder: LSC Communications, Inc.
Cover Printer: LSC Communications, Inc.

PEARSON, ALWAYS LEARNING, and REVEL are exclusive trademarks in the United States and/or other countries owned by Pearson Education, Inc., or its affiliates.

Unless otherwise indicated herein, any third-party trademarks that may appear in this work are the property of their respective owners and any references to third-party trademarks, logos, or other trade dress are for demonstrative or descriptive purposes only. Such references are not intended to imply any sponsorship, endorsement, authorization, or promotion of Pearson's products by the owners of such marks, or any relationship between the owner and Pearson Education, Inc., or its affiliates, authors, licensees, or distributors.

Library of Congress Cataloging-in-Publication Data

Names: Schaefer, Richard T., author.
Title: Race and ethnicity in the United States / Richard T. Schaefer.
Description: 9th edition. | Hoboken, N.J. : Pearson Higher Education, 2019. |
   Includes bibliographical references and index.
Identifiers: LCCN 2017044960 | ISBN 9780134732824 ((student edition) : alk. paper) |
ISBN 9780134736648 (the exam copy (irc) : alk. paper) | ISBN 9780134736747 (ala carte edition : alk. paper) | ISBN 9780134736426 (the revel instant access : alk. paper) | ISBN 9780134736419 (the revel access card : alk. paper)
Subjects: LCSH: Minorities—United States. | Prejudices—United States. |
   United States—Ethnic relations. | United States—Race relations.
Classification: LCC E184.A1 S25 2019 | DDC 305.800973—dc23
LC record available at https://lccn.loc.gov/2017044960

Copyright © 2019, 2016, 2013 by Pearson Education, Inc. All Rights Reserved. Printed in the United States of America. This publication is protected by copyright, and permission should be obtained from the publisher prior to any prohibited reproduction, storage in a retrieval system, or transmission in any form or by any means, electronic, mechanical, photocopying, recording, or otherwise. For information regarding permissions, request forms and the appropriate contacts within the Pearson Education Global Rights & Permissions Department, please visit www.pearsoned.com/permissions/.

Rental Edition:
ISBN 10: 0-134-73282-0
ISBN 13: 978-0-134-73282-4

Instructor's Review Copy:
ISBN 10: 0-134-73664-8
ISBN 13: 978-0-134-73664-8

1 18

Revel Access Code Card:
ISBN 10: 0-134-73641-9
ISBN 13: 978-0-134-73641-9

A la Carte:
ISBN 10: 0-134-73674-5
ISBN 13: 978-0-134-73674-7

Pearson

www.pearsonhighered.com

To my grandchildren, Matilda and Reuben:
May they grow to flourish
in our multicultural society

Brief Contents

1 Exploring Race and Ethnicity 1

2 Prejudice 38

3 Discrimination 68

4 Immigration 96

5 Ethnicity, Whiteness, and Religion 127

6 The Nation as a Kaleidoscope 164

Contents

Preface ix

1 Exploring Race and Ethnicity 1

How Are We Grouped? 5
   Types of Minority Groups 7
      RACIAL GROUPS 7 • ETHNIC GROUPS 7
      • RELIGIOUS GROUPS 8
■ **Speaking Out** The Problem of the Color Line 9
      GENDER GROUPS 9 • OTHER
      SUBORDINATE GROUPS 10
The Social Construction of Race 10
   Biological Meaning 10
      ABSENCE OF PURE RACES 10 • INTELLIGENCE
      TESTS 11
   Race as a Social Construction 12
   Biracial and Multiracial Identity: Who Am I? 13
■ **Research Focus** Multiracial Identity 14
Sociology and the Study of Race and Ethnicity 16
   Stratification by Class and Gender 16
   Theoretical Perspectives 17
      FUNCTIONALIST PERSPECTIVE 17 • CONFLICT
      PERSPECTIVE 18 • LABELING THEORY 19
The Creation of Subordinate-Group Status 21
   Migration 21
   Annexation 22
   Colonialism 22
   The Spectrum of Intergroup Status 23
The Consequences of Subordinate-Group Status 23
   Extermination 23
   Expulsion 24
   Secession 25
   Segregation 25
   Fusion 28
   Assimilation 29
   The Pluralist Perspective 30
Resistance and Change 31
Intersectionality 33

Conclusion 34
   Summary of Learning Objectives 36 • Key
   Terms 36 • Review Questions 37 • Critical
   Thinking 37

2 Prejudice 38

Prejudice and Discrimination 41
   Merton's Typology 41
■ **Research Focus** Virtual Prejudice and
Anti-Prejudice 42
White Privilege 43
Theories of Prejudice 45
   Scapegoating Theory 45
   Authoritarian Personality Theory 46
   Exploitation Theory 46
   Normative Approach 47
Stereotypes 47
   What Are Stereotypes? 48
   Stereotyping in Action: Racial Profiling 48
Color-Blind Racism 50
The Mood of the Oppressed 51
   Intergroup Hostility 54
Reducing Prejudice 56
   Education 57
   Mass Media 57
   Intergroup Contact: Avoidance Versus
   Friendship 59
      THE SOCIAL DISTANCE SCALE 59 • EQUAL
      STATUS CONTACT 59 • AVOIDANCE VIA THE
      INTERNET 60
   Corporate Response: Diversity Training 61
■ **Speaking Out** What Can I Do at Work? 62
Conclusion 65
   Summary of Learning Objectives 66 • Key
   Terms 67 • Review Questions 67 • Critical
   Thinking 67

3 Discrimination 68

Relative Versus Absolute Deprivation 70
Hate Crimes 70
   What Are Hate Crimes? 71
■ **Speaking Out May America Be True to Her Dream** 72
   Why Do Hate Crimes Carry Harsher Penalties? 73
Institutional Discrimination 73
Discrimination Today 76
   Discrimination Hits the Wallet 76
   Eliminating Discrimination 79
■ **Research Focus The Sharing Economy—Another Way to Discriminate** 81
   Wealth Inequality: Discrimination's Legacy 82
Environmental Justice 83
Affirmative Action 85
   Affirmative Action Explained 86
   The Legal Debate 87
   Reverse Discrimination 89
The Glass Ceiling 90
Conclusion 93
Summary of Learning Objectives 93 • Key Terms 94 • Review Questions 94 • Critical Thinking 95

4 Immigration 96

Patterns of Immigration to the United States 98
   The Early Immigrants 99
   The Anti-Chinese Movement 101
Restrictionist Sentiment Increases 103
   The National Origin System 103
   The Immigration and Nationality Act 104
Contemporary Social Concerns 106
   The Brain Drain 107
   Population Growth 108
   Mixed-Status Families 109
   Language Barriers 109
■ **Speaking Out My Parents Were Deported** 110
   The Economic Impact 113
Illegal Immigration 115

Naturalization: The Path to Citizenship 117
■ **Research Focus Arranged Marriages in America** 119
The Global Economy and Immigration 120
Refugees 121
   Policies 121
   Concerns About the Refugee Program 122
Conclusion 124
Summary of Learning Objectives 125 • Key Terms 125 • Review Questions 126 • Critical Thinking 126

5 Ethnicity, Whiteness, and Religion 127

Unpacking Ethnicity 129
   Studying Whiteness 129
   Rediscovering Ethnicity 131
      BLENDED IDENTITY 132 • THE PRINCIPLE OF THIRD-GENERATION INTEREST 133 • THE ETHNIC PARADOX 133 • SYMBOLIC ETHNICITY 133
■ **Speaking Out The Next Americans** 134
The German Americans 136
   Settlement Patterns 136
   German Americans in the Twenty-First Century 137
The Irish Americans 139
   Irish Immigration 139
   Becoming White 140
   The Contemporary Picture 141
The Italian Americans 142
   Early Immigration 142
   Constructing Identity 143
■ **Research Focus Immigrants: Yesterday and Today** 145
   The Contemporary Picture 145
The Polish Americans 146
   Early Immigration 147
   Polonia 147
   The Contemporary Picture 148
Religious Pluralism 149
   Diversity Among Roman Catholics 154
   Diversity Among Protestants 155

Religion and the Courts	157
Company Exemptions	158
School Prayer	158
Secessionist Minorities	159
Creationism and Intelligent Design	160
Public Displays	160
Conclusion	161
Summary of Learning Objectives 162 • Key Terms 163 • Review Questions 163 • Critical Thinking 163	

6 The Nation as a Kaleidoscope   164

The Glass Half Empty	167
Is There a Model Minority?	167
The Family	168
Educational Levels	169
■ Research Focus Tiger Mothers	**170**
Economic Status	171
Acting White, Acting Black, or Neither	174
The Persistence of Inequality	175
■ Speaking Out Black Picket Fences	**176**
Talking Past One Another	178
Talking Face-to-Face	178
Communicating Online	181
Conclusion	183
Summary of Learning Objectives 184 • Key Terms 184 • Review Questions 185 • Critical Thinking 185	
Glossary	186
References	190
Index	204

Preface

The first two decades of the twenty-first century have witnessed significant social changes. The Latino population in the United States is now larger than the African American population, with the Asian Pacific American population growing faster than either. Meanwhile, White non-Hispanic youth have become a numerical minority when compared to other racial and ethnic groups. Alongside these demographic changes, a series of events have underscored the diversity of the American people.

People cheered on May 1, 2011, upon hearing that Osama bin Laden had been found and killed. However, many American Indian people were troubled to learn that the military had assigned the code name "Geronimo" to the infamous terrorist. The Chiricahua Apache of New Mexico were particularly disturbed to learn that their freedom fighter's name was used in this manner.

Barack Obama, the son of an immigrant, became the first African American president, but Mr. Obama also recognizes other aspects of his ethnicity. On an official state visit to Ireland while president, he made a side trip to the village of Moneygall in County Offaly. His great-great-grandfather Falmouth Kearney, a shoemaker's son, came to the United States from County Offaly in 1850.

Race and ethnicity are an important part of the national landscape and the national agenda. Forty years ago, when writing the first edition of this book, I noted that race is not a static phenomenon. Although race is always a part of the social reality, specific aspects of race and ethnicity change. In the first edition, I noted the presence of a new immigrant group, the Vietnamese, and described the early efforts to define affirmative action. Today, in an increasingly diverse society, we seek to describe the growing presence of Salvadorans, Haitians, Nigerians, Tongans, Somalis, Hmong, and Arab Americans in the United States.

Specific issues may change over time, but they continue to play out against a backdrop of discrimination that is rooted in the social structure and changing composition of the population as influenced by immigration and reproduction patterns. In addition, the breakup of the Soviet Union and changes in Middle Eastern governments have made ethnic, language, and religious divisions even more significant sources of antagonism between and within nations. The old ideological debates about communism and capitalism have been replaced by emotional divisions over religious dogma and cultural traditions.

New to the Ninth Edition

This edition of *Race and Ethnicity in the United States* continues to take full advantage of the most recent data releases from the U.S. Census Bureau through the annual American Community Survey (ACS). The ACS allows each new edition of the text to include updated information (without the ACS, data would be updated only once a decade, based on the results of the ten-year census). Thanks to the ACS, readers will find updated and revised tables, figures, maps, and Internet sources throughout the ninth edition. As one example of the thorough updating, we note that more than 30 percent of the citations in the references are new since the last edition.

Chapter-by-Chapter Changes

As with all previous editions, every line, every source, and every number have been checked for their currency. The goal of *Race and Ethnicity in the United States* has always been to provide the most current information. The following list details the major changes in each chapter.

Chapter 1, Exploring Race and Ethnicity

- New opening examples
- Latest American Community Survey 2014–2015 data update all statistics in the chapter
- Expulsion example of Muslim and Nepali-speaking Bhutanese; also noted in their resettling in Manchester, New Hampshire, in chapter-opening example
- 2014 report on trends in school segregation
- Resistance example added of #BlackLives Matter movement
- Intersectionality coverage added
- Key Terms added: *colorism, eugenics, Eurocentrism, intersectionality*

Chapter 2, Prejudice

- New figure on the rise of hate groups
- Latest census data update all income and wealth statistics
- White privilege illustrated by recent study of bus drivers granting or not granting free bus rides
- Latest reports on racial profiling in traffic stops and New York City ending surveillance program in Muslim neighborhoods
- Recent data on minority representation on television and in motion pictures
- New Research Focus: Virtual Prejudice and Anti-Prejudice
- New Speaking Out: "What Can I Do at Work?" by Southern Poverty Law Center
- Updated figure on foreign-born workers
- Key Term added: *microaggressions*

Chapter 3, Discrimination

- New material on restricting voting rights through banning ex-felons and requiring photo ID
- Latest data on income and wealth by race, ethnicity, and gender
- Latest data on ID voting requirements
- New Research Focus: The Sharing Economy—Another Way to Discriminate
- New Speaking Out: "May America Be True to Her Dream," by Nihad Awad
- The water supply in Flint, Michigan, as an example of the need for environmental justice
- 2016 *Fisher v. University of Texas at Austin* Supreme Court decision
- Impact of the Great Recession on Black home ownership
- Key Term added: *sharing economy*

Chapter 4, Immigration

- New opener describing immigration in three towns
- Two figures and map on immigration updated through 2015
- New Speaking Out: "My Parents Were Deported," by Diane Guerrero
- Proposed "DREAMers" policy outlined
- Updated table on immigration benefits and concerns
- New cartoon on immigration reform
- New Research Focus: Arranged Marriages in America
- Expanded section on refugees
- Table on refugees updated to 2015 and contrasted with 2005

Preface   xi

- Specific suggestions on how one can help refugees
- Key Terms added: *arranged marriage, sanctuary city*

Chapter 5, Ethnicity, Whiteness, and Religion

- Chapter title rephrased to reflect emphasis on concept of Whiteness
- Initial section "Unpacking Ethnicity" reorganized
- New table on religious groups and political party affiliations
- Impact of recent immigration on Roman Catholicism and Protestantism in the United States
- New section on company exemptions within discussion of the courts and religion
- Key Term added: *respectable bigotry*

Chapter 6, The Nation as a Kaleidoscope

- New table: lists of top ten states with largest concentrations of minorities
- Updated figures on minority school population, changes in schooling, income, and life expectancy
- New Speaking Out: "Black Picket Fences," by Mary Pattillo
- Expanded material on interaction to include online communication

Features to Aid Students

Several features are included in the text to facilitate student learning. **Learning Objectives** at the start of each chapter provide a road map for previewing and mastering chapter content, and an introductory section alerts students to important issues and topics to be addressed in the chapter. Periodically throughout the book, the **Spectrum of Intergroup Relations**, first presented in Chapter 1, is repeated to reinforce major concepts while addressing the unique social circumstances of individual racial and ethnic groups.

Each chapter ends with a **Conclusion** and a **Summary of Learning Objectives**. **Key Terms** are highlighted in boldface when they are introduced and are listed again at the end of each chapter. This edition also includes Review Questions and Critical Thinking Questions at the end of each chapter. The **Review Questions** test students on their understanding of the chapter's major points; the **Critical Thinking Questions** encourage students to think more deeply about some of the major issues raised in the chapter. An extensive illustration program, which includes maps and political cartoons, expands the text discussion and provokes thought. An end-of-book **Glossary** provides definitions of Key Terms.

Revel™

Revel is an interactive learning environment that deeply engages students and prepares them for class. Media and assessment integrated directly within the authors' narrative lets students read, explore interactive content, and practice in one continuous learning path. Thanks to the dynamic reading experience in Revel, students come to class prepared to discuss, apply, and learn from instructors and from each other.

Learn more about Revel
http://www.pearson.com/revel

Ancillary Materials

This book is accompanied by an extensive learning package to enhance the experience of instructors and students.

INSTRUCTOR'S MANUAL AND TEST BANK Each chapter in the Instructor's Manual offers a variety of resources: Chapter Summary, Chapter Outline, Learning Objectives, Critical Thinking Questions, Activities for Classroom Participation, Key Terms, Suggested Readings, and Suggested Films. Designed to make your lectures more effective and to save preparation time, this extensive resource gathers useful activities and strategies for teaching your course.

Also included in this manual is a test bank offering multiple-choice, true/false, fill-in-the-blank, and/or essay questions for each chapter. The Instructor's Manual and Test Bank are available to adopters at www.pearsonhighered.com/irc.

MYTEST This computerized software allows instructors to create their own exams, to edit any or all of the existing test questions, and to add new questions. Other special features of MyTest include random generation of test questions, creation of alternate versions of the same test, scrambling question sequence, and test preview before printing. For easy access, this software is available at www.pearsonhighered.com/irc.

POWERPOINT PRESENTATIONS The PowerPoint presentations are informed by instructional and design theory. You have the option in every chapter of choosing from Lecture and Illustration PowerPoints. The Lecture PowerPoint slides follow the chapter outline and feature images from the textbook integrated with the text. The Illustration PowerPoint slides include each chapter's figures, maps, and images. They are available to adopters via www.pearsonhighered.com/irc.

Acknowledgments

The ninth edition was improved by the suggestions of:

Tonja Conerly, San Jacinto College–South

Catherine Felton, Central Piedmont Community College

Rebecca Hornung, Carthage College

Lori Lundell, Purdue University

Andrea L. Moore, Sacramento State University

Alicia M. Raia-Hawrylak, Rutgers University

The truly exciting challenge of writing and researching has always been for me an enriching experience, mostly because of the supportive home I share with my wife, Sandy. She knows so well my appreciation and gratitude, now as in the past and in the future.

Richard T. Schaefer
schaeferrt@aol.com

About the Author

Richard T. Schaefer grew up in Chicago at a time when neighborhoods were going through transitions in ethnic and racial composition. He found himself increasingly intrigued by what was happening, how people were reacting, and how these changes were affecting neighborhoods and people's jobs. In high school, he took a course in sociology. His interest in social issues caused him to gravitate to more sociology courses at Northwestern University, where he eventually received a B.A. in sociology. He later received his M.A. and Ph.D. in sociology from the University of Chicago.

Dr. Schaefer is the author of the fifteenth edition of *Racial and Ethnic Groups* (Pearson, 2019) and *Racial and Ethnic Diversity in the USA* (Pearson, 2014). He is the general editor of the three-volume *Encyclopedia of Race, Ethnicity, and Society* (2008). He is also the author of the thirteenth edition of *Sociology: A Brief Introduction* (2019), the fourth edition of *Sociology: A Modular Approach* (2015), and the seventh edition of *Sociology Matters* (2018). He coauthored with William Zellner the ninth edition of Extraordinary Groups (2015). Schaefer's books have been translated into Chinese, Japanese, Portuguese, and Spanish as well as adapted for use in Canadian colleges and universities.

Chapter 1
Exploring Race and Ethnicity

Learning Objectives

1.1 Explain how people are placed in groups.
1.2 Explain the social construction of race.
1.3 Describe how sociology helps us understand race and ethnicity.
1.4 Explain how subordinate groups are created.
1.5 Summarize the consequences of subordinate-group status.
1.6 Describe how resistance and change occur in racial and ethnic relations.
1.7 Define and describe intersectionality.

"Please pass the momos." That's not something you hear very often, unless you're in Bhutan, a small Asian country tucked in the Himalayas—or in Manchester, New Hampshire. In that New England state capital, one finds a growing population of Bhutanese who love their momos—steamed dumplings filled with pork or chicken, which substitutes for the yak or water buffalo meat used back in Bhutan. This refugee group and their children in Manchester are followers of Hinduism and speakers of Nepali. They were forced out of Bhutan in the 1990s by the Buddhist-controlled monarchy.

It was not a quick journey. Most of the over 100,000 Bhutanese refugees spent 20 years in refugee camps before being relocated, with the majority coming to the United States in 2008, just in time for the Great Recession. Initial adjustment in Manchester was challenging, and the reception by locals was not always warm. Within just three years, the 2,000 new arrivals had higher employment rates, higher high-school graduation rates, and lower welfare rates than long-term residents in this city of 110,000. On a rundown street, the Himalayan General Store sells cracked corn, mango pickles, flattened rice, and bags of shiny black kalonji seeds. These Bhutanese Americans will never be the same, and neither will Manchester.

St. Paul, the capital of Minnesota, would seem an unlikely place for racial strife—after all, isn't Minnesota supposed to be the home of liberals and easygoing, friendly people? Yet, in 2016, Philando Castile, a 32-year old African American school nutritionist, was shot dead in his car by a police officer named Jeronimo Yanez, a 28-year-old Mexican American. Castile's death came after he told the officer he was licensed to carry a weapon and was carrying one in his pants pocket. Castile's girlfriend, who was a passenger in the car, along with their four-year-old daughter, recorded much of the incident. Eventually the officer was charged with manslaughter, but not before many protest marches, some of which came close to the governor's mansion. During the period of protests, many were surprised to learn that neighborhood and school segregation in St. Paul have escalated over the past 20 years. Rates of Black incarceration were among the highest in the nation. The number of African Americans living in high-poverty areas in St. Paul increased by 50 percent from 2000 to 2012.

Trying to make sense of the divide and calm frantic people, African American artist Jeremiah Ellison stepped in. The night after the shooting, he mobilized community residents to create murals on the side of an abandoned warehouse to honor the slain Castile. Deciding to become even more involved in finding solutions, he decided to run for city council in 2017. He grew up in a politically aware household—his father is U.S. Congressman Keith Ellison, the first Muslim to be elected to the House of Representatives.

Hamdi Ulukaya is a Turkish immigrant of Kurdish descent. He arrived in the United States in 1994 and started to make and sell feta cheese based on a family recipe. In 2005, using a Small Business Administration loan, he took over a shuttered yogurt plant in upstate New York and transformed and expanded it into the company now known as Chobani. The company employs 2,000 people and has annual sales of $1.5 billion. It is estimated that Ulukaya, the CEO, is worth close to $2 billion.

At a time when many people in the United States were growing suspicious of Muslims—especially Muslim immigrants—Ulukaya decided that he and his company would facilitate immigrant resettlement. His

Hamdi Ulukaya has made a name for himself both as a successful businessman (he is the founder of the successful Chobani yogurt business) and for being an outspoken supporter of immigrants and refugees.

company actively recruits refugees and offers them English-language classes, along with translators in 11 languages. Despite strong criticism from anti-immigrant activists, Ulukaya has held to his position, pointing to the success of the immigrants working for him. Ulukaya joined Bill Gates and other wealthy people in 2015 by signing the Giving Pledge, which commits them to giving away at least half their money to philanthropic causes (Gelles 2016; Halpern and McKibben 2014; Rhee 2016).

Households upended, suspicion of newcomers, starting over in a new land, violence, community action, hard work, and economic success for immigrants are all aspects of race and ethnicity in the United States today.

One aspect of the struggle for equality is the continuing effort to identify strategies and services to assist minorities in their struggle to overcome prejudice and discrimination. Among the beneficiaries of programs aimed at racial and ethnic minorities are White Americans, many of whom are far from affluent and have also experienced challenges in their lives.

The election and reelection of the nation's first African American president, Barack Obama (who incidentally carried three states of the former Confederacy), presents the temptation to declare that racial inequality is a thing of the past or that racism in the United States is limited to a few troublemakers. Progress has been made, and expressions of explicit racism are rarely tolerated, yet challenges remain for immigrants of any color and for racial, ethnic, and religious minorities (Massey 2011).

The United States is a diverse nation and is becoming even more so, as Table 1.1 shows. In 2015, approximately 41 percent (more than one-third) of the U.S. population were racial minorities or Hispanic.

As Figure 1.1 shows, between 2014 and 2060, the Black, Hispanic (or Latino), Asian Pacific Americans, and Native American population is expected to increase to about 56 percent of the U.S.

Figure 1.1 U.S. Population by Race and Ethnicity, 2014 and 2060 (Projected)

According to projections by the Census Bureau, the proportion of U.S. residents who are White non-Hispanics will decrease significantly by the year 2060. By contrast, the proportion of both Hispanic Americans and Asian Pacific Americans will rise significantly.

SOURCE: Author estimates based on U.S. Census data in Colby and Ortman, 2015:9.

2014
- Two or more races 2.5%
- African Americans 12.0%
- Hispanic 17.4%
- Asian Pacific Americans 5.0%
- American Indian 0.9%
- White non-Hispanic 62.2%

2060 (projected)
- Hispanic 28.6%
- White non-Hispanic 43.6%
- African Americans 13%
- Asian Pacific Americans 7.7%
- American Indian 0.9%
- Two or more races 6.2%

Table 1.1 Racial and Ethnic Groups in the United States, 2015

Classification	Number in Thousands	Percentage of Total Population
RACIAL GROUPS		
Whites (non-Hispanic)	188,568	58.7
Blacks/African Americans	40,695	12.7
Native Americans, Alaskan Natives	2,597	0.8
Asian Pacific Americans	21,118	7.0
Chinese	4,761	1.5
Asian Indians	3,982	1.2
Filipinos	3,899	1.2
Vietnamese	1,980	0.6
Koreans	1,822	0.6
Japanese	1,411	0.2
Pacific Islanders, Native Hawaiians	555	0.1
Other Asian Americans	2,708	0.5
Arab Americans	1,963	0.6
Two or more races	9,982	3.1
ETHNIC GROUPS		
White ancestry	144,960	
Germans	45,526	14.2
Irish	32,713	10.2
English	23,959	7.5
Italians	17,070	5.3
Poles	9,231	2.9
Scottish and Scots-Irish	8,492	2.6
French	7,969	2.5
Jews	7,200	1.8
Hispanics (or Latinos)	56,496	17.6
Mexican Americans	35,797	11.1
Puerto Ricans	5,373	1.7
Salvadorans	2,172	0.7
Cubans	2,107	0.7
Dominicans	1,873	0.6
Guatemalans	1,378	0.4
Colombians	1,082	0.3
Other Hispanics	6,764	2.1
TOTAL (ALL GROUPS)	321,419	

Note: Arab American population excluded from White total. All data are for 2015. Percentages do not total 100 percent, and when subcategories are added, they do not match totals in major categories because of overlap between groups (e.g., Polish American Jews or people of mixed ancestry such as Irish and Italian). Only the seven largest White ancestry groups listed.

SOURCE: American Community Survey 2016a: Tables B02001, B02018, B03001, B03001, B04006; Steinhardt Social Research Institute 2016.

population. This trend toward "majority-minority" became particularly noticeable in 2011, when Latino and non-White babies outnumbered White newborns for the first time in the United States (Bureau of the Census 2012d).

How Are We Grouped?

1.1 Explain how people are placed in groups.

In every society, not all groups are treated or viewed equally. Identifying a subordinate group or a minority in a society seems to be a simple task. In the United States, the groups readily identified as minorities—Blacks and Native Americans, for example—are outnumbered by non-Blacks and non-Native Americans. However, having minority status is not necessarily a result of being outnumbered. A social minority need not be a mathematical one. A **minority group** is a subordinate group whose members have significantly less control or power over their own lives than do the members of a dominant or majority group. In sociology, *minority* means the same as *subordinate*, and *dominant* is used interchangeably with *majority*.

Confronted with evidence that a particular minority in the United States is subordinate to the majority, some people respond, "Why not? After all, this is a democracy, so the majority rules." However, the subordination of a minority group involves more than its inability to rule over society. A member of a subordinate or minority group experiences a narrowing of life's opportunities—for success, education, wealth, the pursuit of happiness—that goes beyond any personal shortcoming he or she may have. A minority group does not share in proportion to its numbers what a given society, such as the United States, defines as valuable.

Being superior in numbers does not guarantee a group has control over its destiny or ensure majority status. In 1920, the majority of people in Mississippi and South Carolina were African Americans. Yet African Americans did not have as much control over their lives—let alone control of the states in which they lived—as did Whites. Throughout the United States today are counties or neighborhoods in which the majority of people are African American, Native American, or Hispanic, but White Americans are the dominant force. Nationally, 50.7 percent of the population is female, but men still dominate positions of authority and wealth well beyond their numbers.

A minority or subordinate group has five characteristics: unequal treatment, distinguishing physical or cultural traits, involuntary membership, awareness of subordination, and in-group marriage (Wagley and Harris 1958):

1. Members of a minority experience unequal treatment and have less power over their lives than members of a dominant group have over theirs. Prejudice, discrimination, segregation, and even extermination create this social inequality.

2. Members of a minority group share physical or cultural characteristics such as skin color or language that distinguish them from the dominant group. Each society has its own arbitrary standard for determining which characteristics are most important in defining dominant and minority groups.

3. Membership in a dominant or minority group is not voluntary: People are born into the group. A person does not choose to be African American or White.

4. **Minority-group members have a strong sense of group solidarity.** William Graham Sumner, writing in 1906, noted that people make distinctions between members of their own group (the in-group) and everyone else (the out-group). When a group is the object of long-term prejudice and discrimination, the feeling of "us versus them" often becomes intense.

5. **Members of a minority generally marry others from the same group.** A member of a dominant group often is unwilling to join a supposedly inferior minority by marrying one of its members. In addition, the minority group's sense of solidarity encourages marriage within the group and discourages marriage to outsiders.

Although "minority" status is not about numbers, there is no denying that the White American majority is diminishing in size relative to the growing diversity of racial and ethnic groups, as Figure 1.2 illustrates.

Using available population projections, which are heavily influenced by estimating future immigration patterns, the White population will be outnumbered by other racial groups and Hispanics by 2044. The move to a more diverse nation—one in which no group is the numerical minority—will have social impact in everything from marriage patterns to housing, politics, health care delivery, and education (Colby and Ortman 2015:13).

Figure 1.2 Minority Population by County

In four states (California, Hawai'i, New Mexico, and Texas) and the District of Columbia, as well as in about one out of every nine counties, minorities constitute the numerical majority.

SOURCE: Data from Jones-Puthoff, 2013, slide 5.

Percent minority
- 50.0 or more
- 25.0 to 49.9
- 10.0 to 24.9
- 5.0 to 9.9
- Less than 5.0

Types of Minority Groups

There are four types of minority or subordinate groups. All four, except where noted, have the five properties previously outlined. The four criteria for classifying minority groups are race, ethnicity, religion, and gender.

RACIAL GROUPS The term **racial group** is reserved for minorities and the corresponding majorities that are socially set apart because of obvious physical differences. Notice the two crucial words in the definition: *obvious* and *physical*. What is obvious? Hair color? Shape of an earlobe? Presence of body hair? To whom are these differences obvious, and why? Each society defines what it finds obvious.

In the United States, skin color is one obvious difference. People in the United States have learned informally that skin color is important. We will return periodically in this book to the social importance that people attach to skin color. **Colorism** is the ranking or judging of individuals based on skin tone. In the United States, a binary categorization is often invoked of "Black" or "White," in which White people are usually advantaged. However, even within same-race categories, judgments are often made about people as being lighter or darker (Banton 2012; Norwood 2014).

Other societies use skin color as a standard but may have a more elaborate system of classification. In Brazil, where hostility between races is less prevalent than it is in the United States, numerous categories identify people on the basis of skin color or tone. In the United States, a person is Black or White. In Brazil, a variety of terms such as *cafuso*, *mazombo*, *preto*, and *escuro* are used to describe various combinations of skin color, facial features, and hair texture.

The designation of a racial group emphasizes physical differences such as skin tone, as opposed to cultural distinctions. In the United States, minority races include Blacks, Native Americans (or American Indians), Japanese Americans, Chinese Americans, Arab Americans, Filipinos, Hawaiians, and other Asian peoples. The issue of race and racial differences has been an important one, not only in the United States but also throughout the entire sphere of European influence. We should not forget that Whites are a race, too. As we consider in Chapter 4, who is White has been subject to change over history; at one time, certain European groups were considered not worthy of being considered White. Partly to compete against a growing Black population, the "Whiting" of some European Americans has occurred. In Chapter 5, we consider how Italians and Irish, for all intents and purposes, were once considered not to be White by others.

Some racial groups also may have unique cultural traditions, as we can readily see in the many Chinatowns throughout the United States. For racial groups, however, the physical distinctiveness and not the cultural differences generally prove to be the barrier to acceptance by the host society. For example, Chinese Americans who are faithful Protestants and know the names of all the members of the Baseball Hall of Fame may be bearers of American culture. Yet these Chinese Americans are still part of a minority because they are seen as physically different.

ETHNIC GROUPS Ethnic minority groups are differentiated from the dominant group on the basis of cultural differences such as language, attitudes toward marriage and parenting, and food habits. **Ethnic groups** are groups set apart from others because of their national origin or distinctive cultural patterns.

Ethnic groups in the United States include a grouping that we call *Hispanics* or *Latinos*, which, in turn, includes Mexican Americans, Puerto Ricans, Cubans, and other

Latin American residents of the United States. Hispanics can be either Black or White, as in the case of a dark-skinned Puerto Rican who may be taken as Black in central Texas but may be viewed as Puerto Rican in New York City. The ethnic group category also includes White ethnic groups such as Irish Americans, Polish Americans, and Norwegian Americans.

The cultural traits that make groups distinctive usually originate from their homelands or, for Jews, from a long history of being segregated and prohibited from becoming a part of a host society. In the United States, an immigrant group may maintain distinctive cultural practices through associations, clubs, and worship. Ethnic enclaves such as a Little Haiti or a Greektown in urban areas also perpetuate cultural distinctiveness.

Ethnicity and race have been long recognized as important sources of differentiation. More than a century ago, African American sociologist W. E. B. Du Bois, addressing an audience at a world antislavery convention in London in 1900, called attention to the overwhelming importance of the color line throughout the world. The Speaking Out feature reprints remarks by Du Bois, who was the first Black person to receive a doctorate from Harvard and later helped to organize the National Association for the Advancement of Colored People (NAACP). Du Bois's observations give us a historic perspective on the struggle for equality. We can look ahead, knowing how far we have come and speculating on how much farther we have to go.

We also should appreciate the context of Du Bois's insights. He spoke of his "color-line" prediction in light of then-contemporary U.S. occupation of the Philippines and the relationship of "darker to lighter races" worldwide. So today, he would see race matters not only in the sporadic hate crimes we hear about but also in global conflicts (Roediger 2009).

RELIGIOUS GROUPS Association with a religion other than the dominant faith is the third basis for minority-group status. In the United States, Protestants, as a group, outnumber members of all other religions. Roman Catholics form the largest minority religion. For people who are not a part of the Christian tradition, such as followers of Islam, allegiance to their faith often is misunderstood and used to stigmatize them. This stigmatization became especially widespread and legitimated by government action in the aftermath of the attacks of September 11, 2001.

Religious minorities include groups such as the Church of Jesus Christ of Latter-day Saints (the Mormons), Jehovah's Witnesses, Amish, and Buddhists. Cults or sects associated with practices such as animal sacrifice, doomsday prophecies, demon worship, or the use of snakes in a ritualistic fashion also constitute religious minorities. Jews are excluded from this category

The changing landscape of the United States is hard to miss, but not all people equally embrace it.

Speaking Out

The Problem of the Color Line

W. E. B. Du Bois

In the metropolis of the modern world, in this the closing year of the nineteenth century, there has been assembled a congress of men and women of African blood, to deliberate solemnly upon the present situation and outlook of the darker races of mankind. The problem of the twentieth century is the problem of the color line, the question as to how far differences of race—which show themselves chiefly in the color of the skin and the texture of the hair—will hereafter be made the basis of denying to over half the world the right of sharing to their utmost ability the opportunities and privileges of modern civilization....

To be sure, the darker races are today the least advanced in culture according to European standards. This has not, however, always been the case in the past, and certainly the world's history, both ancient and modern, has given many instances of no despicable ability and capacity among the blackest races of men.

In any case, the modern world must remember that in this age when the ends of the world are being brought so near together, the millions of black men in Africa, America, and Islands of the Sea, not to speak of the brown and yellow myriads elsewhere, are bound to have a great influence upon the world in the future, by reason of sheer numbers and physical contact. If now the world of culture bends itself towards giving Negroes and other dark men the largest and broadest opportunity for education and self-development, then this contact and influence is bound to have a beneficial effect upon the world and hasten human progress. But if, by reason of carelessness, prejudice, greed, and injustice, the black world is to be exploited and ravished and degraded, the results must be deplorable, if not fatal—not simply to them, but to the high ideals of justice, freedom and culture which a thousand years of Christian civilization have held before Europe....

Let the world take no backward step in that slow but sure progress which has successively refused to let the spirit of class, of caste, of privilege, or of birth, debar from life, liberty, and the pursuit of happiness a striving human soul.

Let not color or race be a feature of distinction between White and Black men, regardless of worth or ability....

Thus we appeal with boldness and confidence to the Great Powers of the civilized world, trusting in the wide spirit of humanity, and the deep sense of justice of our age, for a generous recognition of the righteousness of our cause.

W. E. B. Du Bois

Source: Du Bois 1900 [1969a]: 20–21, 23.

---

and placed among ethnic groups. Culture is a more important defining trait for Jewish people worldwide than is religious doctrine. Jewish Americans share a cultural tradition that goes beyond theology. In this sense, it is appropriate to view them as an ethnic group rather than as members of a religious faith.

GENDER GROUPS Gender is another attribute that creates dominant and subordinate groups. Men are the social majority; women, although numerous, are relegated to the position of the social minority. Women are considered a minority even though they do not exhibit all the characteristics outlined earlier (e.g., there is little in-group marriage). Women encounter prejudice and discrimination and are physically distinguishable from men. Group membership is involuntary, and many women have developed a sense of sisterhood.

Women who are members of racial and ethnic minorities face special challenges to achieving equality. They suffer from greater inequality because they belong to two separate minority groups: a racial or ethnic group plus a subordinate gender group.

OTHER SUBORDINATE GROUPS This book focuses on groups that meet a set of criteria for subordinate status. People encounter prejudice or are excluded from full participation in society for many reasons. Racial, ethnic, religious, and gender barriers are the main ones, but there are others. Age, disability status, physical appearance, and sexual identity are among the factors that are used to subordinate groups of people.

The Social Construction of Race

1.2 Explain the social construction of race.

We see people all around us—some of whom may look quite different from us. Do these differences matter? The simple answer is no, but because so many people have for so long acted as if differences in physical characteristics, geographic origin, and shared culture do matter, distinct groups have been created in people's minds. Race has many meanings for many people. Often these meanings are inaccurate and based on theories that scientists discarded generations ago. As we will see, race is a socially constructed concept (Young 2003).

Biological Meaning

The term *race* as applied to human beings lacks any scientific basis. Distinctive physical characteristics for groups of human beings cannot be identified in the same way that scientists distinguish one animal species from another. The idea of **biological race** is based on the mistaken notion of a genetically isolated human group.

ABSENCE OF PURE RACES Even past proponents of the belief that sharp scientific divisions exist among humans had endless debates over what the world's races were. Given people's frequent migration, exploration, and invasions, pure genetic types have not existed for some time, if they ever did. There are no mutually exclusive races. Skin tone among African Americans varies tremendously, as it does among White Americans. There is even an overlapping of dark-skinned Whites and light-skinned African Americans. If we grouped people by genetic resistance to malaria and by fingerprint patterns, then Norwegians and many African groups would be the same race. If we grouped people by lactose intolerance, some Africans, Asians, and southern Europeans would belong to one group, and West Africans and northern Europeans would belong to another (Leehotz 1995; Shanklin 1994).

Biologically, no pure, distinct races exist. Despite this scientific fact, people at different times have advocated **eugenics**, the belief that human genetic quality can be improved by selective breeding. Eugenics has taken many forms, including sterilizing people with mental illnesses, banning interracial marriages, and, as in the Holocaust, attempting to exterminate entire groups of people judged to be inferior.

Research as a part of the Human Genome Project mapping human deoxyribonucleic acid (DNA) has served to confirm genetic diversity only, with differences *within* traditionally regarded racial groups (e.g., Black Africans) much greater than those *between* groups (e.g., between Black Africans and Europeans). Contemporary studies of DNA on a global basis have determined that about 90 percent of human genetic variation is within "local populations," such as within the French or within the Afghan people. The remaining 10 percent of total human variation is what we think of today as constituting races and accounts for skin tone, hair texture, and nose shape (Cohen 2016; Feldman 2010).

It is no surprise that the question of whether races have different innate levels of intelligence has led to some of the most explosive controversies (Bamshad and Olson 2003; El-Haj 2007).

INTELLIGENCE TESTS Typically, intelligence is measured as an **intelligence quotient (IQ)**, which is the ratio of a person's mental age to his or her chronological age, multiplied by 100, with 100 representing average intelligence and higher scores representing greater intelligence. It should be noted that there is little consensus over just what intelligence is, other than as defined by such IQ tests. Intelligence tests are adjusted for a person's age so that 10-year-olds take a different test than 20-year-olds. Although research shows that certain learning strategies can improve a person's IQ, generally IQ remains stable as one ages.

A great deal of debate rages over the accuracy of IQ tests. Are they biased toward people who come to the tests with knowledge similar to that of the test writers? Skeptics argue that questions in IQ tests do not truly measure intellectual potential. The question of cultural bias in tests remains a concern. The most recent research shows that differences in intelligence scores between Blacks and Whites are almost eliminated when adjustments are made for social and economic characteristics (Lindsey 2013).

Back in 1994, an 845-page book unleashed another national debate on the issue of IQ. The research efforts of psychologist Richard J. Herrnstein and social scientist Charles Murray, published in *The Bell Curve* (1994), concluded that 60 percent of IQ is inheritable and that racial groups offer a convenient means to generalize about differences in intelligence. Unlike most other proponents of the race–IQ link, the authors offered policy suggestions that included ending welfare to discourage births among low-IQ poor women and changing immigration laws so that the average IQ in the United States is not diminished. Herrnstein and Murray even made generalizations about IQ levels among Asians and Hispanics—two groups that often intermarry—in the United States.

In spite of *The Bell Curve* "research," it is not possible to generalize about absolute differences between groups, such as Latinos versus Whites, when almost half of Latinos in the United States marry non-Hispanics.

More than a decade later, the mere mention of the "bell curve" still signals a belief in a racial hierarchy, with Whites toward the top and Blacks near the bottom. The research presented then and repeated today points to the difficulty in definitions: What is intelligence, and what constitutes a racial group, given generations (and sometimes centuries) of intermarriage? How can we speak of definitive inherited racial differences if there have been intermarriages between people of every color? Furthermore, as people on both sides of the debate have noted, regardless of the findings, we would still want to strive to maximize the talents of each individual. All research shows that the differences within a group are much greater than any alleged differences between group averages.

Why does such IQ research occasionally reemerge when it is clear that the data are subject to different interpretations? The argument that "we" are superior to "them" is appealing to the dominant group. It justifies receiving opportunities that are denied to others. We can anticipate that the debate over IQ and the allegations of significant group differences will continue. Policymakers need to acknowledge the difficulty in treating race as a biologically significant characteristic.

Race as a Social Construction

If race does not distinguish humans from one another biologically, then why does it seem to be so important? It is important because of the social meaning people have attached to it. The 1950 (UNESCO) Statement on Race maintains that race is not a biological phenomenon (Montagu 1972:118).

Race is a social construction that benefits the oppressor, who defines which groups of people are privileged and which groups are not. The acceptance of race in a society as a legitimate category allows racial hierarchies to emerge to the benefit of the dominant "races." For example, inner-city drive-by shootings, which are mostly carried out by people of color, are viewed as a race-specific problem to be remedied by local officials cleaning up troubled neighborhoods. Yet school shootings, which are largely carried out by Whites, are viewed as a societal concern and placed on the national agenda.

People could speculate that if human groups have obvious physical differences, then they could also have corresponding mental or personality differences. No one disagrees that people differ in temperament, potential to learn, and sense of humor, among other characteristics. In its social sense, race implies that groups that differ physically also bear distinctive emotional and mental abilities or disabilities. These beliefs are based on the notion that humankind can be divided into distinct groups. We have already seen the difficulties associated with pigeonholing people into racial categories. Despite these difficulties, belief in the inheritance of behavior patterns and in an association between physical and cultural traits is widespread. When this belief is coupled with the belief that certain groups or races are inherently superior to others, the result is racism. **Racism** is a doctrine of racial supremacy that sees one race as superior to another (Bash 2001; Bonilla-Silva 1996).

We disproved the biological significance of race in the previous section. In modern, complex industrial societies, we find little adaptive usefulness in the presence or absence of prominent chins, the epicanthic eye fold associated with eastern and central Asian peoples, or the comparative amount of melanin in the skin. It is of little importance that people are genetically different; what is important is that they approach one another with dissimilar perspectives. It is in the social setting that race is decisive. Race is significant because people have given it significance.

Race definitions are crystallized through what Michael Omi and Howard Winant (2015) called **racial formation**, a sociohistorical process by which racial categories are created, inhabited, transformed, and destroyed. Those in power define groups of people in a way that depends on a racist social structure. As in the United States, these definitions can become systematic and embedded in many aspects of society for a significant length of time. No one escapes the extent and frequency to which we are subjected to racial formation. The creation of the reservation system for Native Americans in the late 1800s is an example of racial formation. The federal American Indian policy treated previously distinctive tribes as a single group.

With rising immigration from Latin America in the latter part of the twentieth century, the fluid nature of racial formation is evident. As if it happened in one day, people in the United States have spoken about the Latin Americanization of the United States or stated that the biracial order of Black and White has been replaced with a *triracial* order of Black, White, and Hispanic. Yet even this assertion is overly simplistic given the presence of tribal groups and growing numbers of Asian Pacific Americans. We examine the social context of the changing nature of diversity to understand how scholars have sought to generalize about intergroup relations in the United States and elsewhere (Bonilla-Silva and Dietrich 2011; Biagas Jr. and Bianchi 2015).

In the southern United States, the social construction of race was known as the "one-drop rule." This tradition stipulated that if a person had even a single drop of "Black blood," that person was defined and viewed as Black. Today, children of biracial or multiracial marriages try to build their own identities in a country that seems intent on placing them in a single, traditional category—a topic we examine next.

Biracial and Multiracial Identity: Who Am I?

People are now more willing to accept and advance identities that do not fit neatly into mutually exclusive categories. That is, increasing numbers of people are identifying themselves as biracial or multiracial or, at the very least, explicitly viewing themselves as reflecting a diverse racial and ethnic identity. Barack Obama is perhaps the most visible person with a biracial background. President Obama has explicitly stated he sees himself as a Black man, although his mother was White and his White grandparents largely raised him. In 2010, he chose to check the "Black, African American, or Negro" box on his household's census form. Obviously, *biracial* does not mean *biracial identity*.

The diversity of the United States today has made it more difficult for many people to place themselves on the country's traditional and inflexible racial and ethnic landscape. This difficulty reminds us that racial formation continues to take place. As we have seen, the racial and ethnic landscape is constructed not naturally but socially and, therefore, is subject to change and different interpretations. Although our focus is on the United States, almost every nation faces the same challenges.

The United States tracks people by race and ethnicity for myriad reasons, ranging from attempting to improve the status of oppressed groups to diversifying classrooms. But how can we measure the growing number of people whose ancestry is mixed by anyone's definition? In the Research Focus feature, we consider how the U.S. Bureau of the Census deals with this issue.

Research Focus

Multiracial Identity

Approaching Census 2000, a movement began among those who were frustrated by government questionnaires that forced them to identify themselves by only one race. Take the case of Stacey Davis in New Orleans. The young woman's mother is Thai and her father is Creole, a blend of Black, French, and German. People often think Stacey is a Latina, Filipina, or Hawaiian. Officially, she has been "White" all her life because she looks White. Census 2000 for the first time gave people the option to check off one or more racial groups. (However, "biracial" or "multiracial" was not an option.) In other words, Census 2000 was the first time the U.S. government officially recognized different social constructions of racial identity—for example, that a person could be Asian American *and* White.

Most people did select one racial category in Census 2000 and again in 2010. Overall, approximately 9 million people, or 2.9 percent of the total population, selected two or more racial groups in 2010. As Figure 1.3 shows, White and African American was the most common multiple identity, with about 1.8 million people selecting that response. As a group, American Indians were the most likely to select a second category, and Whites were the least likely—further evidence that race is socially defined.

The possible real size of the multiracial population is significantly larger. A 2015 research report found that when one considers the background of grandparents and parents, the size of the U.S. multiracial population is closer to 7 percent, not 2.9 percent.

Complicating the situation is the fact that the Census asks people separately whether they are Hispanic or non-Hispanic. So a Hispanic person can be any race. In the 2010 Census, 94 percent of Hispanics indicated they were one race, but 6 percent indicated two or more races; this proportion was twice as high as it was among non-Hispanics. Therefore, Latinos are more likely than non-Hispanics to indicate a multiracial ancestry.

Changes in measuring race and ethnicity are not necessarily over. For Census 2020, bureau officials are considering adding categories for people of Middle Eastern, North African, or Asian descent. "Hispanic" may even be added as a "race category" along with White, African American, Asian, American Indian/Alaska Native, and Pacific Islander.

Regardless of government definitions, we know that some people do change their racial identity over time, choosing to self-identify as something different. This fluidity in individual self-definition could increase if the nation as a whole appears to be more accepting of biracial and multiracial categories.

The Census Bureau's decision does not necessarily resolve the frustration of hundreds of thousands of people, such as Stacey Davis, who daily face people trying to place them in some convenient racial or ethnic category. However, it does underscore the complexity of social construction and trying to apply arbitrary definitions to the diversity of the human population. A symbol of this social construction of race can be seen in Barack Obama, born of a White woman and a Black immigrant from Kenya. Although he has always identified himself as a Black man, it is worth noting that he was born in Hawai'i, a state in which 23.6 percent of people see themselves as more than one race, compared to the national average of 2.9 percent.

Sources: DaCosta 2007; Humes, Jones, and Ramirez 2011: 2–11; Pew Research Center 2015; Saperstein and Penner 2012; Saulny 2011; Welch 2011; Williams 2005.

Figure 1.3 Multiple-Race Choices in Census 2010

This figure shows the percentage distribution of the 9 million people who chose two or more races (out of the total U.S. population of 309 million).

SOURCE: Data from Humes, Jones, and Ramirez 2011:10.

- "White and Black or African American" — 20.4%
- "White and Asian" — 18.0%
- "White and American Indian or Alaska Native" — 15.9%
- "Black or African American and American Indian or Alaska Native" — 3.0%
- All other combinations of two races — 34.4%
- Three or more races — 8.3%

Besides the increasing respect for biracial identity and multiracial identity, group names undergo change as well. Within little more than a generation during the twentieth century, labels that were applied to subordinate groups changed from *Negroes* to *Blacks* to *African Americans*, from *American Indians* to *Native Americans* or *Native Peoples*. However, more Native Americans prefer the use of their tribal name, such as *Seminole*, instead of a collective label. The old 1950s statistical term of "people with a Spanish surname" has long been discarded, but there is disagreement over a new term: *Latino* or *Hispanic*. Like Native Americans, Hispanic Americans avoid such global terms and prefer their native names, such as *Puerto Ricans* or *Cubans*. People of Mexican ancestry indicate preferences for a variety of names, such as *Mexican American*, *Chicano*, or simply *Mexican*.

In the United States and other multiracial, multiethnic societies, **panethnicity**, the development of solidarity among related ethnic subgroups, has emerged. The coalition of tribal groups as Native Americans or American Indians to confront outside forces, notably the federal government, is one example of panethnicity. Hispanics or Latinos and Asian Americans are other examples of panethnicity. Although it is rarely recognized by the dominant society, the very terms *Black* and *African American* represent the descendants of many different ethnic or tribal groups, such as African groups of Fulani and Yoruba, as well as Afro Caribbeans (Brown and Jones 2015).

Is panethnicity a convenient label for "outsiders" or a term that reflects a mutual identity? Certainly, many people outside the group are unable or unwilling to recognize ethnic differences and prefer umbrella terms such as *Asian Americans*. For some small groups, combining with others is emerging as a useful way to make themselves heard, but there is always a fear that their own distinctive culture will become submerged. Although many Hispanics share the Spanish language and many are united by Roman Catholicism, only one in four native-born people of Mexican, Puerto Rican, or Cuban descent prefers a panethnic label to nationality or ethnic identity. Yet the growth of a variety of panethnic associations among many groups, including Hispanics, continues into the twenty-first century (Espiritu 1992; Mora 2014).

Another challenge to identity is **marginality**: the status of being between two cultures, as in the case of a person whose mother is a Jew and whose father a Christian. A century ago, Du Bois (1903) spoke eloquently of the "double consciousness" that Black Americans feel—being citizens of the United States but viewed as something quite apart from the dominant social groups in society. Incomplete assimilation by immigrants also results in marginality. Although a Filipina woman migrating to the United States may take on the characteristics of her new host society, she may not be fully accepted and may, therefore, feel neither Filipina nor American. Marginalized individuals often encounter social situations in which their identities are sources of tension, especially when the expression of multiple identities is not accepted, and they find themselves being perceived differently in different environments, with varying expectations (Park 1928; Stonequist 1937; Townsend, Markos, and Bergsieker 2009).

Yet another type marginality is that experienced by children of biracial or multiracial parental backgrounds and children adopted by parents of a different racial or ethnic background. For these children or adolescents, developing their racial or ethnic identity requires them to negotiate society's desire to put labels on them (Fryer et al. 2012).

As we seek to understand diversity in the United States, we must be mindful that ethnic and racial labels are just that: labels that have been socially constructed. Yet these social constructs can have a powerful impact, whether they are self-applied or applied by others.

Sociology and the Study of Race and Ethnicity

1.3 Describe how sociology helps us understand race and ethnicity.

Before proceeding further with our study of racial and ethnic groups, let us consider several sociological perspectives that provide insight into dominant–subordinate relationships. **Sociology** is the systematic study of social behavior and human groups, so it is well suited to enlarging our understanding of intergroup relations. The study of race relations has a long, valuable history in sociology. Admittedly, it has not always been progressive; indeed, at times it has reflected the prejudices of society. In some instances, sociology scholars who are members of racial, ethnic, and religious minorities, as well as women, have not been permitted to make the contributions they are capable of making to the field.

Stratification by Class and Gender

That some members have unequal amounts of wealth, prestige, or power is a characteristic of all societies. Sociologists observe that entire groups may be assigned less or more of what a society values. The hierarchy that emerges is called stratification. **Stratification** is the structured ranking of entire groups of people that perpetuates unequal rewards and power in a society.

Much discussion of stratification identifies the **class**, or social ranking, of people who share similar wealth, according to sociologist Max Weber's classic definition. Mobility from one class to another is not easy to achieve. Movement into classes of greater wealth may be particularly difficult for subordinate-group members faced with lifelong prejudice and discrimination (Banton 2008; Gerth and Mills 1958).

Recall that the first property of subordinate-group standing is unequal treatment by the dominant group in the form of prejudice, discrimination, and segregation.

Stratification is intertwined with the subordination of racial, ethnic, religious, and gender groups. Race has implications for the way people are treated; so does class. One also must add the effects of race and class together. For example, being poor and Black is not the same as being either one by itself. A wealthy Mexican American is not the same as an affluent Anglo American or Mexican Americans as a group.

Public discussion of issues such as housing or public assistance often is disguised as a discussion of class issues, when, in fact, the issues are based primarily on race. Similarly, some topics such as the poorest of the poor or the working poor are addressed in terms of race when the class component should be explicit. Nonetheless, the link between race and class in society is abundantly clear (Winant 2004).

Another stratification factor that we need to consider is gender. How different is the situation for women as contrasted with men? Returning again to the first property of minority groups—unequal treatment and less control—women do not receive the same treatment as men. Whether the issue is jobs or poverty, education or crime, women typically have more difficult experiences. In addition, the situations women face in areas such as health care and welfare raise different concerns than they do for men. Just as we need to consider the role of social class to understand race and ethnicity better, we also need to consider the role of gender.

Theoretical Perspectives

Sociologists view society in different ways. Some see the world as a stable and ongoing entity. They note the endurance of a Chinatown, the general sameness of male–female roles over time, and other common aspects of intergroup relations. Other sociologists see society as composed of many groups in conflict, competing for scarce resources. Within this conflict, some people or even entire groups may be labeled or stigmatized in a way that blocks their access to what a society values. We examine three theoretical perspectives that are widely used by sociologists today: the functionalist, conflict, and labeling perspectives.

FUNCTIONALIST PERSPECTIVE In the view of a functionalist, a society is like a living organism in which each part contributes to the survival of the whole. The **functionalist perspective** emphasizes how the parts of society are structured to maintain its stability. According to this approach, if an aspect of social life does not contribute to a society's stability or survival, then it will not be passed on from one generation to the next.

It seems reasonable to assume that bigotry between races offers no such positive function, and so we ask: Why does it persist? Although agreeing that racial hostility is hardly to be admired, the functionalist would point out that it serves some positive functions from the perspective of the racists. We can identify five functions that racial beliefs have for the dominant group:

1. Racist ideologies such as the belief in the inherent inferiority of entire groups of people provide a moral justification for maintaining a society that routinely deprives a group of its rights and privileges.
2. Racist beliefs discourage subordinate people from attempting to question their lowly status and why they must perform "the dirty work"; to do so is to question the very foundation of the society.

3. Racial ideologies not only justify existing practices but also serve as a rallying point for social movements, as seen in the rise of the Nazi party or present-day Aryan movements.
4. Racist myths encourage support for the existing order. Some argue that if there were any major societal change, the subordinate group would suffer even greater poverty, and the dominant group would suffer lower living standards.
5. Racist beliefs relieve the dominant group of the responsibility to address the economic and educational problems faced by subordinate groups.

As a result, racial ideology grows when a value system (e.g., that underlying a colonial empire or slavery) is being threatened (Levin and Nolan 2011:115–145; Nash 1962).

Prejudice and discrimination also cause definite dysfunctions. **Dysfunctions** are elements of society that may disrupt a social system or decrease its stability. Racism is dysfunctional to a society, including to its dominant group, in six ways:

1. A society that practices discrimination fails to use the resources of all individuals. Discrimination limits the search for talent and leadership to the dominant group.
2. Discrimination aggravates social problems such as poverty, delinquency, and crime, and it places the financial burden of alleviating these problems on the dominant group.
3. Society must invest a good deal of time and money to defend the barriers that prevent the full participation of all members.
4. Racial prejudice and discrimination undercut goodwill and friendly diplomatic relations between nations. They also negatively affect efforts to increase global trade.
5. Social change is inhibited because change may assist a subordinate group.
6. Discrimination promotes disrespect for law enforcement and for the peaceful settlement of disputes.

That racism has costs for the dominant group as well as for the subordinate group reminds us that intergroup conflict is exceedingly complex (Bowser and Hunt 1996; Feagin, Vera, and Batur 2000; Rose 1951).

CONFLICT PERSPECTIVE In contrast to the functionalists' emphasis on stability, conflict sociologists see the social world as being in continual struggle. The **conflict perspective** assumes that the social structure is best understood in terms of conflict or tension between competing groups. The result of this conflict is significant economic disparity and structural inequality in education, the labor market, housing, and health care. Specifically, society is in a struggle between the privileged (the dominant group) and the exploited (the subordinate group). Such conflicts need not be physically violent and may take the form of immigration restrictions, real-estate practices, or disputes over cuts in the federal budget.

The conflict model is often used today to examine race and ethnicity because it readily accounts for the presence of tension between competing groups. According to the conflict perspective, competition takes place between groups with unequal amounts of economic and political power. The minorities are exploited or, at best, ignored by the dominant group. The conflict perspective is more radical and activist than functionalism because conflict theorists emphasize social change and the redistribution of resources.

Those who follow the conflict approach to race and ethnicity have remarked repeatedly that the subordinate group is criticized for its low status. That the dominant group is responsible for subordination is often ignored. William Ryan (1976) calls this phenomenon **blaming the victim**: portraying the problems of racial and ethnic minorities as their fault rather than recognizing society's responsibility.

Conflict theorists consider the costs that come with residential segregation. Besides the more obvious cost of reducing housing options, racial and social class isolation reduces for people (including Whites) all available options in schools, retail shopping, and medical care. People, however, can travel to access services and businesses, and it is more likely that racial and ethnic minorities will have to make that sometimes costly and time-consuming trip.

LABELING THEORY Related to the conflict perspective and its concern over blaming the victim is **labeling theory**, a concept introduced by sociologist Howard Becker to explain why certain people are viewed as deviant while others engaging in the same behavior are not. Students of crime and deviance have relied heavily on labeling theory. According to labeling theory, a youth who misbehaves may be considered and treated as a delinquent (deviant) if he or she comes from the "wrong kind of family." Another youth from a middle-class family who commits the same misbehavior might be given another chance before being punished.

From the conflict perspective, the emphasis should not be primarily on the attributes of the individual (i.e., blaming the victim) but on structural factors such as the labor market, affordable housing, and availability of programs to assist people with addiction or mental-health issues.

The labeling perspective directs our attention to the role that negative stereotypes play in race and ethnicity. The image that prejudiced people maintain of a group toward which they hold ill feelings is called a stereotype. **Stereotypes** are unreliable generalizations about all members of a group that do not take individual differences into account. The warrior image of Native American (American Indian) people is perpetuated by the frequent use of tribal names or even names such as "Indians" and "Redskins" for sports teams. This labeling is not limited to racial and ethnic groups, however. For instance, age can be used to exclude a person from an activity in which he or she is qualified to engage. Groups are subjected to stereotypes and discrimination in such a way that their treatment resembles that of social minorities. Social prejudice as a result of stereotyping exists toward ex-convicts, gamblers, alcoholics, transgender people, lesbians, gay men, prostitutes, people with AIDS, and people with disabilities, to name a few.

The labeling approach points out that stereotypes, when applied by people in power, can have negative consequences for people or groups. A crucial aspect of the relationship between dominant and subordinate groups is the prerogative of the dominant group to define society's values. U.S. sociologist William I. Thomas (1923), an early critic of racial and gender discrimination, saw that the "definition of the situation" could mold the personality of the individual. In other words, Thomas observed that people respond not only to the objective features of a situation (or person) but also to the meaning these features have for them. So, for example, a lone walker seeing a young Black man walking toward him may perceive the situation differently than if the oncoming person is an older woman. Sociologist Elijah Anderson (2011) has long seen passersby scrutinize him and other African American males more closely and suspiciously than they would women or White males. In other words, people can create false images, definitions, or stereotypes that have real social consequences.

In certain situations, we may respond to negative stereotypes and act on them, with the result that false definitions become accurate. This result is known as a **self-fulfilling prophecy**. A person described as having particular characteristics begins to display the very traits attributed to him or her. Thus, a child who is praised for being a natural comic may focus on learning to become funny to gain approval and attention. In other words, dominant-group definitions of minority groups may have a self-validating effect.

Self-fulfilling prophecies can be devastating for minority groups. For example, as Figure 1.4 shows, the subordinate-group individual may attend a poorly financed school that leaves him or her unequipped to perform jobs that offer high status and pay. He or she then gets a low-paying job and must settle for a much lower standard of living. The rationale of the dominant society is that these minority people lack the ability to perform in more important and lucrative positions. Training to become scientists, executives, or physicians is denied to many subordinate-group individuals

Figure 1.4 Self-Fulfilling Prophecy

White taxpayers do not want to waste money → SGI attends poorly financed school → or: SGI drops out / SGI pushed out / SGI performs poorly on exams → SGI has less job opportunity → SGI earns less money → SGI 1. Has poor health 2. Shops at less attractive stores with higher prices 3. Has poor housing 4. Is more likely to be a crime victim → (Judged by himself or herself) → SGI has self-doubt and self-hate → (Judged by others) → SGI is inferior by cultural measures of success → (back to White taxpayers do not want to waste money)

SGI = subordinate-group individual

(SGIs), who are then locked into society's inferior jobs. As a result, the false definition of the self-fulfilling prophecy becomes real. The subordinate group becomes inferior because it was defined at the start as inferior and was, therefore, prevented from achieving the levels attained by the majority.

Because of this vicious circle, talented SGIs may come to see the fields of entertainment and professional sports as their only hope for achieving wealth and fame. Thus, it is no accident that successive waves of Irish, Jewish, Italian, African American, and Hispanic performers and athletes have made their mark on culture in the United States. Unfortunately, these very successes may convince the dominant group that its original stereotypes were valid—that these are the only areas of society in which subordinate-group members can excel. Furthermore, athletics and the arts are highly competitive areas. For every LeBron James and Jennifer Lopez who makes it, many, many more SGIs will end up disappointed.

The Creation of Subordinate-Group Status

1.4 **Explain how subordinate groups are created.**

Three situations are likely to lead to the formation of a relationship between a subordinate group and the dominant group. A subordinate group can emerge through migration, annexation, and/or colonialism.

Migration

People who emigrate to a new country often find themselves a minority in that new country. Cultural or physical traits or religious affiliation may set the immigrant apart from the dominant group. Immigration from Europe, Asia, and Latin America has been a powerful force in shaping the fabric of life in the United States. **Migration** is the general term used to describe any transfer of population. **Emigration** (by emigrants) means leaving a country to settle in another country. **Immigration** (by immigrants) denotes coming into the new country. As an example, from Vietnam's perspective, the "boat people" were emigrants from Vietnam to the United States, but in the United States they were counted as U.S. immigrants.

Although some people migrate because they want to, leaving one's home country is not always voluntary. Millions have been transported as slaves against their will. Conflict and war have displaced people throughout human history. The twentieth century saw huge population movements caused by two world wars; revolutions in Spain, Hungary, and Cuba; the partition of British India; conflicts in Southeast Asia, Korea, and Central America; and confrontations between Arabs and Israelis. Involuntary migration guarantees a subordinate role for the migrating group. Although enslavement has a long history, all industrialized societies today prohibit slavery. Of course, many contemporary societies, including the United States, bear the legacy of slavery.

In all types of movement, even when a U.S. family moves from Ohio to Florida, but especially regarding emigration, two sets of forces operate: push factors and pull factors. *Push factors* discourage a person from remaining where he or she lives. Religious persecution and economic factors such as dissatisfaction with employment opportunities are common push factors. *Pull factors* encourage a person to move to a new location. Pull factors that attract an immigrant to a particular country include a better standard of living, friends and relatives who have already emigrated, and a promised job.

Migration has taken on new significance in the twenty-first century partly because of **globalization**, or the worldwide integration of government policies, cultures, social movements, and financial markets through trade and the exchange of ideas. The increased movement of people and money across borders has made the distinction between temporary and permanent migration less meaningful. Even after they have relocated, people maintain global linkages to their former country and with a global economy (Richmond 2002).

Annexation

Nations, particularly during wars or as a result of war, incorporate or attach land through the process of **annexation**. This new land is contiguous to the nation's existing border, as in the German annexation of Austria and Czechoslovakia in 1938 and 1939 and in the U.S. Louisiana Purchase of 1803. The Treaty of Guadalupe Hidalgo, which ended the Mexican-American War in 1848, gave the United States California, Utah, Nevada, most of New Mexico, and parts of Arizona, Wyoming, and Colorado. The indigenous peoples in some of this huge territory were dominant in their society one day, only to become minority-group members the next.

When annexation occurs, the dominant power generally suppresses the language and culture of the minority. Such was the practice of Russia with the Ukrainians and Poles, and of Prussia with the Poles. Minorities often try to maintain their cultural integrity despite annexation. In the twentieth century, Poles inhabited an area divided into territories ruled by three countries but maintained their own culture across political boundaries.

Colonialism

Colonialism has been the most common way for one group of people to dominate another. **Colonialism** is the maintenance of political, social, economic, and cultural dominance over people by a foreign power for an extended period (Bell 1991). Colonialism is rule by outsiders, but unlike annexation, it does not involve actual incorporation into the dominant people's nation. The long-standing control that was exercised by the British Empire over much of North America, parts of Africa, and India is an example of colonial domination.

Societies gain power over a foreign land through military strength, sophisticated political organization, and investment capital. The extent of power may also vary according to the dominant group's scope of settlement in the colonial land. Relations between the colonizing nation and the colonized people are similar to those between a dominant group and exploited subordinate groups. Colonial subjects generally are limited to menial jobs and the wages from their labor. The natural resources of their land benefit the members of the ruling class.

By the 1980s, colonialism, in the sense of political rule, had become largely a phenomenon of the past, yet industrial countries of North America and Europe still dominated the world economically and politically. Drawing on the conflict perspective, sociologist Immanuel Wallerstein (1974) described today's global economic system as very similar to the economic system that prevailed at the height of colonialism.

Figure 1.5 Spectrum of Intergroup Relations

EXPULSION	SEGREGATION	ASSIMILATION

INCREASINGLY UNACCEPTABLE → MORE TOLERABLE

EXTERMINATION or genocide | **SECESSION** or partitioning | **FUSION** or amalgamation or melting pot | **PLURALISM** or multiculturalism

Wallerstein advanced the **world systems theory**, which views the global economic system as divided between nations that control wealth and those that provide natural resources and labor. The limited economic resources available in developing nations worsen many of the ethnic, racial, and religious conflicts noted at the beginning of this chapter. In addition, the presence of massive inequality between nations only serves to encourage immigration generally and, more specifically, the movement of many of the most skilled workers from developing nations to the industrial nations.

The Spectrum of Intergroup Status

Relationships between and among racial, ethnic, and religious groups, as well as other dominate-subordinate relationships, are not static. These relations change over time, sometimes in one's own lifetime. To illustrate this idea, we can use the Spectrum of Intergroup Relations in Figure 1.5. These relationships can be viewed along a continuum from those largely unacceptable to the subordinate group (such as extermination and expulsion) to those that are more tolerated (such as assimilation and pluralism).

The Consequences of Subordinate-Group Status

1.5 Summarize the consequences of subordinate-group status.

A group with subordinate status faces several consequences. These differ in their degree of harshness, ranging from physical annihilation to absorption into the dominant group. In this section, we examine seven consequences of subordinate-group status: extermination, expulsion, secession, segregation, fusion, assimilation, and pluralism.

Extermination

The most extreme way to deal with a subordinate group is to eliminate it. **Genocide** is the deliberate, systematic killing of an entire people or nation. This term is often used in reference to the Holocaust, Nazi Germany's extermination of 12 million European Jews and other ethnic minorities during World War II. The **Holocaust** was the state-sponsored systematic persecution and annihilation of European Jews by Nazi Germany and its collaborators. The move to eliminate Jews from the European continent started slowly, with Germany gradually restricting the rights of Jews: for example, by preventing them from voting, living outside the Jewish ghetto, and owning businesses. Much anti-Semitic cruelty was evident before the beginning of the war. *Kristallnacht*, or the "Night of Broken Glass," in Berlin on November 9, 1938, was a turning point toward genocide. Ninety Berlin Jews were murdered, hundreds of homes and synagogues were set on fire or ransacked, and thousands of windows were broken in Jewish-owned stores. Despite the obvious intolerance they faced, Jews desiring to immigrate were often turned back by government officials in Europe and the Americas. In 1994, a genocidal war between the Hutu and Tutsi people in Rwanda left 300,000 school-age children orphaned (Chirot and Edwards 2003; Naimark 2004; Institute for Jewish and Community Research 2008; DellaPergola 2007).

The term **ethnic cleansing** refers to the forced deportation of people, accompanied by systematic violence, including death. The term was introduced in 1992 when ethnic Serbs instituted a policy intended to "cleanse"—eliminate—Muslims from parts of Bosnia.

Genocide also appropriately describes White policies toward Native Americans in the nineteenth century. In 1800, the American Indian population in the United States was approximately 600,000; by 1850, it had been reduced to 250,000 through warfare with the U.S. Army, disease, and forced relocation to inhospitable environments, all of which led to the death of many Native Americans.

In 2008, the Australian government officially apologized for its past brutality toward and neglect of its native people, the Aboriginal population. The government's policies led to a quarter of Aboriginal children, the so-called lost generation, being taken from their families and placed in orphanages or foster homes, or being put up for adoption by White Australians, until the policies were finally abandoned in 1969 (Johnston 2008).

Expulsion

Dominant groups may choose to force a specific subordinate group to leave certain areas or even vacate a country. Expulsion, therefore, is another extreme consequence of minority-group status. European colonial powers in North America and eventually the U.S. government itself drove almost all Native Americans off their tribal lands and into unfamiliar territory.

In the 1990s, the monarchy in Bhutan, which was sympathetic to Buddhists, expelled 107,000 Nepali-speaking Hindus from the southern part of the country. Languishing for nearly 20 years in refugee camps, they eventually were resettled. Some went to Australia or Canada, but the majority (approximately 70,000) came to the United States to communities like Manchester, New Hampshire, as described at the beginning of this chapter.

Stigmatizing and expelling minority groups are not actions of the distant past. Here, police in Paris round up Roma (Gypsies) for subsequent expulsion from the country.

More recently, beginning in 2009, France expelled over 10,000 ethnic Roma (Gypsies), forcing them to return to their home countries of Bulgaria and Romania. This expulsion appeared to violate the European Union's (EU) ban against targeting ethnic groups, as well as the EU's policy of "freedom of movement." In 2011, the EU withdrew its threat of legal action against France when the government said it would no longer expel Roma in particular but only those living in "illegal camps," which many observers see as a technicality that allows France to get around long-standing human-rights policies.

Secession

A group ceases to be a subordinate group when it secedes to form a new nation or moves to an already-established nation, where it becomes dominant. After Great Britain withdrew from Palestine, Jewish people achieved a dominant position in 1948, attracting Jews from throughout the world to the new state of Israel. Similarly, Pakistan was created in 1947 during the Indian partition. The predominantly Muslim areas in the north became Pakistan, making India predominantly Hindu.

Throughout the twentieth century, minorities repudiated dominant customs, and they continue to do so. For example, the Estonian, Latvian, Lithuanian, and Armenian peoples, not content to be merely tolerated by the majority, all seceded to form independent states after the demise of the Soviet Union in 1991. In 1999, ethnic Albanians fought bitterly for their cultural and political recognition in the Kosovo region of Yugoslavia.

Some African Americans have called for secession. Suggestions dating back to the early 1700s supported the return of Blacks to Africa as a solution to racial problems. The American Colonization Society suggested resettling Blacks in Liberia, but proposals were also advanced to establish settlements in other areas. Territorial separatism and the emigrationist ideology were recurrent and interrelated themes among African Americans from the late nineteenth century well into the 1980s. The Black Muslims, or Nation of Islam, once expressed the desire for complete separation in their own state or territory within the modern borders of the United States.

Segregation

Segregation is the physical separation of two groups in residence, workplace, and social functions. Generally, the dominant group imposes segregation on a subordinate group. Segregation is rarely complete, however. Intergroup contact inevitably occurs even in the most segregated societies.

Sociologists Douglas Massey and Nancy Denton wrote *American Apartheid* (1993), which described segregation in U.S. cities on the basis of 1990 census data. The title of their book was meant to indicate that segregation in U.S. neighborhoods resembled **apartheid**, the rigid government-imposed racial segregation that prevailed for so long in the Republic of South Africa.

Analysis of census data shows continuing segregation in the United States despite the country's racial and ethnic diversity. Scholars use a *segregation index* to measure separation. This index ranges from 0 (complete integration) to 100 (complete segregation), where the value indicates the percentage of the minority group that needs to move for the minority group to be distributed exactly like Whites. Thus a segregation index of 60 for Blacks–Whites would mean that 60 percent of all African Americans would have to move to have the same residential pattern as Whites.

Table 1.2 lists the most segregated metropolitan areas with large African American, Latino, and Asian American populations. Blacks and Whites are most separated from each other in Milwaukee/Waukesha/West Allis. The Los Angeles/Long Beach/Anaheim metropolitan area finds Whites and Latinos most living apart, and the Edison/New Brunswick, New Jersey, area is where Asians and Whites are most segregated from each other. Typically half to three-quarters of the people would have to move to achieve even distribution throughout the city and surrounding suburbs.

Table 1.2 Segregated Metro America

BLACK–WHITE

1. Milwaukee/Waukesha/West Allis	81.0
2. New York/Newark/Jersey City	77.0
3. Chicago/Naperville/Elgin	76.0
4. Detroit/Warren/Dearborn	74.0
5. Cleveland/Elyria	73.0
6. Buffalo/Cheektowaga/Niagara Falls	73.0
7. St. Louis	72.0
8. Los Angeles/Long Beach/Anaheim	68.0

HISPANIC–WHITE

1. Los Angeles/Long Beach/Anaheim	61.0
2. New York/Newark/Jersey City	61.0
3. Providence/Warwick, RI	60.0
4. Boston/Cambridge/Newton, MA	60.0
5. Hartford/West Hartford/East Hartford, CT	58.0
6. Milwaukee/Waukesha/West Ellis	57.0
7. Miami/Ft. Lauderdale/West Palm Beach	56.0
8. Chicago/Naperville/Elgin	56.0

ASIAN–WHITE

1. Edison/New Brunswick, NJ	53.7
2. New York/White Plains	49.5
3. Houston	48.7
4. Los Angeles/Long Beach	47.6
5. Boston	47.4
6. Sacramento, CA	46.8
7. San Francisco	46.7
8. Warren/Farmington Hills, MI	46.3

Note: The higher the value, the more segregated the metropolitan area. Data are 2011–2015 except for Asian–White data, which are for 2010.

SOURCE: Frey 2016; Logan and Stults 2011.

Over the past 40 years, Black–White segregation has declined modestly. Hispanic–White segregation, while lower, has not grown over the last 40 years. Asian–White segregation is even a bit lower but also has been mostly unchanged. Even when we consider social class, the patterns of minority segregation persist. Despite the occasional multiracial neighborhood, segregation prevails (Massey 2016; Rugh and Massey 2014).

This focus on metropolitan areas should not cause us to ignore the continuing legally sanctioned segregation of Native Americans on reservations. Although the majority of our nation's first inhabitants live outside these tribal areas, the reservations play a prominent role in the identity of Native Americans. Although it is easier to maintain tribal identity on the reservation, economic and educational opportunities are more limited in these areas, which are segregated from the rest of society.

A particularly troubling pattern has been the emergence of **resegregation**, or the physical separation of racial and ethnic groups reappearing after a period of relative integration. Resegregation has occurred in neighborhoods and schools after a transitional period of desegregation. For example, in 1954, only one in 100,000 Black students attended a majority White school in the South. Thanks to the civil rights movement and a series of civil rights measures, by 1968, Black student attendance in White-majority schools rose to 23 percent and then to 47 percent by 1988. The latest analysis, however, shows continuing racial isolation. A 2014 report documents that nationwide, school segregation prevails. As the minority population has grown, such as in the suburbs recently, segregation has soared (Orfield and Frankenberg 2014).

Given segregation patterns, many Whites in the United States have limited contact with people of other racial and ethnic backgrounds. One study of 100 affluent powerful White men looked at their experiences, past and present, and determined that they had lived in a "White bubble"—their neighborhoods, schools, elite colleges, and workplaces were overwhelmingly White. The continuing pattern of segregation in the United States means our diverse population grows up in very different nations. For many urban Blacks and Latinos, segregation in neighborhoods with limited job opportunities is a social fact (Bonilla-Silva and Embrick 2007; Feagin and O'Brien 2003; Massey 2012).

Segregation by race, ethnicity, religion, tribal or clan affiliation, and sometimes even language grouping occurs throughout the world. The most dramatic government-engineered segregation in recent history was in South Africa. In 1948, Great Britain granted South Africa its independence, and the National Party, dominated by a White minority, assumed control of the government. The rule of White supremacy, well under way as the custom in the colonial period, became more and more formalized into law. To deal with the multiracial population, the Whites devised a policy called apartheid to ensure their dominance. *Apartheid* (in Afrikaans, the language of the White Afrikaners, it means *separation* or *apartness*) came to mean a policy of separate development, euphemistically called *multinational development* by the government. Black South Africans were relegated to impoverished urban townships or rural areas, and their mobility within the country was strictly regulated. Events took a significant turn in 1990, when the South African prime minister legalized once-banned Black organizations and freed Nelson Mandela, leader of the African National Congress (ANC), after 27 years of imprisonment. Soon afterward, Mandela became head of the government, and a half-century of apartheid came to an end.

Fusion

Fusion occurs when a minority and a majority group combine to form a new group. This combining can be expressed as A + B + C → D, where A, B, and C represent the groups present in a society and D signifies the result, an ethnocultural–racial group that shares some of the characteristics of each initial group. Mexican people are an example of fusion, originating as they do from the mixing of Spanish and indigenous Indian cultures. Theoretically, fusion does not entail intermarriage, but it is very similar to **amalgamation**, the process by which a dominant group and a subordinate group combine through intermarriage into a new people. In everyday speech, the words *fusion* and *amalgamation* are rarely used, but the concept is expressed in the notion of a human **melting pot** in which diverse racial or ethnic groups form a new creation, a new cultural entity (Newman 1973).

The analogy of the cauldron, the "melting pot," was first used to describe the United States by the French observer Crèvecoeur in 1782. The phrase dates back to the Middle Ages, when alchemists attempted to change less-valuable metals into gold and silver. Similarly, the idea of the human melting pot implied that the new group would represent only the best qualities and attributes of the different cultures contributing to it. The belief in the United States as a melting pot became widespread in the early twentieth century. This belief suggested that the United States had an almost divine mission to destroy artificial divisions and create a single kind of human. However, the dominant group had indicated its unwillingness to welcome such groups as Native Americans, Blacks, Hispanics, Jews, Asians, and Irish Catholics into the melting pot. It is a mistake to think of the United States as an ethnic melting pot. Although superficial signs of fusion are present, as in a cuisine that includes sauerkraut and spaghetti, most contributions of subordinate groups are ignored (Gleason 1980).

Marriage patterns indicate the resistance to fusion. People are unwilling, in varying degrees, to marry outside their own ethnic, religious, and racial groups. Until relatively recently, interracial marriage was outlawed in much of the United States. At the time that President Barack Obama's White mother and Black father were married in Hawai'i, their union would have been illegal in 22 other states. Surveys show that 20 to 50 percent of various White ethnic groups report single ancestry. When White ethnics do cross boundaries, they tend to marry within their religion and social class. For example, Italians are more likely to marry Irish, who are also Catholic, than they are to marry Protestant Swedes.

Although it may seem that interracial matches are everywhere, there is only modest evidence of a fusion of races in the United States. Nonetheless, racial

While still not typical, more couples are crossing racial and ethnic boundaries in the United States today than in any previous generation. Clearly, this trend will increase the potential for their children to identify as biracial or multiracial rather than in a single category.

intermarriage has been increasing. In 1980, there were 651,000 interracial marriages, but by 2010, there were 5.4 million. By 2015, about 10 percent of people married someone of a different race or ethnicity. Among unmarried couples, the number rises to 14 percent and among same-sex couples to 15 percent.

Among couples in which at least one member is Hispanic, marriages with a non-Hispanic partner account for 28 percent. Taken together, all interracial and Hispanic–non-Hispanic marriages account for 10 percent of married opposite-sex couples today. But this number includes people who have been married for decades. Among new couples, about 17 percent of marriages are between people of different races or between Hispanics and non-Hispanics (Bialik 2017; Bureau of the Census 2010a: Table 60; Lofquist et al. 2012).

Assimilation

Assimilation is the process by which a subordinate individual or group takes on the characteristics of the dominant group and is eventually accepted as part of that group. Assimilation is a majority ideology in which A + B + C → A. The majority (A) dominates in such a way that the minorities (B and C) become indistinguishable from the dominant group. Assimilation dictates conformity to the dominant group, regardless of how many racial, ethnic, or religious groups are involved (Newman 1973:53).

To be complete, assimilation must entail an active effort by the minority-group individual to shed all distinguishing actions and beliefs and the unqualified acceptance of that individual by the dominant society. In the United States, dominant White society encourages assimilation. The assimilation perspective tends to devalue alien culture and to treasure the dominant. For example, assimilation assumes that whatever is admirable among Blacks was adapted from Whites and that whatever is bad is inherently Black. The assimilation solution to Black–White conflict has been typically defined as the development of a consensus around White American values.

Assimilation is very difficult. The person being assimilated must forsake his or her cultural tradition to become part of a different, often antagonistic culture. However, cross-border movement is often preceded by adjustments and awareness of the culture that awaits the immigrant. Furthermore, the dominant group, White Americans in this case, totally defines what is an acceptable level of assimilation (Schachter 2016, Skrentny 2008).

Assimilation does not occur at the same pace for all groups or for all individuals in the same group. Typically, the assimilation process is not completed by the first generation—the new arrivals.

One aspect of assimilation is immigrants' attempt to learn the language of the host society, as shown in this adult bilingual education class.

Assimilation is not a smooth process (Warner and Srole 1945) and tends to take longer under the following conditions:

- The differences between the minority and the majority are large.
- The majority is not receptive, or the minority retains its own culture.
- The minority group arrives over a short period of time.
- The minority-group residents are concentrated rather than dispersed.
- The arrival is recent, and the homeland is accessible.

Segmented assimilation describes the outcome of immigrants and their descendants moving into different classes of the host society. It emphasizes that there is not a single, uniform lifestyle in the United States and that much assimilation is into the working or even lower classes. For a very small number of people, such as high-level and elite engineers and other professionals, the movement might be into the higher reaches of class divisions. However, for many, assimilation may be into a lower class than that enjoyed in their home country and may represent downward mobility even while assimilation progresses (Haller, Portes, and Lynch 2011).

Many people view assimilation as unfair or even dictatorial. However, most members of the dominant group believe it is reasonable that subordinate people shed their distinctive cultural traditions. In public discussions today, assimilation is the ideology of the dominant group in forcing people how to act. Consequently, the social institutions in the United States—the educational system, economy, government, religion, and medical establishment—all push toward assimilation, with only occasional references to the pluralist approach, which we discuss next.

The Pluralist Perspective

Thus far, we have concentrated on how subordinate groups cease to exist (removal) or take on the characteristics of the dominant group (assimilation). The alternative to these relationships between the majority and the minority is pluralism. **Pluralism** implies that various groups in a society have mutual respect for one another's culture, a respect that allows minorities to express their own culture without suffering prejudice or discrimination. Whereas the assimilationist or integrationist seeks the elimination of ethnic boundaries, the pluralist believes in maintaining many of them.

There are limits to cultural freedom. A Romanian immigrant to the United States cannot expect to avoid learning English and still move up the occupational ladder. To survive, a society must have a consensus among its members on basic ideals, values, and beliefs. Nevertheless, there is still plenty of room for variety. Earlier, fusion was described as $A + B + C \rightarrow D$ and assimilation as $A + B + C \rightarrow A$. Using this same scheme, we can think of pluralism as $A + B + C \rightarrow A + B + C$, with groups coexisting in one society (Manning 1995; Newman 1973; Simpson 1995).

In the United States, cultural pluralism is more an ideal than a reality. Although there are instances of cultural pluralism—in the various ethnic neighborhoods in major cities, for instance—the general progression has been for subordinate groups to assimilate. Yet as the minority becomes the numerical majority, the ability to live one's identity becomes a bit easier. African Americans, Hispanics, American Indians, and Asian Pacific Americans already outnumber Whites in most of the largest U.S. cities.

The trend is toward even greater diversity. Nonetheless, the cost of cultural integrity throughout the nation's history has been high. The various Native American tribes have succeeded to a large extent in maintaining their heritage, but the price has been bare subsistence on federal reservations.

The United States is experiencing a reemergence of ethnic identification by groups that had previously expressed little interest in their heritage. Groups that make up the dominant majority also are reasserting their ethnic heritages. Various nationality groups are rekindling interest in almost-forgotten languages, customs, festivals, and traditions. In some instances, this expression of the past has taken the form of a protest against exclusion from the dominant society. For example, some Chinese youths chastise their elders for forgetting the old ways and accepting White American influence and control.

The most visible expression of pluralism is language use. As of 2015, more than one in every five people in the United States (21.5 percent) over age five spoke a language other than English at home (American Community Survey 2016a: Table B16001).

Facilitating a diverse and changing society affects just about every aspect of that society. Yet another nod to pluralism, although not nearly so obvious to the general population as language, are the changes within the funeral industry. Where Christian and Jewish funeral practices once dominated, funeral home professionals are now being trained to accommodate a variety of practices. Latinos often expect 24-hour viewing of their deceased, whereas Muslims may wish to participate in washing the deceased before burial in a grave pointing toward Mecca. Hindu and Buddhist requests to participate in cremation are now being respected (Brulliard 2006).

Resistance and Change

1.6 Describe how resistance and change occur in racial and ethnic relations.

By virtue of wielding power and influence, the dominant group may define the terms by which all members of society operate. This power is particularly evident in a slave society, but even in contemporary industrialized nations, the dominant group has a disproportionate role in shaping immigration policy, school curricula, and media content.

Subordinate groups do not merely accept the definitions and ideology proposed by the dominant group. A continuing theme in dominant–subordinate relations is the minority group's challenge to its subordination. Resistance by subordinate groups is well documented as they seek to promote change that will bring them more rights and privileges, if not true equality. Often, traditional notions of racial formation are overcome not only through panethnicity but also because Black people, along with Latinos and sympathetic Whites, join in the resistance to subordination (Moulder 1996; Winant 2004).

Resistance can be seen in efforts by racial and ethnic groups to maintain their identity through newspapers and organizations and in today's technological age through cable television stations, blogs, and Internet sites. Resistance manifests itself in social movements such as the civil rights movement, the feminist movement, and gay rights efforts. The passage of such legislation as the Age Discrimination Act or the Americans with Disabilities Act marks the success of oppressed groups in lobbying on their own behalf.

Through recent efforts of collective action, African Americans and others sympathetic to the #BlackLivesMatter campaign have drawn attention to violence against Black youth, as in this demonstration in Tampa in 2016.

Resistance efforts may begin with small actions. For example, residents of an American Indian reservation may question why a toxic waste dump is to be located on their land. Although the dump may bring in money, the reservation's residents question the wisdom of such a move. Their concerns lead to further investigations of the extent to which American Indian lands are used disproportionately as containment areas for dangerous materials. This action in turn leads to a broader investigation of the ways in which minority-group people often find their neighborhoods "hosting" dumps and incinerators. These local efforts eventually lead the Environmental Protection Agency to monitor the disproportionate placement of toxic facilities in or near racial and ethnic minority communities.

Social media platforms provide a new vehicle for resistance and change. For example, the 2013 acquittal of a man who shot to death Trayvon Martin, an unarmed African American youth, mobilized Blacks and other groups concerned about violence against Black youth. A national survey at the time showed that only 9 percent of African Americans were "satisfied" with the verdict, compared to 25 percent of Hispanics and 49 percent of Whites. Some 60 percent of Whites felt that race was got more attention than it deserved in news coverage of the story.

People throughout the United States organized to call attention to the perceived indiscriminate shooting deaths of Black youths. An activist movement using the hashtag #BlackLivesMatter surfaced and continued to gain strength with each ensuing incident that seemingly showed that a Black life did not matter to a law-enforcement officer. One such incident was the death of Philando Castile in St. Paul, Minnesota, described at the beginning of this chapter (Pew Research Center for the People and the Press 2013).

Change has occurred. At the beginning of the twentieth century, lynching of Blacks was practiced in many parts of the country. At the beginning of the twenty-first century, laws punishing hate crimes are increasingly common and cover a variety of stigmatized groups. Although this social progress should not be ignored, the nation still must focus concern on the significant social inequalities that remain.

An even more basic form of resistance is to question societal values. In this book, we avoid using the term *American* to describe people of the United States because geographically, Brazilians, Canadians, and El Salvadorans are Americans as well. It is easy to overlook how members of the dominant group and social institutions have shaped our understanding of history. African American studies scholar Molefi Kete Asante (2007, 2008, 2015) has called for an **Afrocentric perspective** that emphasizes the customs of African cultures and how they have pervaded the history, culture, and behavior of Blacks in the United States and around the world. Afrocentrism seeks to balance **Eurocentrism** and works toward a multiculturalist or pluralist orientation in which no viewpoint is suppressed. The Afrocentric approach could become part of our school curriculum, which has not adequately acknowledged the importance of this heritage (King and Swartz 2015).

The Afrocentric perspective has attracted much attention in education. Opponents view it as a separatist view of history and culture that distorts both past and present. Its supporters counter that African peoples everywhere can come to full self-determination only when they are able to overthrow the dominance of White or Eurocentric intellectual interpretations (Conyers 2004).

The remarkable efforts by members of racial and ethnic minorities working with supportive White Americans beginning in the 1950s through the early 1970s successfully targeted overt racist symbols, as well as racist and sexist actions. Today's targets are more intractable and tend to emerge from institutional discrimination. Sociologist Douglas Massey (2011) argued that a central goal must be to reform the criminal justice system by demanding repeal of the following: the three-strikes law, mandatory minimum sentencing, and harsher penalties for crack than for powdered cocaine. Such targets are quite different from laws that prevented Blacks and women from serving on juries.

Intersectionality

1.7 Define and describe intersectionality.

Race and ethnicity, as well as other social identifiers, are important and define relationships of power (or lack of power). Yet they do not exist in isolation. Rather, they coexist with religion, gender, age, disability status, and sexual identity (among other identities). **Intersectionality** refers to the overlapping and interdependent system of advantage and disadvantage that positions people in society on the basis of race, class, gender, and other characteristics (Collins and Bilge 2016; Crenshaw 1989).

Awareness of intersectionality grew as female scholars noted that an emphasis on race could ignore other related processes of domination. For example, many women experience social inequality not only because of their gender but also because of their race and ethnicity. These citizens face a double or triple subordinate status based on their intersecting identities. A disproportionate share of this low-status group also is poor. African American feminist Patricia Hill Collins (2000, 2013:232–234) views intersectionality as creating a *matrix of domination* (Figure 1.6). Whites dominate non-Whites, men dominate women, and the affluent dominate the poor—race, class, and gender are interconnected.

Gender, race, and social class are not the only systems of oppression, but they do profoundly affect women and people of color in the United States. Other forms of categorization and stigmatization can also be included in this matrix. If we turn to the global stage, we can add citizenship status and being perceived as a "colonial subject" even long after colonialism has ended.

Critics argue that intersectionality is all about people who are obsessed with "identity politics" and who form alliances based on allegedly shared social groupings. Yet intersectionality is not so much about the identities themselves but rather how society uses and abuses these identities to exclude and privilege different groups. Addressing exclusion and acknowledging privilege are not easy; they require change (Crenshaw 2015).

Figure 1.6 Intersectionality and the Matrix of Domination

Intersectionality illustrates how several social factors—including gender, social class, language spoken, and race and ethnicity—intersect and overlap to create a cumulative impact on a person's social standing.

Feminists have addressed themselves to the needs of minority women, but the oppression of these women because of their sex is overshadowed by the subordinate status that White men and White women impose on them because of their race or ethnicity. The question for the Latina (Hispanic woman), African American woman, Asian Pacific American woman, Native American woman, and so on appears to be whether she should unify with her brothers against racism or challenge them for their sexism. The answer is that society cannot afford to let up on the effort to eradicate sexism, racism, and the other forces that create social inequality.

Conclusion

One hundred years ago, sociologist and activist W. E. B. Du Bois took another famed Black activist, Booker T. Washington, to task for saying that the races could best work together apart, like fingers on a hand. Du Bois felt that Black people had to be a part of all social institutions and not create their own. With an African American having been elected and reelected to the presidency of the United States, Whites, African Americans, and other groups continue to debate what form society should take. Should we seek to bring everyone together into an integrated whole? Or do we strive to maintain as much of our group identities as possible while working as cooperatively as necessary?

In considering the inequalities present today, as we do in the chapters that follow, it is easy to forget how much change has taken place and how much progress has been made. Much of the resistance to prejudice and discrimination in the past, either to slavery or to women's prohibition from voting, came from the members of the dominant group. The indignities still experienced by subordinate groups continue to be resisted as subordinate groups and their allies in the dominant group seek further change.

In this chapter, we have attempted to organize our approach to subordinate–dominant relations in the United States. We observed that subordinate groups do not necessarily contain fewer members than the dominant group. Subordinate groups are classified into racial, ethnic, religious, and gender groups. Biological differences of race are not supported by scientific data. Yet as the continuing debate over standardized tests demonstrates, attempts to establish a biological meaning of race have not been swept entirely into the dustbin of history. The social meaning attached to physical differences remains very significant. The dominant group has defined racial differences in such a way as to encourage or discourage the progress of certain groups.

Subordinate-group members' reactions include the seeking of an alternative avenue to acceptance and success: "Why should we give up what we are, to be accepted by them?" In response to this question, individual ethnic identification remains strong. As a result of this maintenance of ethnic and racial identity, complementary and occasionally competing images of what it means to be a productive member of a single society persist. Pluralism describes a society in which several different groups coexist, with no dominant or subordinate groups. People individually choose which cultural patterns to keep and which to let go.

Subordinate groups have not and do not always accept their second-class status passively. They may protest, organize, revolt, and resist society as defined by the dominant group. Patterns of race and ethnic relations are changing, not stagnant. Indicative of the changing landscape, biracial and multiracial children present us with new definitions of identity emerging through a process of racial formation, reminding us that race is socially constructed. In addition, we assume or have placed upon us multiple social identities that intersect in a manner that may lead to social inequality.

Society is not static, but dynamic and evolving. In the twenty-first century, we are facing new challenges to cooperation. There has been such a marked increase in the population of minority racial and ethnic groups in the United States that these groups will be in the majority well before today's college students reach 40 years of age. Little wonder that scholars are now talking about "super-diversity" and considering whether past notions of race and ethnicity are passé (Bobo 2013).

Continuing immigration and the explosive growth of the Hispanic population—which has more than doubled since 1990—fuel this growth. Latinos are now such a significant portion of the U.S. population that the Spanish-language Telemundo network has introduced English-language subtitles to ensure that its Latino viewers can fully comprehend its programming.

Barack Obama's presidency was a significant period in U.S. history. The fact that he was the first African American (and also the first non-White man) to serve as president demonstrates how much progress the United States has achieved with regard to race relations. It also underscores how long it has taken to make this progress and how much more needs to be accomplished before the United States can truly be "a more perfect union," as stated in the Constitution.

Yet the issues are exceedingly complex. The #BlackLivesMatter movement has brought attention to wrongful deaths of African Americans at the hands of law enforcement and to the needs of the less powerful to be heard. As African American writer Ralph Ellison wrote, "I am invisible, understand, simply because people refuse to see me." Black filmmaker Spike Lee supports the movement but believes we must also talk about the "self-inflicted genocide" of Black-on-Black crime (Smith 2015).

The problems are complex, as are the solutions, but this reality should not freeze us into inaction. The two significant forces that are absent in a truly pluralistic society are prejudice and discrimination. In an assimilation society, prejudice disparages out-group differences, and discrimination financially rewards those who shed their past. In the next two chapters, we explore the nature of prejudice and discrimination in the United States.

Summary of Learning Objectives

1.1 Explain how people are placed in groups.

1. When sociologists define a minority group, they are concerned primarily with the economic and political power, or powerlessness, of the group.
2. A racial group is set apart from others primarily by physical characteristics; an ethnic group is set apart primarily by national origin or cultural patterns.

1.2 Explain the social construction of race.

3. People cannot be sorted into distinct racial groups, so race is best viewed as a social construct that is subject to different interpretations over time.
4. A small but still significant number of people in the United States—more than 9 million—readily see themselves as having a biracial or multiracial identity.

1.3 Describe how sociology helps us understand race and ethnicity.

5. The study of race and ethnicity in the United States often considers the role played by class and gender.
6. We can use three sociological schools of thought to gain insight into racial and ethnic groups and their relationships to the dominant society: the functionalist perspective, the conflict perspective, and labeling theory.

1.4 Explain how subordinate groups are created.

7. Subordinate-group status has emerged through migration, annexation, and colonialism.
8. The Spectrum of Intergroup Relations illustrates the patterns between racial and ethnic groups ranging from those that are extremely harsh to those that are more tolerated.

1.5 Summarize the consequences of subordinate-group status.

9. The social consequences of subordinate-group status include extermination, expulsion, secession, segregation, fusion, assimilation, and pluralism.

1.6 Describe how resistance and change occur in racial and ethnic relations.

10. Racial, ethnic, and other minorities maintain a long history of resisting efforts to restrict their rights.

1.7 Define and describe intersectionality.

11. The intersectionality of overlapping identities plays a role in placing a person in a society's hierarchy.

Key Terms

Afrocentric perspective, *page 32*
amalgamation, *page 28*
annexation, *page 22*
apartheid, *page 25*
assimilation, *page 29*
biological race, *page 10*
blaming the victim, *page 19*
class, *page 16*
colonialism, *page 22*

colorism, *page 7*
conflict perspective, *page 18*
dysfunction, *page 18*
emigration, *page 21*
ethnic cleansing, *page 24*
ethnic group, *page 7*
eugenics, *page 10*
Eurocentrism, *page 33*
functionalist perspective, *page 17*
fusion, *page 28*
genocide, *page 23*
globalization, *page 22*
Holocaust, *page 23*
immigration, *page 21*
intelligence quotient (IQ), *page 11*
intersectionality, *page 33*
labeling theory, *page 19*
marginality, *page 15*
melting pot, *page 28*
migration, *page 21*
minority group, *page 5*
panethnicity, *page 15*
pluralism, *page 30*
racial formation, *page 13*
racial group, *page 7*
racism, *page 12*
resegregation, *page 27*
segmented assimilation, *page 30*
segregation, *page 25*
self-fulfilling prophecy, *page 20*
sociology, *page 16*
stereotype, *page 19*
stratification, *page 16*
world systems theory, *page 23*

Review Questions

1. What are the characteristics of subordinate and minority groups?
2. Distinguish between racial groups and ethnic groups.
3. How do biracial and multiracial categories call into question traditional groupings in the United States?
4. How do the conflict, functionalist, and labeling approaches apply to the social construction of race?
5. How do subordinate groups emerge?
6. Characterize the range of intergroup relations from those that are most tolerated to those that are most unacceptable to minority groups. Provide a brief definition of each point along the spectrum of intergroup relations.
7. What roles do subordinate groups play in their own destiny?
8. What is meant by "intersectionality"?

Critical Thinking

1. How do the concepts of "biracial" and "multiracial" relate to W. E. B. Du Bois's notion of a "color line"?
2. How diverse is your town or city? Can you see evidence that some group is being subordinated? What social construction of categories do you see that may be different in your community compared to elsewhere?
3. Select a racial or ethnic group and apply the Spectrum of Intergroup Relations. Can you provide an example today or in the past where each relationship occurs?
4. Identify some protest and resistance efforts by subordinated groups in your area. Have they been successful? Even though some people say they favor equality, why may they be uncomfortable with such efforts? How can people unconnected with such efforts either help or hinder such protests?
5. How does intersectionality enhance our understanding of race and ethnicity?

Chapter 2
Prejudice

Photo credit: Timothy Jacobsen/AP Images

Learning Objectives

2.1 Differentiate between prejudice and discrimination.

2.2 Explain White privilege.

2.3 Summarize the theories of prejudice.

2.4 Define and explain stereotyping.

2.5 Understand color-blind racism.

2.6 Discuss how members of subordinate groups respond to prejudice.

2.7 Explain the ways prejudice can be reduced.

Finding a job with a living wage can be a challenge. Government funds to help the jobless get by while they look for work or training opportunities are limited. So, imagine you are in charge of allocating government assistance, and you want the money to be effective.

A recent study gave a nationwide sample of 1,000 participants the choice to extend $1,500 of assistance to applicants—some with an excellent work ethic, others with a poor work ethic—based on a completed questionnaire. Study participants also had the alternative not to spend the money and thereby help to reduce the state's budget deficit—another very real challenge. Oh, and the study participants received another piece of information besides the assessment of the person's work ethic: the applicants' names—either Laurie and Latoya or Emily and Keisha.

The results of the study were clear. Not surprisingly, hard workers were given more assistance than those judged to be low-quality workers. Faced with a "lazy" recipient, the hypothetical decision-makers were more likely to use the money to offset the budget deficit. However, what seemed to make the real difference was the name on the application. Hardworking Emily was given ten times as much money as hardworking Keisha. Similarly, lazy Laurie received much more than lazy Latoya. In fact, money allocated to the lazy applicant with the White-sounding name came close to what the hardworking Black could expect to be awarded.

In summary, Keisha and Latoya were not evaluated as positively as Emily and Laurie, and the applicants with Black-sounding names were more likely to have assistance withheld (DeSante 2013).

Prejudice is so prevalent that it is tempting to consider it inevitable or, even more broadly, part of human nature. Such a view ignores its variability from individual to individual and from society to society. Not everyone punished Keisha and rewarded Emily. People learn prejudice as children before they exhibit it as adults. Therefore, prejudice is a social phenomenon, an acquired characteristic. A truly pluralistic society would lack unfavorable distinctions caused by prejudicial attitudes toward and among racial and ethnic groups.

Holding ill feelings based on a person's race or ethnicity is cause for concern because the United States is so increasingly diverse. Figure 2.1 shows the increase in minority presence in the first decade

Figure 2.1 Change in Minority Population by County, 2000–2010

The minority population has grown across the United States, even in many areas that previously had few racial and ethnic minorities.

SOURCE: Data from Humes, Jones, and Ramirez 2011:21.

Percentage change
- 57.6 or more
- 28.8 to 57.5
- 0.0 to 28.7
- −9.9 to −0.1
- Less then −9.9
- Fewer than 1,000 minority
- Not comparable

of the twenty-first century. Many counties far removed from urban centers, as well as areas with historically large Black and Latino populations, saw minority population increases between 2000 and 2010. The likelihood that prejudices will be expressed, dealt with, or hidden increases and becomes a nationwide phenomenon as more and more communities experience majority-minority interaction.

Ill feeling among groups of different races, ethnicities, or cultures may result from **ethnocentrism**, the tendency to believe that one's culture and way of life are superior to all others. The ethnocentric person judges other groups and other cultures by the standards of his or her own group. This attitude makes it quite easy for people to view other cultures as inferior. Within the United States, we see a woman wearing a veil and may regard her as strange and backward, yet we are baffled when other societies think U.S. women in short skirts are dressed inappropriately. Ethnocentrism and other expressions of prejudice are often voiced, and such expressions sometimes become the motivation for criminal acts.

A very troubling part of contemporary life in the United States and elsewhere is the rise of organized hate groups. Research indicates a fluctuating but larger number of hate groups than a decade ago (Figure 2.2). The Internet and social media platforms give these groups visibility far beyond their numbers. Hate groups include White supremacists, neo-Confederates, and neo-Nazis, as well as anti-White, anti-Jewish Black supremacist minority groups. Collectively, these hate groups target Muslims, immigrants, racial and ethnic groups, and the lesbian, gay, bisexual, and transgender (LGBT) community (Potok 2016; Wines and Saul 2015).

Figure 2.2 Active Hate Groups, 1999–2016

The number of hate and extremist groups has fluctuated over the past 15 years but has remained at well over 750 for several years.

SOURCE: Data from Southern Poverty Law Center 2017.

Prejudice and Discrimination

2.1 Differentiate between prejudice and discrimination.

Prejudice and discrimination are related concepts but are not the same. **Prejudice** is a negative attitude toward an entire category of people. The important components in this definition are *attitude* and *entire category*. Prejudice involves attitudes, thoughts, and beliefs—not actions. Prejudice often is expressed using **ethnophaulisms**, or ethnic slurs, which include derisive nicknames such as *honky, gook,* and *wetback*. Ethnophaulisms also include speaking to or about members of a particular group in a condescending way, such as saying, "José does well in school for a Mexican American" or referring to a middle-aged woman as "one of the girls."

A prejudiced belief leads to categorical rejection. Prejudice does not mean you dislike someone because you find his or her behavior objectionable; rather, it means you dislike an entire racial or ethnic group, even if you have had little or no contact with that group. A college student is not prejudiced because he requests a room change after three weeks of enduring his roommate's sleeping all day, playing loud music all night, and piling garbage on his desk. However, he is displaying prejudice if he requests a change after arriving at school and learning that his new roommate is of a specific nationality.

Even short-lived expressions of prejudice can be very hostile. **Microaggressions** are the commonplace daily verbal indignities that members of a minority group experience—for example, calling on a Latina classmate or coworker to comment on immigration policy, or telling a prospective Black job candidate, "I believe the most qualified person should get the job. Regardless of race." Microaggressions can be intentional or unintentional, and the perpetrator is often unaware of the insult (Sue 2010).

Prejudice is a belief or attitude; discrimination is action. **Discrimination** is the denial of opportunities and equal rights to individuals and groups as a result of prejudice or for other arbitrary reasons. Unlike prejudice, discrimination involves *behavior* that excludes members of a group from certain rights, opportunities, or privileges. Like prejudice, it is categorical, with a few rare exceptions. If an employer refuses to hire an illiterate Italian American as a computer analyst, that is not discrimination. If an employer refuses to hire all Italian Americans because he thinks they are incompetent and makes no effort to determine if an Italian American applicant is qualified, that is discrimination.

Prejudice is a complicated aspect of human behavior and has been extensively researched. For a sample of some fascinating research on prejudice, consider the Research Focus, "Virtual Prejudice and Anti-Prejudice," which explores online expressions of prejudice.

Merton's Typology

Prejudice does not necessarily coincide with discriminatory behavior. In exploring the relationship between negative attitudes and negative behavior, sociologist Robert Merton (1949, 1976) identified four major categories (Figure 2.3). The label added to each of Merton's categories may more readily identify the type of person described:

1. The unprejudiced nondiscriminator—or all-weather liberal
2. The unprejudiced discriminator—or reluctant liberal

Research Focus

Virtual Prejudice and Anti-Prejudice

Increasingly larger portions of our daily lives are spent not directly talking with or seeing other people but rather online, in front of our phones, iPads, and computers. Sometimes we indirectly communicate with friends through social media, but many Americans also spend a large amount of time in some virtual world (such as Second Life) separated from reality. What impact can online activities have on reinforcing or undercutting prejudice?

Researchers have looked at video games and found that minorities are vastly underrepresented, and when they do appear it is usually as thugs or athletes. In addition, White players are more likely to recall Black characters as violent and aggressive.

Nonetheless, virtual society can seek to have a positive impact on race and ethnic relations. User-generated video sites (such as YouTube) abound with videos reflecting favorable representations of racial and ethnic groups. For example, one study found that images of American Indians tend to evoke positive responses in online comments. However, viewers seemed most positive when videos were historical rather than dealing with present-day situations. And if ill treatment toward contemporary Native Americans was central to the video, negative comments began to escalate.

The complexity of online representations and prejudice is highlighted in a May 2013 Cheerios advertisement. In the 30-second spot, a White mom tells her biracial daughter that Cheerios is heart-healthy. The six-year-old then scampers into the next room, spilling Cheerios on her Black father's chest while he is napping on the living-room couch. The comments were 10–1 favorable toward the biracial household, but General Mills was forced to disable the comment section because of all the racist remarks that were posted.

Researchers of online prejudice admit the depth of hostility is difficult to assess because many commercial venues and news outlets monitor comments (often at considerable expense) and selectively delete offensive comments, thus giving the casual online user an inaccurate view of how the general public is responding to racially charged topics. It also appears that many who wish to express racist views are retreating to Web sites where such rhetoric will not be challenged. As in everyday life, one cannot assume that the absence of overt prejudice means tolerance.

In the United States, with its historical support and constitutional safeguards for freedom of speech, the government is largely uninvolved in trying to limit online bigotry. However, this is not true everywhere. Germany limits anti-Semitic or pro-Nazi sentiments, and German lawmakers demanded in 2016 that Facebook do more to monitor and censor online hate speech.

Sources: Burgess et al. 2011; Hughley and Daniels 2013; Kenji America 2013; Kopacz and Lawton 2013; Nudd 2013; Scott and Eddy 2016.

---

3. The prejudiced nondiscriminator—or timid bigot
4. The prejudiced discriminator—or all-weather bigot

As the term is used in types 1 and 2, *liberals* are committed to equality among people. The all-weather liberal believes in equality and practices it. Merton was quick to observe that all-weather liberals may be far removed from any real contact with subordinate groups such as African Americans or women. Furthermore, such people may be content with their own behavior and do little to change it. The reluctant liberal is not completely committed to equality between groups. Social pressure may

Figure 2.3 Prejudice and Discrimination
As Robert Merton's typology shows, prejudice and discrimination are related but are not the same.

	Nondiscriminator	Discriminator
Unprejudiced	Type 1 — All-weather liberal	Type 2 — Reluctant liberal
Prejudiced	Type 3 — Timid bigot	Type 4 — All-weather bigot

cause such a person to discriminate. For example, fear of losing employees may lead a manager to avoid promoting women to supervisory capacities. Equal-opportunity legislation may be the best way to influence a reluctant liberal.

Types 3 and 4 do not believe in equal treatment for racial and ethnic groups, but they vary in their willingness to act. The timid bigot, type 3, will not discriminate if discrimination costs money or reduces profits, or if peers or the government apply pressure against engaging in discrimination. The all-weather bigot acts without hesitation on the prejudiced beliefs he or she holds.

White Privilege

2.2 Explain White privilege.

Being White is not the same as being Black or Latino. Being White in the United States may not ensure success and wealth, but it does limit encounters with intolerance.

White privilege refers to the rights or immunities granted as a particular benefit or favor for being White. This advantage exists unconsciously and is often invisible to the White people who enjoy it (Ferber 2008). Returning to the research described at the beginning of the chapter, we saw how easily Emily and Laurie were privileged over Latoya and Keisha in being awarded government assistance.

Scholar Peggy McIntosh of the Wellesley College Center for Research on Women looked at the privilege that comes from being White and the added privilege of being male. The other side of racial oppression is the privilege enjoyed by dominant groups. Being White or being successful in establishing a White identity carries with it distinct advantages. Among those that McIntosh (1988) identified were the following:

- Being considered financially reliable when using checks, credit cards, or cash
- Taking a job without having coworkers suspect that employment came about because of race
- Never having to speak for all the people of your race
- Watching television or reading a newspaper and seeing people of your own race widely represented
- Speaking effectively in a large group without being called a credit to your race
- Assuming that if legal or medical help is needed, your race will not work against you

Privilege being automatically extended to White people is not an exclusively U.S. phenomenon. Researchers in Australia conducted more than 1,500 observations of young adults, some White and some Black. The young adults boarded a public bus and tried to use a fare card that was out of money to reach a bus stop a mile or two away. In every case, the rider said, "I do not have any money, but I need to get to that stop." Overall, 72 percent of the White would-be riders were allowed to ride free, compared to 36 percent of the people of color. Curiously, even Black bus drivers extended the privilege to Whites, though they were a bit more likely to extend the same opportunity (to ride the bus for free) to Blacks. However, we do not know what the bus drivers were thinking. Were they more likely to view non-White riders with suspicion? Did they consider the White passengers more honest (Mujcic and Frijters 2013)?

Typically, White people do not see themselves as privileged in the way many African Americans and Latinos see themselves as disadvantaged. When asked to comment on their "Whiteness," they are unaware that they go about their daily lives without experiencing microaggressions. White people most likely see themselves as devoid of ethnicity ("no longer Irish," for example), stigmatized as racist, and victims of reverse discrimination. In short, many White people are unaware of the White privilege that informs their lives.

White privilege in action: A recent study showed that bus drivers in Australia were twice as likely to allow Whites to board a bus even though they could not pay the fare.

Theories of Prejudice

2.3 Summarize the theories of prejudice.

Prejudice is learned. Friends, relatives, newspapers, books, movies, television, and the Internet all teach it. Awareness of the differences among people that society judges to be important begins at an early age. Several theories have been advanced to explain the rejection of certain groups in a society. We examine four theoretical explanations. The first two, scapegoating and the authoritarian personality, are psychological and emphasize why a particular person harbors ill feelings toward a specific racial or ethnic group. The second two, exploitation theory and the normative approach, are sociological and view prejudice in the context of our interaction in a larger society.

Scapegoating Theory

People use some expressions of prejudice to blame others and to refuse to accept responsibility. **Scapegoating theory** says that prejudiced people believe they are society's victims.

The term *scapegoat* comes from a biblical injunction in which God told the Hebrews to send a goat into the wilderness to symbolically carry away the people's sins. Similarly, the theory of scapegoating suggests that rather than accepting guilt for some personal failure, a prejudiced person transfers the blame for failure to a vulnerable group.

In the major tragic twentieth-century example, Adolf Hitler used the Jews as scapegoats for all German social and economic ills in the 1930s. This scapegoating led to the passage of laws restricting Jewish life in pre–World War II Germany and eventually escalated into the mass extermination of Europe's Jews. Scapegoating of Jews persists today. A national survey in 2009 showed that one out of four people in the United States blame "the Jews" for the financial crisis that launched the Great Recession that began in 2008. **Anti-Semitism**—anti-Jewish prejudice and discrimination—remains a very real phenomenon (Malhotra and Margalit 2009).

Today in the United States, both legal and illegal immigrants often are blamed for "real" Americans' failure to secure jobs or desirable housing. The immigrant becomes the

The changing racial and ethnic composition in the United States means that the groups who are viewed as scapegoats or who are exploited changes as well. In the 2008 motion picture *Gran Torino*, Clint Eastwood portrays a bitter retired auto worker who is suspicious of his Hmong neighbors in Detroit but comes to appreciate their willingness to help and their strong family values. The Hmong ethnic group came to the United States as refugees from Laos and Cambodia, fearing reprisals for assisting the United States during the Vietnam War.

scapegoat for one's own lack of skills, planning, or motivation. It is so much easier to blame someone else.

Authoritarian Personality Theory

Prejudice may be influenced by one's upbringing and the lessons taught—and learned—early in life. Several efforts have been made to detail the prejudiced personality, but the most comprehensive effort culminated in a book titled *The Authoritarian Personality* (Adorno et al. 1950). Using a variety of tests and relying on more than 2,000 respondents ranging from middle-class Whites to inmates of San Quentin State Prison (in California), the authors claimed they had isolated the characteristics of the authoritarian personality.

In Adorno and colleagues' view, the **authoritarian personality** has basic characteristics that make him or her likely to be prejudiced. The authoritarian personality adheres to conventional values, practices uncritical acceptance of authority, and is concerned with power and toughness. The authoritarian personality is also characterized by aggressiveness toward people who do not conform to conventional norms or obey authority. According to the researchers, this personality type develops from the experience of harsh discipline in early childhood. A child with an authoritarian upbringing is obedient to authority figures and then later treats others as he or she had been raised to treat them.

This study has been widely criticized, but the very existence of such wide criticism indicates the study's influence. Critics have attacked the study's equation of authoritarianism with right-wing politics (because liberals also can be rigid); its failure to recognize that prejudice is more closely related to other individual traits, such as social class, than to authoritarianism as it was defined; the research methods used; and the emphasis on extreme racial prejudice rather than on more common expressions of hostility.

Despite these concerns about the study, which was completed more than 60 years ago, annual conferences continue to draw attention to how authoritarian attitudes contribute to racism, sexism, and even torture (Kinloch 1974; O'Neill 2008).

Exploitation Theory

Racial prejudice is often used to justify keeping a group in a subordinate economic position. Conflict theorists, in particular, stress the role of racial and ethnic hostility as a way for the dominant group to keep its status and power intact. Indeed, even the less affluent White working class uses prejudice to minimize competition from upwardly mobile minorities.

This **exploitation theory** is part of the Marxist tradition in sociological thought. Nineteenth-century philosopher Karl Marx emphasized exploitation of the lower class as an integral part of capitalism. Similarly, the exploitation or conflict approach explains how racism can stigmatize a group as inferior to justify the exploitation of that group. As developed by Oliver Cox (1942), exploitation theory saw prejudice against Blacks as an extension of the inequality faced by the entire lower class.

The exploitation theory of prejudice is persuasive. Japanese Americans were the object of little prejudice until they began to enter occupations that brought them into competition with Whites. The movement to keep Chinese out of the United States became strongest during the late nineteenth century, when Chinese immigrants and Whites fought over dwindling numbers of jobs. Both the enslavement of African Americans and the forced westward movement of Native Americans were economically motivated to a significant degree.

Table 2.1 Theories of Prejudice

No single explanation of why prejudice exists is satisfactory, but several approaches taken together offer insight.

Theory	Explanation	Example
Scapegoating	People blame others for their own failures.	An unsuccessful applicant assumes that a minority member or a woman got "his" job.
Authoritarian Personality	Authoritarian parents lead their children to develop intolerance.	A rigid person dislikes people who are different.
Exploitation Theory	People use others unfairly for economic advantage.	A minority member is hired at a lower wage level.
Normative Approach	Peer and social influences encourage tolerance or intolerance.	A person from an intolerant household is more likely to be openly prejudiced.

Normative Approach

Although personality factors are important contributors to prejudice, normative or situational factors also play a role. The **normative approach** takes the view that prejudice is influenced by societal norms and situations that encourage or discourage the tolerance of minorities.

Analysis reveals how societal influences shape a climate for tolerance or intolerance. Societies develop social norms that dictate not only what foods are desirable (or forbidden) but also what racial and ethnic groups are to be favored (or despised). Social forces operate in a society to encourage or discourage tolerance. The force may be widespread, such as the pressure on White Southerners to oppose racial equality even when slavery or segregation was the norm, which would seem to make concerns about equality irrelevant. The influence of social norms may be limited, such as when one man finds himself becoming more sexist as he competes with three women for a position in a prestigious law firm.

The four approaches to prejudice, summarized in Table 2.1, are not mutually exclusive. Social circumstances provide cues regarding the attitudes that a person should adopt; personality determines the extent to which people follow social cues and the likelihood that they will encourage others to do the same. Societal norms may promote or deter tolerance; personality traits suggest the degree to which a person will conform to norms of intolerance. To understand prejudice, we must use all four approaches together.

Stereotypes

2.4 Define and explain stereotyping.

On Christmas Day 2001, Arab American Walied Shater boarded an American Airlines flight from Baltimore to Dallas carrying a gun. The cockpit crew refused to let him fly, fearing that Shater would take over the plane and use it as a weapon of mass destruction. However, Shater carried documentation identifying him as a Secret Service agent, and calls to Washington, D.C., confirmed that he was flying to join a presidential protection force at President George W. Bush's ranch in Texas. Nevertheless, the crew could not get past the stereotype of Arab American men posing a lethal threat (Leavitt 2002).

What Are Stereotypes?

In Chapter 1, we saw that stereotypes play a powerful role in how people come to view dominant and subordinate groups. **Stereotypes** are unreliable generalizations about all members of a group and do not take individual differences into account. Numerous scientific studies have been conducted on these exaggerated images. This research has shown people's willingness to assign positive and negative traits to entire groups of people, which are then applied to particular individuals. Stereotyping causes people to view Blacks as superstitious, Whites as uncaring, and Jews as shrewd. Over the past 80 years of research, social scientists have found that people have become less willing to express such views openly, but prejudice persists (Quillian 2006).

If stereotypes are exaggerated generalizations, then why are they so widely held, and why are some traits assigned more often than others? Evidence for traits may arise out of real conditions. For example, more Puerto Ricans live in poverty than Whites, so the prejudiced mind associates Puerto Ricans with laziness. According to the New Testament, some Jews were responsible for the crucifixion of Jesus, so to the prejudiced mind, all Jews are Christ killers. Some activists in the women's movement are lesbians, so all feminists are seen as lesbians. From a kernel of fact, faulty generalization creates a stereotype.

Labeling individuals with negative stereotypes has strong implications for the self-fulfilling prophecy (discussed in Chapter 1). Studies show that people are all too aware of the negative images others have of them. When asked to estimate the prevalence of hard-core racism among Whites, one in four Blacks agrees that more than half of White people "personally share the attitudes of groups like the Ku Klux Klan toward Blacks." Only one Black in ten says "only a few" White people hold such views. Stereotypes not only influence how people feel about themselves but also affect how people interact with others. If people feel that others hold incorrect, disparaging attitudes toward them, then harmonious relations become increasingly unlikely (Sigelman and Tuch 1997).

Although explicit expressions of stereotypes are becoming less common, it is much too soon to write the obituary of racial and ethnic stereotypes. In addition, stereotyping is not limited to racial and ethnic groups. Other groups are subjected to stereotyping. Probably the most common stereotypes in daily life and the mass media are sexist stereotypes. **Sexism** is the ideology that one sex (male) is superior to the other (female). Images and descriptions of women and even girls often reinforce sexism. **Homophobia**, the fear of and prejudice toward homosexuals, is present in every facet of life: the family, organized religion, the workplace, and the mass media. Like the myths and stereotypes of race and gender, those about homosexuality keep gay men and lesbians oppressed as a group and may also prevent sympathetic members of the dominant group, the heterosexual community, from supporting them. We next consider the use of stereotypes in the contemporary practice of racial profiling.

Stereotyping in Action: Racial Profiling

In recent years, the government has given its attention to a social phenomenon with a long history: racial profiling. According to the Department of Justice, **racial profiling** is any police-initiated action based on race, ethnicity, or national origin rather than the person's behavior. Generally, profiling occurs when law-enforcement officers, including customs officials, airport security, and police, assume that people fitting certain descriptions are likely to be engaged in an illegal activity.

Racial profiling has become a more visible part of the national discussion in recent years. Two developments have been especially important. First is the #BlackLivesMatter (BLM) movement, which emerged to call attention to the shooting deaths of African Americans, especially men, usually by police officers. BLM organized in 2013 after a neighborhood watch coordinator in Florida, George Zimmerman, shot and killed Trayvon Martin, an unarmed Black 17-year-old. Zimmerman's acquittal was broadly viewed as a miscarriage of justice. Defensively, some counter the phrase "Black lives matter" with "All lives matter" and call attention to the dangerous position in which police officers often find themselves on a daily basis. However, cameras on bystanders' smartphones and mounted on the dashboards of police vehicles have led to a video record of law-enforcement encounters with African American civilians that many interpret as an excessive, and sometimes lethal, show of force. Not surprisingly, a 2015 national survey showed that only 8 percent of African Americans, compared to 42 percent of Whites, felt that Whites and Blacks have the same chance of receiving fair treatment from the police.

Second are the strident calls for greater scrutiny of Muslims, including Muslim Americans, in the wake of terrorist episodes by Islamic extremists. Rhetoric that links all terrorist events to followers of Islam, as well as viewing most or even all Muslims as extremists, constitutes **Islamophobia**, which refers to a range of negative feelings toward Muslims and their religion. Those feelings range from generalized intolerance to hatred. The current xenophobic expressions against Muslims are strikingly different than earlier expressions of xenophobia because, in the twenty-first century, they have taken on a decidedly patriotic fervor; that is, many people who overtly express anti-Muslim or anti-Arab feelings also believe themselves to be pro-American (Halstead 2008). For example, in 2015 then–presidential candidate Donald Trump called for a ban on all Muslims entering the United States pending thorough background checks. A national survey of all likely voters at the time showed that over one-third supported Trump's proposal. However, this singling out of people on the basis of their religion received strong condemnation from other political leaders. The broad level of support nonetheless underscores the persistent temptation to use profiling, whether racial or religious, as a shortcut to maintaining public safety (McCormick 2015; Marist Poll 2015: Question 7F).

Racial profiling persists despite overwhelming evidence that it is not effective in identifying potential troublemakers. Whites are more likely to be found with drugs in the areas in which minority group members are disproportionately targeted. A federal study made public in 2005 found little difference nationwide in the likelihood of being stopped by law-enforcement officers on the basis of one's race or nationality, but African Americans were twice as likely as Whites to have their vehicles searched, and Latinos were five times more likely than Whites. In addition, a 2015 study considering the states with the most accurate data tracking "stop and frisk" encounters found that African American drivers were much more likely to be stopped but, except in Rhode Island, were always less likely than Whites to have contraband such as drugs or firearms.

A similar pattern emerged in the likelihood of force being used against drivers: It was three times more likely for Latinos and Blacks than for White drivers. A study of New York City police officers describing some 4.43 million stops between 2004 and mid-2012 found that Blacks and Latinos accounted for 83 percent of people who were stopped

The majority of people in the United States think that ethnic and religious profiling should be permitted to maintain national security. In 2010, 53 percent of Americans favored "ethnic and religious profiling," even for U.S. citizens, and wanted Arab Americans to undergo more intensive security checks before boarding planes in the United States (Zogby 2010).

and frisked, and a related study found that Whites were 50 percent more likely to be carrying weapons (Center for Constitutional Rights 2011; Apuzzo and Goldstein 2014; Herbert 2010; LaFraniere and Lehren 2015; Tomaskovic-Devey and Warren 2009).

Back in the 1990s, increased attention to racial profiling led not only to special reports and commissions but also to talk of legislating against it. Enacting such legislation proved difficult. The U.S. Supreme Court in *Whren v. United States* (1996) upheld the constitutionality of using a minor traffic infraction as an excuse to stop and search a vehicle and its passengers. Nonetheless, states and other government units are discussing policies and training that would discourage racial profiling. At the same time, most law-enforcement agencies reject the idea of compiling racial data on traffic stops, arguing that it would be a waste of money and staff time.

Efforts to stop racial profiling came to an abrupt end after the September 11, 2001, terrorist attacks on the United States. Suspicions about Muslims and Arabs in the United States became widespread. Foreign students from Arab countries were summoned for special questioning. Legal immigrants identified as Arab or Muslim were scrutinized for any illegal activity and were prosecuted for routine immigration violations that were ignored for people of other ethnic backgrounds and religious faiths.

Calls to end profiling resumed after the Trayvon Martin case. Around the same time, the New York Police Department abandoned its program "The Demographic Unit," which dispatched officers to Muslim neighborhoods to eavesdrop on residents on the street and in mosques and to create detailed files on Muslim Americans (Apuzzo and Goldstein 2014).

Color-Blind Racism

2.5 Understand color-blind racism.

Over the past three generations, nationwide surveys have consistently shown growing support by Whites for integration, interracial dating, and members of minority groups attaining political office, including president of the United States. How can we reconcile the results of these surveys when thousands of hate crimes occur annually?

Color-blind racism refers to the use of race-neutral principles to defend the racially unequal status quo. For example, color-blind racism may entail believing that "no discrimination for college admission" should exist—despite the fact that the disparity in educational experiences means that formal college admissions criteria will privilege White high-school graduates. Color-blind racism has also been called *laissez-faire racism, postracialism,* or *aversive racism,* but the common theme is that racial discrimination is a thing of the past. Notions of racial inferiority are rarely expressed despite the fact that proceeding color-blind into the future will perpetuate inequality.

An important aspect of color-blind racism is the recognition that race is rarely invoked in public debates on social issues. Instead, people emphasize lower social class, lack of citizenship, or immigration status; these descriptions serve as proxies for race. Furthermore, the emphasis is on individuals failing rather than on recognizing patterns of groups being disadvantaged. Together, these aspects of color-blind racism lead many White people to declare that they are not racist and do not know anyone who is racist. They also lead to the mistaken conclusion that more progress has been made toward racial and ethnic equality and tolerance than has really taken place.

Prejudice or commemoration? In 2015, the Supreme Court upheld Texas's refusal to allow the Confederate flag on a specialty license plate in honor of the Sons of Confederate Veterans. Eight states continue to offer a license plate similar to the rejected Texas sample plate shown here.

When we survey White attitudes toward African Americans, three conclusions are inescapable. First, attitudes are subject to change; during periods of dramatic social upheaval, dramatic shifts can occur within one generation. Second, less progress was made in the late twentieth century and early twenty-first century than was made in the relatively brief period of the 1950s and 1960s. Third, the pursuit of a color-blind agenda has created lower levels of support for policies that could reduce racial inequality if implemented.

Economically less-successful groups such as African Americans and Latinos have been associated with negative traits to the point that issues such as urban decay, homelessness, welfare, and crime are viewed as race issues even though race is rarely mentioned explicitly. In addition to making it harder to solve difficult social problems, this discourse is another instance of blaming the victim (defined in Chapter 1). These perceptions come at a time when the government's willingness to address domestic ills is limited by increasing opposition to new taxes and continuing commitments to fight terrorism here and abroad. The color line remains, even if more people are unwilling to accept its divisive impact on everyone's lives (Bonilla-Silva 2006; Bonilla-Silva and Embrick with Seamster 2011; Mueller 2017; Omi and Winant 2015:257).

The Mood of the Oppressed

2.6 Discuss how members of subordinate groups respond to prejudice.

Sociologist W. E. B. Du Bois relates an experience from his youth in a largely White community in Massachusetts. He tells how, on one occasion, the boys and girls were exchanging cards, and everyone was having a lot of fun. One girl, a newcomer, refused his card as soon as she saw that Du Bois was Black. He wrote:

> *Then it dawned upon me with a certain suddenness that I was different from others... shut out from their world by a vast veil. I had therefore no desire to tear down that veil, to creep through; I held all beyond it in common contempt and lived above it in a region of blue sky and great wandering shadows. (1903:2)*

In using the image of a veil, Du Bois describes how members of subordinate groups learn they are being treated differently. In his case and that of many others, the result is a feeling of contempt toward all Whites that continues for a lifetime.

Opinion pollsters have been interested in White attitudes on racial issues longer than they have measured the views of subordinate groups. This neglect of minority attitudes reflects, in part, the bias of the White researchers. It also stems from the contention that the dominant group is more important to study because it is in a better position to act on its beliefs.

The results of a nationwide survey conducted in the United States offer insight into sharply different views on the state of race relations today (Figure 2.4). Latinos,

Figure 2.4 What Is the State of Race Relations? Three Views
Note: Answers mean respondent chose "very important problem" or "strongly agree" regarding the statements listed. Based on 1,105 interviews in August–September 2007, with bilingual questioners used as necessary.

SOURCE: Data from New America Media 2007: 6, 12, 14, 24, 26.

African Americans, and Asian Americans all have strong reservations about the state of race relations in the United States. They are skeptical about the level of equal opportunity and perceive a lot of discrimination. It is interesting to note that Hispanics and Asian Americans, overwhelmingly immigrants, are more likely to believe they will succeed if they work hard. And the majority of all three groups had a positive outlook for the next ten years (New America Media 2007; Preston 2007).

We have focused so far on what comes to mind when we think about prejudice: one group hating another group. But there is another form of prejudice that has been proposed in the past: A group may come to hate itself. Members of groups held in low esteem by society may, as a result, either hate themselves or have low self-esteem, as many social scientists once believed. Research literature of the 1940s through the 1960s emphasized the low self-esteem of minorities. Usually, the subjects were African Americans, but the argument has been generalized to include any subordinate racial, ethnic, or nationality group.

This view of group self-hatred is no longer accepted. We should not assume that minority status influences personality traits in either a good or a bad way. First, such assumptions may create a stereotype. We cannot describe a Black personality any more accurately than we can a White personality. Second, the characteristics of minority-group members are not entirely the result of subordinate racial status; they also are influenced by low incomes, poor neighborhoods, and other factors. Third, many studies of personality imply that certain values are normal or preferable, but the values chosen are those of dominant groups.

If assessments of a subordinate group's self-regard are so prone to misjudgments, then why has the belief in low self-esteem been so widely held? Much of the research rests on studies with preschool-age Black children who were asked to express their preferences for dolls with different facial colors. Indeed, one such study by psychologists Kenneth and Mamie Clark was cited in the arguments before the U.S. Supreme Court in the landmark 1954 case *Brown v. Board of Education*, which led to desegregation in public schools. The Clarks' study showed that Black children preferred White dolls, a finding that suggested the children had developed a negative self-image. Although subsequent doll studies have sometimes shown Black children's preference for white-faced dolls, other social scientists contend that this preference shows a realization of what most commercially sold dolls look like rather than low self-esteem (Bloom 1971; Powell-Hopson and Hopson 1988).

How do children develop an image of themselves? Toys and playthings have an important role, and many children of racial and ethnic minorities find it difficult to find dolls that look like them. In 2005, a new doll was released: Fulla—an Arab who reflects modesty, piety, and respect, yet underneath her traditional garb she wears chic clothes that a Muslim woman might wear in private.

Because African American children, as well as the children of other subordinate groups, realistically see that Whites have more power and resources and, therefore, rate them higher does not mean that the children feel inferior. However, children who experience overt discrimination are more likely to display feelings of distress and anxiety later in life. Other studies show that when the self-images of middle-class or affluent African Americans are measured, their feelings of self-esteem are more positive than those of comparable Whites (Coker et al. 2009; Gray-Little and Hafdahl 2000).

Intergroup Hostility

Prejudice is as diverse as the nation's population. It exists not only between dominant and subordinate peoples but also among specific subordinate groups. Unfortunately, until recently, little research existed on this subject except for a few social distance scales (discussed later in this chapter) administered to racial and ethnic minorities.

Do different groups get along with one another? Although this question often is framed in terms of the relationships between White Americans and other racial and ethnic groups, we should recognize that prejudice exists among minority groups. In a national survey, people were asked whether they could generally get along with members of other groups. In Figure 2.5, we can see that Whites felt they had the most difficulty getting along with Hispanics. We also see the different views that Blacks, Latinos, Asian Americans, and American Indians hold toward other groups.

It is curious that some minority groups get along better with Whites than with other minority groups. Why would that be? Often, low-income people compete daily with other low-income people and do not readily see the larger societal forces that contribute to their low status. The survey results reveal that many Hispanics are more likely to believe Asian Americans are getting in their way than the White Americans who are the real decision makers in their community.

Research into hostility among marginalized groups has begun to focus on how recent immigrants fit into a complicated picture of multidirectional prejudice. Immigrants themselves bring with them their culture, which includes its own distinctive brand of prejudice that many immigrants then harbor in their new home. Many of the new immigrants to the United States are Black people who have come from either Africa or the Caribbean. They harbor and receive a unique mixture of acceptance and avoidance by U.S.-born Black Americans and display mixed attitudes toward U.S.-born Blacks (Roth and Kim 2013; Waters, Kasinitz, and Asad 2014).

Intergroup hostility sometimes becomes violent. Ethnic and racial tensions among African Americans, Latinos, and immigrants may manifest themselves in hate crimes. Violence can surface in neighborhoods where people compete for scarce resources such as jobs and housing. Gangs become organized along racial lines, much like private clubs "downtown." In recent years, Los Angeles has been particularly concerned about rival Black and Hispanic gangs. Conflict theorists see gang violence as resulting from larger structural forces, but for the average person in such areas, life itself becomes more of a challenge as a result of gang activity (Archibold 2007).

Prejudice 55

Figure 2.5 Do We Get Along?

The bars represent the percentage of each group—Whites, Blacks, Hispanics, Asians, and American Indians—that says how well each group gets along with other groups ("Don't Knows" excluded).[1]

[1]Sample size for American Indians is very small and subject to large sample variance.

Note: The wording of the question was: "We hear a lot these days about how various groups in society get along with each other. I'm going to mention several groups and ask whether you think they generally get along with each other or generally do not get along with each other." So, in the "Asked of White Respondents" graph, Whites are asked how Whites get along with each ethnic group; in the "Asked of Black Respondents" graph, Blacks are asked how Blacks get along with each ethnic group, and so on.

SOURCE: Smith, Tom W. 2006:65. Taking America's Pulse III. Intergroup Relations in Contemporary America. Chicago: National Opinion Research Center, University of Chicago. Reprinted by permission of the author.

Asked of White Respondents
- Blacks: 77
- Hispanics: 75
- Asians: 87
- American Indians: 86

Asked of Black Respondents
- Whites: 64
- Hispanics: 82
- Asians: 67
- American Indians: 85

Asked of Hispanic Respondents
- Whites: 71
- Blacks: 63
- Asians: 66
- American Indians: 77

Asked of Asian Respondents
- Whites: 95
- Blacks: 65
- Hispanics: 78
- American Indians: 90

Asked of American Indian Respondents[1]
- Whites: 91
- Blacks: 86
- Hispanics: 76
- Asians: 83

Reducing Prejudice

2.7 **Explain the ways prejudice can be reduced.**

Focusing on how to eliminate prejudice involves an explicit value judgment: Prejudice is wrong and causes problems for those who are prejudiced and for their victims. As individuals, we can act to stop prejudice. Table 2.2 summarizes ten ways to fight prejudice. The important thing to remember is not to ignore prejudice when you witness it.

The obvious way to eliminate prejudice is to eliminate its causes: the desire to exploit, the sense of being threatened, the need to blame others for one's own failure. Individuals might use personal therapy to help them eliminate these causes, but therapy, even if it works for every individual, is not a solution for an entire society in which prejudice is a part of everyday life.

The answer appears to rest with programs directed at society as a whole. Prejudice is attacked indirectly when discrimination is attacked. Despite prevailing beliefs to the contrary, we *can* legislate against prejudice: Legal statutes and decisions do affect attitudes. In the past, people firmly believed that laws could not overcome norms, especially racist norms. Recent history, especially after the civil rights movement began in 1954, has challenged that once-common belief. Laws and court rulings have mandated equal treatment of Blacks, and Whites have led people to reevaluate their beliefs about

---

Table 2.2 Ways to Fight Prejudice

1. *Act.* Do something. In the face of hatred, apathy will be taken as acceptance, even by the victims of prejudice themselves.
2. *Unite.* Call a friend or coworker. Organize a group of like-thinking friends from your school, place of worship, or club. Create a coalition that is diverse and includes the young, the old, law-enforcement representatives, and the media.
3. *Support the victims.* Victims of hate crimes are especially vulnerable. Let them know you care in person, or by e-mail or text message. If you or someone you know is a victim of a hate crime, report it to the police or campus authorities.
4. *Do your homework.* If you suspect a hate crime has been committed, do your research to document it.
5. *Create an alternative.* Never attend a rally where hate is a part of the agenda. Find another outlet for your frustration, whatever the cause.
6. *Speak up.* You, too, have First Amendment rights. Denounce the hatred, the cruel jokes. If you see a news organization misrepresenting a group, speak up.
7. *Lobby leaders.* Persuade policymakers, business leaders, community leaders, and executives of media outlets to take a stand against hate.
8. *Look long term.* Participate in or organize events such as annual parades or cultural fairs to celebrate diversity and harmony. Supplement it with a Web site that can be a 24/7 resource.
9. *Teach acceptance.* Prejudice is learned, and parents and teachers can influence the content of a school's curriculum. In a first-grade class in Seattle, children paint self-portraits, mixing colors to match their skin tone.
10. *Dig deeper.* Look into the issues that divide us—social inequality, immigration, and sexual orientation. Work against prejudice. Dig deep inside yourself to identify the prejudices and stereotypes you may embrace. Find out what is happening and act!

SOURCE: Southern Poverty Law Center 2010; Willoughby 2004.

what is right and wrong. The increasing tolerance by Whites during the civil rights era from 1954 to 1965 supports this conclusion.

Much research has determined how to change negative attitudes toward groups of people. The most encouraging findings point to education, mass media, intergroup contact, and workplace training programs.

Education

Research on education and prejudice considers two key areas: (1) special programs aimed at promoting mutual respect and (2) the general effect of formal schooling on expressions of bigotry.

Most research studies show that well-constructed school programs have a positive effect on reducing prejudice, at least temporarily. The reduction is rarely as much as one might want, however. The difficulty is that a single program is insufficient to change lifelong habits, especially if little is done to reinforce the program's message once it ends. Persuasion to respect other groups does not operate in a clear field because, in their ordinary environments, people are still subjected to situations that promote prejudicial feelings. Children and adults are encouraged to laugh at Polish jokes and cheer for a team named the *Redskins*. Peers may discourage Black adolescents from befriending a White youth. All of these realities undermine the effectiveness of prejudice-reduction programs (Allport 1979).

Studies document that increased formal education, regardless of content, is associated with racial tolerance. Research data show that highly educated people are more likely to indicate respect and liking for groups different from themselves. Why might more education have this effect? It might promote a broader outlook and make a person less likely to endorse myths that sustain racial prejudice. Formal education teaches the importance of qualifying statements such as "even though they have lower test scores, you need to remember the neighborhoods from which they come." Education introduces the learner to the almost infinite diversity of social groups and the need to question and reject rigid categorizations. Colleges increasingly require students to complete a course that explores diversity or multiculturalism. Another explanation is that education does not reduce intolerance but instead makes people more careful about revealing it. Formal education may simply instruct people in the appropriate responses. Whatever the mechanism, the continued trend toward a better-educated population in the United States will likely contribute to a reduction in overt prejudice.

However, college education may not reduce prejudice uniformly. For example, some White students might believe that minority students did not earn their admission into college but rather were admitted based on affirmative action programs. Students may feel threatened as they watch large groups of people of different racial and cultural backgrounds congregating and forming their own groups. Therefore, some aspects of the college experience may foster "we" versus "they" attitudes (Schaefer 1986, 1996).

Mass Media

The mass media may work to reduce prejudice. Television, radio, motion pictures, newspapers, magazines, and the Internet present only a portion of real life, but what effect do they have on prejudice if the content is racist or antiracist, sexist or antisexist? We can reach only a tentative answer to this question, but overall the evidence points to a measurable effect.

Today, over 56 percent of all youth less than 14 years of age in the United States are children of color, but only recently have we seen television reflect their race or cultural heritage. By the 2016–2017 television season, diversity on broadcast television had improved, with 20 percent of the 595 series regular characters played by African Americans, although they were disproportionately male (62 percent). Asian Pacific Americans have gradually grown in prominence on programs such as *The Big Bang Theory, Master of None,* and *The Mindy Project,* perhaps spurred on by the success of the 2005 motion picture *Slumdog Millionaire.*

We still do not see across-the-board diversity in the mass media, however. Less than 5 percent of regular series characters were identified as gay, lesbian, or transgender—although this number is significantly higher than it was a few years earlier. Cable networks are improving representation of previously ignored segments of the nation's diversity, including the LGBT community (Amazon's *Transparent*), multiracial casts (AMC's *The Walking Dead* and Netflix's *Orange Is the New Black*), and Latinos (USA's *Queen of the South*). Other cable outlets such as HBO and the Hallmark Channel are more uneven in their representation of diversity. Niche cable networks now target specific groups; BET, OWN, and TV One focus on African Americans, and El Rey focuses on English-speaking Latinos.

Muslims and Arabs have become the new villains of choice in visual media, which threatens to reinforce prejudicial beliefs. In past generations, Arabs and Muslims were shown in mystical ways (as in the Aladdin mythology), but increasingly they have become the perennial bad guys, and another common character is the suffering Muslim woman waiting to be rescued (Matar 2015; Soltas and Stephens-Davidowitz 2015).

It is easy to focus merely on the visual content of the mass media but more difficult to assess the representation of racial and ethnic minority groups behind the scenes, especially in the important policymaking roles. Behind the camera, minority representation in television is low, with only 19 percent of directors and 13 percent of writers being Black, Hispanic, or Asian Pacific American (Blas 2016; GLAAD 2016; Keveney 2016; Ryan 2016; Thakore 2014).

Motion pictures are even less diverse in their representations than television. Less than 29 percent of speaking characters were female during the period 2007 to 2015. Most *Star Wars* fans can easily name all the women who spoke more than a dozen lines in the eight movies released so far—there are just four such female characters. Only 3.4 percent of directors, 10.8 percent of writers, and about one-quarter of top film executives are female. On the big screen, about one in four speaking roles are by a minority actor compared to minorities' 40 percent share of the population (Smith, Choueiti, and Pieper 2016).

Reality or unscripted television programs have dominated prime-time television for the past few years. Because these shows are popular with consumers and relatively inexpensive to produce, broadcast and cable networks have launched shows that

"I'm here at the Academy Awards, otherwise known as the White People's Choice Awards." So began comedian Chris Rock's opening monologue of the 2016 Oscar ceremony, acknowledging that once again only White performers were nominated in all acting categories. This underrepresentation of minority groups led to the #OscarsSoWhite movement. In 2017, two African American actors won Oscars, and *Moonlight* became the first-ever movie with an all-Black cast to win the Best Picture Oscar.

Xinhua/Alamy Stock Photo

feature everyday people or C-list celebrities in some type of competition. While these unscripted shows have been routinely criticized on artistic grounds, they do represent the diversity of the population. They are a significant exception to television dominated by White actors and actresses.

In one area of unscripted television, the color line remains in place. Reality shows that promote creation of romantic partnerships such as *The Bachelor* and *The Bachelorette* do so in an overwhelming all-White dating gallery—at least that has been the case for all seasons through 2016—except for one African American male most remembered for his anti-gay comments (C. Kelly 2016).

Intergroup Contact: Avoidance Versus Friendship

Is prejudice reduced or intensified when people cross racial and ethnic boundaries in their friendships? To answer this question, researchers and theorists have followed two parallel paths of inquiry: social distance and the contact hypothesis.

THE SOCIAL DISTANCE SCALE Robert Park and Ernest Burgess (1921:440) first defined **social distance** as the tendency to approach or withdraw from a racial group. Emory Bogardus (1968) created a scale to measure social distance empirically. His social distance scale, often called the **Bogardus scale**, is now widely used.

The Bogardus scale asks people how willing they would be to interact with various racial and ethnic groups in specific social situations. The situations describe different degrees of social contact or social distance. For example, people are asked whether they would be willing to work alongside, be a neighbor to, or be related by marriage to someone of a different group. Over the 70-year period in which the tests were administered, certain patterns emerged. In the top third of the hierarchy are White Americans and northern Europeans. Held at greater social distance are eastern and southern Europeans, and generally near the bottom are racial minorities (Bogardus 1968; Song 1991; Wark and Galliher 2007).

Generally, even the respondents who had friends of different racial and ethnic origins were more likely to show greater social distance—that is, they were less likely to have been in each other's homes, shared fewer activities, and were less likely to talk about their problems with each other. This social distance is unlikely to promote mutual understanding.

EQUAL STATUS CONTACT Many research studies have confirmed the **contact hypothesis**, which states that intergroup contact between people of equal status in harmonious circumstances causes them to become less prejudiced and to abandon previously held stereotypes. The importance of *equal status* in interaction cannot be stressed enough. If a Puerto Rican is mistreated by his employer, little interracial harmony is promoted. Similarly, the situation in which contact occurs must be pleasant, making a positive evaluation likely for both individuals. Contact between two nurses, one Black and the other White, who are competing for one vacancy as a supervisor may lead to greater racial hostility. In contrast, being employed together in a harmonious workplace or living in the same neighborhood would work against harboring stereotypes or prejudices (Krysan, Farley, and Couper 2008; Schaefer 1976).

The key factor in reducing hostility, in addition to equal-status contact, is the presence of a common goal. If people are in competition, contact may heighten tension, as already noted.

We often are unaware of all the social situations that allow us to meet people of different ethnic and racial backgrounds. Such interactions may increase understanding.

Segregation in schools, neighborhoods, and the workplace undercuts the impact of the contact hypothesis. If there is no positive contact, then how can we expect a decrease in prejudice? National surveys show prejudice directed toward Muslim Americans, but social contact bridges that prejudice. In a 2006 survey, 50 percent of people who were not acquainted with a Muslim favored special identification for Muslim Americans, but only 24 percent of those who knew a Muslim embraced that same view. Similarly, people who are personally familiar with Muslims are more than one-third less likely to endorse special security checks for Muslims and are less nervous when they share an airplane with Muslim men. Although negative views are common toward Muslim Americans today, such views are much less likely to be held by people who have had intergroup contact (Saad 2006; Zafar and Ross 2015).

As African Americans and other subordinate groups slowly gain access to better-paying jobs with more responsibility, the contact hypothesis takes on greater significance. Usually, the availability of equal-status interaction is taken for granted; yet in everyday life, intergroup contact does not conform to the equal-status ideal of the contact hypothesis. Furthermore, as we have seen, in a highly segregated society such as the United States, contact tends to be brief and superficial, especially between Whites and minorities. Yet there are encouraging signs. For example, more heterosexuals report having a close family member or friend who is gay or lesbian. Recent studies show that the contact hypothesis is working toward lowering prejudice toward members of the LGBT community (Lytle and Levy 2015).

AVOIDANCE VIA THE INTERNET The Internet, smartphones, and social media are often heralded as transforming social behavior, allowing us to network globally. While electronic media do make communication easier, they do not necessarily increase contact among groups. Avoiding racial, ethnic, and religious minorities online is just another way of doing what previous generations did without the Internet.

Take dating, for example. In the past, many avoided people who looked different at social occasions. Internet daters have a new tool for such avoidance. Studies document that people who use Internet dating services typically use filters or respond to background questions to exclude contact with people different from themselves. While many daters use such filters, Whites are least open to dating racial and ethnic groups different from themselves, African Americans are most open, and Latinos and Asian Americans are somewhere between the two extremes (Robnett and Feliciano 2011).

Sometimes the avoidance is not necessarily initiated by people but by the technology itself. In an increasingly wired world, we are actually less likely to benefit from intergroup contacts and friendships. Facebook, Classmates.com, and LinkedIn allow us to reach out to those who are different from ourselves—or do they? The search engines we use to navigate the Internet are personalized. For example, Google uses as many as 57 sources of information, including a person's location and past searches, to make calculated guesses about the sites a person might like to visit. Google searches have been personalized in this way since 2009. Keep in mind that Google accounts for 82 percent of global Internet searches and captures 98 percent of mobile-phone searches. In 2012, Google carried the process one step further by collecting information from the Web sites that people "friend" or "like" through social media, and then using that information to direct their Web searches.

Although Google's approach may at first sound personalized and convenient, critics charge that it can trap users in their own worlds by routing them ever more narrowly in the same direction. In his book *The Filter Bubble*, online political activist Eli Pariser (2011a, 2011b) contends that search-engine filters enclose us in a kind of "invisible bubble" or "walled garden" that limits what we see to what we are already familiar with. Thus, we are not likely to discover people, places, and ideas that are outside our comfort zone. Secure in our online bubble, which we may not even realize is there, we have little interaction with people different from ourselves (Katz 2012; Zittrain 2008).

What is wrong with that? Given a choice, most of us go only to restaurants whose food we enjoy and read and listen to only those books and radio programs we know we like. Yet, wasn't the Internet supposed to open new vistas to us? If we are investigating a major news event, shouldn't we all see the same information when we search for it? Pariser describes what happened when two friends searched for the term "BP" in the spring of 2010, during the Deepwater Horizon oil rig's accidental discharge of crude oil into the Gulf of Mexico. Using the same browser, the two friends got very different results. One saw links to information about the oil spill; the other saw links to information about BP's CEO, intended for investors.

Corporate Response: Diversity Training

Prejudice carries a cost. This cost is not only to the victim but also to any organization that allows prejudice to interfere with its functioning. Workplace hostility can lead to lost productivity and even staff attrition. Furthermore, if left unchecked, an organization—whether it is a corporation, government agency, or nonprofit enterprise—can develop a reputation for having a "chilly climate." If a business has a reputation for being unfriendly to people of color or to women, qualified people are discouraged from applying for jobs there, and potential clients might seek products or services elsewhere.

How do you battle prejudice in the workplace? The Speaking Out feature "What Can I Do at Work?" offers some suggestions from the Southern Poverty Law Center, a well-known anti-prejudice organization.

In an effort to improve workplace relations, most organizations have initiated some form of diversity training. These programs are aimed at eliminating circumstances and relationships that cause groups to receive fewer rewards, resources, or opportunities. Typically, programs aim to reduce ill treatment based on race, gender,

Speaking Out

What Can I Do at Work?

The workplace is, for some, the only place they experience diversity. For those who live in segregated neighborhoods, attend segregated houses of worship, or take part in segregated hobbies or activities, work becomes the only place they interact with people of varied and diverse backgrounds. It often is, for these people, a testing ground.

The workplace often offers built-in grievance procedures, tied to policies or laws, which can be used to respond to some forms of everyday bigotry. You need not file a lawsuit to have such a policy be effective; many roundtable participants spoke of invoking such policies when speaking up, saying the mere mention carries weight.

Power, too, comes into play at the workplace. The dynamic of an employee speaking to a supervisor is very different than that of a supervisor speaking to an employee. Likewise, an executive's tacit acceptance of bigoted remarks can create an atmosphere where bias thrives—just as one powerfully placed comment from that executive can curb everyday bigotry in significant ways. Who sets the tone at your office? And what leverage do you have with that person? If you lack leverage, who has it? And might that person be an ally?

What Can I Do About Casual Comments?

"Have You Had Diction Lessons?"

An African American businesswoman in the South writes: "I was speaking with a white coworker when, midway through the conversation, she smiled and said, 'You speak so clearly. Have you had diction lessons?'—like for an African American to speak clearly, we'd have to have diction lessons."

A manager writes: "One of my employees constantly makes 'jokes' about people being 'bipolar' or 'going postal' or being 'off their meds.' I happen to know that one of our other employees—within earshot of these comments—is on medication for depression. How can I stop the bad behavior without revealing proprietary information?"

One coworker asks another if she wants to go out for lunch. "We're going to get Ping-Pong chicken," she says, faking a vaguely Asian accent.

An Italian American woman's coworker makes daily comments about her heritage. "Are you in the Mafia?" "Are you related to the Godfather?" There are only six colleagues in the office, and the Italian American woman doesn't know whether—or how—to respond

Speaking Up

Core-value statements and other policies sitting on dusty shelves don't establish an office's culture; casual interactions do. Whether you're a staffer, a manager, or an executive, there's a role for you to play in setting a respectful and unbiased tone in the office. Consider these actions:

- **Interrupt early.** Workplace culture largely is determined by what is or isn't allowed to occur. If people are lax in responding to bigotry, then bigotry prevails. Speak up early and often in order to build a more inclusive environment.

- **Use—or establish—policies.** Call upon existing—too often forgotten or ignored—policies to address bigoted language or behavior. Work with your personnel director or human resources department to create new policies and procedures, as needed. Also ask your company to provide anti-bias training.

- **Go up the ladder.** If behavior persists, take your complaints up the management ladder. Find allies in upper management, and call on them to help create and maintain an office environment free of bias and bigotry.

- **Band together.** Like-minded colleagues also may form an alliance and then ask the colleague or supervisor to change his or her tone or behavior.

What Can I Do About Workplace Humor?

"Please Don't Tell It"

A man mentions to a colleague that he is originally from West Virginia. The colleague laughs and says she knows some "jokes" about people from West Virginia.

She begins to tell one, and it's clear that the "joke" will have an offensive punch line.

The man holds up his hand and says, "Don't tell it. Please don't tell it."

She laughs, perhaps thinking he's joking himself, and tells not one but three "jokes," each with an increasingly bigoted punch line.

The man, at a loss for words, simply sits down when she is done.

Don't laugh. Meet a bigoted "joke" with silence, and maybe a raised eyebrow. Use body language to communicate your distaste for bigoted "humor."

Speaking Up

Humor can enliven the workplace, provide people relief from routine tasks, and help foster team spirit. When humor goes sour, however, the work culture suffers and collegiality can be harmed or damaged. When faced with bigoted "jokes" in the office, try this:

- **Interrupt the laughter.** "Why does everyone think that's funny?" Tell your coworkers why the "joke" offends you, that it feels demeaning and prejudicial. And don't hesitate to interrupt a "joke" with as many additional "no" messages as needed.
- **Set a "not in my workspace" rule.** Prohibit bigotry in your cubicle, your office, or whatever other boundaries define your workspace. Be firm, and get others to join in. Allies can be invaluable in helping to curb bigoted remarks and behavior at the workplace.

Provide alternate humor. Learn and share jokes that don't rely on bias, bigotry, or stereotypes as the root of their humor.

Source: Southern Poverty Law Center, At www.splcenter.org under Publications. Speak Up: Responding to Everyday Bigotry. January 25, 2015, pp. 36–38, 40–42. Used with permission.

---

and ethnicity. In addition, diversity training may deal with (in descending order of frequency) age, disability, religion, language, citizenship status, marital status, and parental status (Society for Human Resource Management 2010, 2011).

It is difficult to make broad generalization about the effectiveness of diversity-training programs because they vary so much between organizations. At one extreme are short presentations that seem to have little support from management. People file into the room, feeling that the training is something they need to get through quickly. Such training is unlikely to be effective and may be counterproductive because it heightens social tensions. At the other end of the continuum is a diversity-training program that is integrated into initial job training, reinforced periodically, and presented as part of the organization's overall mission, with full support from all levels of management. In such businesses, diversity is a core value, and management demands a high degree of commitment from all employees.

Remarkably, the adoption of diversity programs in organizations remains slow more than three decades after the diversity-management paradigm was first widely viewed as good for business (only 10 to 30 percent of businesses have such a program). Even inexpensive steps are not widely adopted. Unfortunately, corporations with lower representation of women and minorities are less likely to embrace diversity programs.

Research into different corporate policies has found two that are particularly effective. Diversity task forces that bring together people from different departments to brainstorm about opening up hiring opportunities appear to eventually increase the diversity in upper management. A second successful policy is the presence of

Figure 2.6 Foreign-Born Workers in the United States, by Country, 2015

Nearly 17 percent of the civilian labor force is foreign-born, with Mexico the largest source.

SOURCE: Data for 2011–2015 from American Community Survey 2016b.

- Native born, 83.5%
- Foreign born, 16.5%

Foreign-born breakdown:
- Mexico
- Central America
- Asia
- Europe
- Caribbean
- South America
- Africa
- Other

diversity mentoring programs designed for aspiring women and minorities, as well as White men, to help them achieve their career goals. Unfortunately, research suggests that if White men perceive African Americans as the primary organizers of such efforts, the programs can actually have a negative impact.

As Figure 2.6 shows, the workforce is becoming more diverse, and management is taking notice. An increasing proportion of the workforce is foreign-born, and the numbers of U.S.-born African Americans, Latinos, and Asian Pacific Americans also are growing. Growing research in business and the social sciences documents that diversity is an asset in bringing about creative changes. The benefits of workplace diversity are especially true at management levels, where leadership teams can develop innovative solutions and creative ideas. However, it is troubling to note that organizations that have the least diverse leadership are also less likely to adopt any kind of diversity program (DiTomaso, Post, and Parks-Yancy 2007; Dobbin and Kalev 2013; Dobbin, Kalev, and Kelly 2007; Dobbin, Kim, and Kalev 2011; Gose 2013; Kalev, Dobbin, and Kelly 2006).

It is not in an organization's best interests if employees start to create barriers based on, for example, racial lines. Earlier, we learned that equal-status contact can reduce hostility. However, in the workplace, people compete for promotions, desirable work assignments, and better office space, to name just a few sources of friction. When done well, diversity training removes ill feelings among workers, which often reflect the prejudices present in larger society.

To have a lasting impact, diversity training should not be separated from other aspects of the organization. For example, even the most inspired program will have little effect on prejudice if the organization promotes a sexist or ethnically offensive image in its advertising. The University of North Dakota launched an initiative in 2001 to become one of the top institutions for Native Americans in the nation. Yet at almost the same time, the administration reaffirmed its commitment, despite tribal objections, to have the "Fighting Sioux" as its mascot for athletic teams. In 2005, the National Collegiate Athletic Association began to review logos and mascots that could be considered insulting to Native Americans. Finally, 68 percent of the state's voters voted to abandon the logo. In short, it does little good to offer diversity training if an organization's overt actions propel it in the opposite direction (Kolowich 2015).

Despite the challenges of confronting and eliminating prejudice, an organization with a comprehensive, management-supported program of diversity training can go a long way toward reducing prejudice in the workplace. For the program to be successful, the rest of the organization must also support mutual respect.

Conclusion

This chapter has examined theories of prejudice and measurements of its extent. Prejudice has a long history in the United States. Whispering campaigns suggested that presidents Martin Van Buren and William McKinley were secretly working with the Pope. This whispering emerged into a national debate when John F. Kennedy became the first Roman Catholic to become president. Much more recently, in 2015, 29 percent of Americans believed President Obama to be a Muslim, and only 39 percent believed him to be Christian or Protestant (Barrett 2016).

Are some minority groups now finally being respected? People cheered on May 1, 2011, on hearing that Osama bin Laden had been found and killed. However, the American Indian people were troubled to learn that the military had assigned the code name "Geronimo" to the operation to capture the terrorist. The Chiricahua Apache of New Mexico were particularly disturbed to learn that the name of their freedom fighter was associated with a global terrorist. In response, the U.S. Defense Department said no disrespect was meant to Native Americans. Of course, one can imagine that the operation never would have been named "Operation Lafayette" or "Operation Jefferson" (Dally 2011).

Several theories try to explain why prejudice exists. Theories for prejudice include two that tend to be psychological (scapegoating and authoritarian personality) and emphasize why a particular person harbors ill feelings toward minority groups. Others (exploitation theory and the normative approach) view prejudice in the context of our interaction in a larger society.

Surveys conducted in the United States over the past 60 years point to a reduction of prejudice as measured by the willingness to express stereotypes or maintain social distance. Survey data also show that African Americans, Latinos, Asian Pacific Americans, and American Indians do not necessarily feel comfortable with one another. They have adopted attitudes toward other oppressed groups similar to those held by many White Americans.

The absence of widespread public expression of prejudice does not mean prejudice itself is absent. Recent prejudice aimed at Hispanics, Asian Pacific Americans, and large recent immigrant groups such as Arab Americans and Muslim Americans is well documented. Issues such as immigration and affirmative action reemerge and cause bitter resentment. Furthermore, ill feelings exist between subordinate groups in schools, on the streets, and in the workplace. Color-blind racism allows one to appear to be tolerant while allowing racial and ethnic inequality to persist.

Equal-status contact may reduce hostility between groups. However, in a highly segregated society defined by inequality, such opportunities are not typical. The mass media can help reduce discrimination, but they have not done enough and may even intensify ill feelings by promoting stereotypical images, such as Arab Americans as terrorists or convenience-store clerks, or Latinos as gang members.

Even though we can be encouraged by the techniques available to reduce intergroup hostility, sizable segments of the population still do not want to live in integrated neighborhoods, do not want to work for or be led by someone of a different race, and object to the idea of their relatives marrying outside their own group. People (including minorities) still harbor stereotypes of racial and ethnic minorities.

Reducing prejudice is important because it can lead to support for policy change. There are steps we can take as individuals to confront prejudice and overcome hatred. The ultimate objective is to improve the social condition of oppressed groups in the United States. To consider this challenge, we turn to discrimination in Chapter 3. Discrimination's costs are high to both dominant and subordinate groups. With this fact in mind, we examine some techniques for reducing discrimination.

Summary: Prejudice

Summary of Learning Objectives

2.1 Differentiate between prejudice and discrimination.

1. Prejudice consists of negative attitudes, and discrimination consists of negative behavior toward a group.

2.2 Explain White privilege.

2. White privilege refers to the rights or immunities granted as a particular benefit or favor for being White. Typically unconsciously, White people accept privilege automatically extended to them in everyday life.

2.3 Summarize the theories of prejudice.

3. Among explanations for prejudice are the theories of scapegoating, authoritarian personality, exploitation theory, and the normative approach.

2.4 Define and explain stereotyping.

4. Stereotypes present the content or images that prejudiced people hold and become accepted as reality.

2.5 Understand color-blind racism.

5. Although evidence indicates that the public expression of prejudice has declined, ample evidence exists that people are expressing race-neutral principles (color-blind racism) that perpetuate inequality in society.

2.6 Discuss how members of subordinate groups respond to prejudice.

6. Typically, members of minority groups have a significantly more negative view of social inequality than Whites, but the majority of Blacks, Latinos, and Asian Pacific Americans believe matters will improve over the next ten years. There is also persistent intergroup hostility among the minorities themselves; this hostility may turn violent.

2.7 Explain the ways prejudice can be reduced.

7. Various techniques are used to reduce prejudice, including educational programs, positive portrayals and inclusion in mass media, friendly intergroup contact, and corporate diversity-training programs.

Key Terms

anti-Semitism, *page 45*
authoritarian personality, *page 46*
Bogardus scale, *page 59*
color-blind racism, *page 50*
contact hypothesis, *page 59*
discrimination, *page 41*
ethnocentrism, *page 40*
ethnophaulism, *page 41*
exploitation theory, *page 46*
homophobia, *page 48*
Islamophobia, *page 49*
microaggressions, *page 41*
normative approach, *page 47*
prejudice, *page 41*
racial profiling, *page 48*
scapegoating theory, *page 45*
sexism, *page 48*
social distance, *page 59*
stereotypes, *page 48*
White privilege, *page 43*

Review Questions

1. How are prejudice and discrimination both related and unrelated to each other?
2. If White people are privileged, how do we explain the presence of poverty among Whites?
3. How do theories of prejudice relate to different expressions of prejudice?
4. What is the impact of stereotypes on how we interact with others?
5. How is color-blind racism expressed?
6. What is intergroup hostility?
7. Describe efforts to reduce prejudice through education and the mass media.
8. Explain the role of intergroup contact in reducing prejudice.

Critical Thinking

1. It is said that prejudice is an attitude and discrimination is an action. Can you think of some examples from your experience that draw out people's prejudice toward and discrimination against others?
2. What privileges do you have that you do not give much thought to? Are they in any way related to race, ethnicity, religion, gender, sexuality, or social class?
3. Identify stereotypes associated with a group of people such as older adults or people with physical disabilities.
4. Consider the television programs you watch the most. In terms of race and ethnicity, how well do these programs reflect the diversity of the U.S. population?
5. In what ways do you think interactions over the Internet are promoting prejudice and discrimination? Conversely, do you think the Internet and social media can be used as tools to reduce prejudice and discrimination? If so, how?

Chapter 3
Discrimination

Learning Objectives

3.1 Distinguish between relative and absolute deprivation.

3.2 Define hate crimes.

3.3 Summarize how institutions discriminate.

3.4 Describe the effects of discrimination and the efforts to reduce or eliminate it.

3.5 Explain and discuss environmental justice.

3.6 Explain affirmative action and the legal debate surrounding it.

3.7 Explain the glass ceiling in the workplace.

"I didn't get the job" is a frequent complaint that soon leads to reasons "I" did not get the job for which "I" applied. Sometimes people think they didn't get the job because of their race. Is discrimination common in hiring practices?

A dramatic confirmation of discrimination in hiring came with research begun by sociologist Devah Pager in 2003. She sent White, Black, and Latino men out as trained "testers" in Milwaukee and New York City to look for entry-level jobs that required no experience or special training. Each tester was in his twenties and was college educated, but all of them presented themselves as having only a high-school diploma, and each had a similar job history.

The experiences with potential employers were vastly different. Why? Besides having different racial and ethnic backgrounds, some testers indicated in the job application that they had served 18 months in jail for a felony conviction (possession of cocaine with intent to distribute). So what happened when Black Americans applied?

- Black male applicant, jail time: 5 percent received a callback
- Black male applicant, NO jail time: 14 percent received a callback

Clearly, past felons had a harder time continuing through the employment process. What about when White people made the same queries?

- White male applicant, jail time: 17 percent received a callback
- White male applicant, NO jail time: 34 percent received a callback

Once again, applicants with past jail time were less likely to receive a callback. Yet a White job applicant with a jail record received more callbacks for further consideration than did a Black man with no criminal record. Whiteness has a privilege even when it comes to jail time; race, it seems, was more of a concern to potential employers than a criminal background. It is no surprise that an analysis of labor patterns after release from prison finds that wages grow 21 percent more slowly for Black ex-inmates than for White ex-inmates. In another study, Pager documented that Latino job applicants were at a disadvantage similar to that of the African American testers (Pager 2003; Pager, Western, and Bonikowski 2009; Pager and Western 2012).

"I expected there to be an effect of race, but I did not expect it to swamp the results as it did," Pager told an interviewer. Her finding was especially significant because one in three African American men and one in six Hispanic men are expected to serve time in prison during their lifetime compared to one in 17 White men (Greenhouse 2012; Kroeger 2004).

Pager's research, which was widely publicized, eventually contributed to a change in public policy. In his 2004 State of the Union address, and specifically referring to Pager's work, President George W. Bush announced a $300 million monitoring program for ex-convicts who are attempting to reintegrate into society.

Discrimination has a long history, right up to and including the present, of taking its toll on people. **Discrimination** is the denial of opportunities and equal rights to individuals and groups because of prejudice or other arbitrary reasons. In this chapter, we examine the many faces of discrimination, its many victims, and the many ways scholars have documented its presence today in the United States. We examine not only discrimination in housing but also look at differential treatment in employment opportunities, wages, voting, vulnerability to environmental hazards, and even access to membership in private clubs.

Relative Versus Absolute Deprivation

3.1 Distinguish between relative and absolute deprivation.

People in the United States find it difficult to see discrimination as a widespread phenomenon. "After all," it is often said, "these minorities drive cars, hold jobs, own their homes, and even go to college." But discrimination does exist in the United States, as it does abroad, where its victims include a broad array of groups.

To understand discrimination in modern industrialized societies such as the United States, we must begin by distinguishing between relative and absolute deprivation.

Conflict theorists have correctly observed that it is not absolute, unchanging standards that determine deprivation and oppression. Although minority groups may be viewed as having adequate or even good incomes, housing, health care, and educational opportunities, their position relative to some other group provides evidence of discrimination.

Relative deprivation is the conscious experience of a negative discrepancy between legitimate expectations and present actualities. After settling in the United States, immigrants often enjoy better material comforts and more political freedom than was possible in the countries they left. If they compare themselves with most other people in the United States, however, they will feel deprived because, although their standards have improved, the immigrants still perceive that they are deprived in relation to other groups.

Absolute deprivation, in contrast, implies a fixed standard based on a minimum level of subsistence, often determined by the government. Discrimination does not necessarily mean absolute deprivation. A Japanese American who is promoted to a management position may still be a victim of discrimination if he or she had been passed over for years because of corporate reluctance to place an Asian American in a highly visible position.

Dissatisfaction is likely to arise from feelings of relative deprivation. However, the members of a society who feel most frustrated and disgruntled by the social and economic conditions of their lives are not necessarily worse off in an objective sense. Social scientists have long recognized that the most significant factor in deprivation is how people perceive their situations. As Karl Marx pointed out, the misery of the workers is important in reflecting their oppressed state, but so is their position relative to the ruling class. In 1847, Marx wrote, "Although the enjoyment of the workers has risen, the social satisfaction that they have has fallen in comparison with the increased enjoyment of the capitalist" (Marx and Engels 1955:94).

Marx's assertion explains why the groups or individuals who are most vocal and best organized against discrimination are not necessarily in the worst economic and social situation. However, they are likely to be those who most strongly perceive that, relative to others, they are not receiving their fair share. Resistance to perceived discrimination, rather than the actual amount of absolute discrimination, is the key.

Hate Crimes

3.2 Define hate crimes.

Although prejudice certainly is not new in the United States, it is receiving increased attention as it manifests itself in hate crimes in neighborhoods, at meetings, and on college campuses. The Hate Crime Statistics Act, which became law in 1990, directs the Department of Justice to gather data on hate or bias crimes.

What Are Hate Crimes?

The government elevates an ordinary crime to the status of **hate crime** when offenders choose a victim because of some characteristic—for example, race, ethnicity, religion, sexual orientation, or disability—and provide evidence that hatred prompted them to commit the crime. Hate crimes are sometimes called *bias crimes*.

The Hate Crime Statistics Act created a national mandate to identify such crimes, whereas previously only 12 states had monitored hate crimes. The act has since been amended to include disabilities—physical and mental—as well as sexual orientation as factors that can be considered a basis for hate crimes.

In 2016, law enforcement agencies released hate crime data submitted by police agencies. Even though many hate crimes are not reported (less than one in seven participating agencies reported an incident), a staggering number of offenses that come to law agencies' attention were motivated by hate. While most incidents receive relatively little attention, some grab the headlines and dominate news sites for days. Such was the case in 2015 when a 21-year-old self-described White supremacist walked into a prayer service at a Black church in Charleston, South Carolina, and killed nine people and wounded three others.

Official reports noted more than 5,800 hate crimes and bias-motivated incidents in 2015. As Figure 3.1 indicates, race, ethnicity, and ancestry were the apparent motivation for the bias in approximately 57 percent of the reports, and religion and sexual orientation accounted for 18 to 22 percent each. Vandalism against property and intimidation were the most common crimes, but among the more than 4,400 crimes directed against people, 58 percent involved assault, rape, or murder.

The vast majority of hate crimes are committed by members of the dominant group against those who are, relatively speaking, powerless. Only one in five bias incidents based on race are anti-White. Hate crimes, except for those that are most horrific, generally receive little media attention, and anti-White incidents probably receive even less. Hostility based on race knows no boundaries (Witt 2007).

The official reports of hate or bias crimes appear to be only the tip of the iceberg. Government-commissioned surveys conducted over a national cross-section indicate that 192,000 people annually report they have been victims of hate crimes, but only half reported those crimes to the police. Of these, only one out of ten are confirmed as hate crimes, according to the victims. In short, a considerable amount of racial hostility in this country becomes violent (Harlow 2005; Perry 2003).

National legislation and publicity have made *hate crime* a meaningful term, and we are beginning to recognize the victimization associated with such incidents. A current proposal would make a violent crime a federal crime if it is motivated by racial or religious bias. Although passage is uncertain, the serious consideration of the proposal indicates a willingness to consider a major expansion of federal jurisdiction. Currently, federal law prohibits crimes motivated by race, color, religion, or national origin only if they violate a federally guaranteed right such as voting.

Figure 3.1 Distribution of Reported Hate Crimes

SOURCE: Incidents reported for 2015 by Federal Bureau of Investigation 2016a.

- Disability 1%
- Gender/Gender Identity 2%
- Sexual Orientation 18%
- Religion 22%
- Race/Ethnicity/Ancestry 57%

Victimized groups do more than experience and observe hate crimes and other acts of prejudice. Watchdog organizations play an important role in documenting bias-motivated violence; such groups include the Anti-Defamation League, the National Institute Against Prejudice and Violence, the Southern Poverty Law Center, and the National Gay and Lesbian Task Force.

To further their agenda, established hate groups have even set up propaganda sites online, thus creating opportunities for previously unknown haters and hate groups to promote themselves. However, hate crime legislation does not affect such outlets because of legal questions involving freedom of speech. More recently, enterprising bigots have begun to use directories to target their attacks through instant messages, in much the same way as they placed harassing telephone calls in the past. Even more creative and subtle are people who have constructed Web sites to attract people who are surfing for information on Martin Luther King, Jr., only to find a site that looks educational but savagely discredits the civil rights activist. A close inspection reveals that a White-supremacist organization hosts the site (Davis 2008; Simon Wiesenthal Center 2008; Working 2007).

In the Speaking Out feature, Nihad Awad, national executive director of the Council on American-Islamic Relations (CAIR), the nation's largest civil-rights and advocacy organization, draws parallels between the violence (including hate crimes) experienced by African Americans and anti-Islam incidents.

Speaking Out

May America Be True to Her Dream

Nihad Awad

This Fourth of July weekend, friends and families around the country will gather together to celebrate the freedoms we cherish as Americans, those for which countless generations have struggled and sacrificed so much.

We celebrate our freedom from oppression, freedom to practice our religion, representation in our government, and self-determination.

Yet as recent events targeting African Americans have made abundantly clear, we still have a long way to go to achieve full equality under the flag we will fly high this weekend.

The terror attack on an African Methodist Episcopal Church in Charleston, South Carolina, the abuse of African American teens by a police officer in McKinney, Texas, and police-involved shootings and mistreatment of men, women, and children of color across our nation point to the lingering structural racism in our society. These troubling incidents must be honestly addressed before we can truly be the nation President Abraham Lincoln described as "conceived in Liberty, and dedicated to the proposition that all men are created equal."

While much was accomplished through the civil rights movement during the '50s and '60s, much still remains to be done.

No less corrosive to the American values on which our country was founded is the pervasive hate to which American Muslims have increasingly found themselves subjected.

Recent, and largely unreported, incidents of anti-Muslim hate include a Texas road rage shooting in which the alleged gunman reportedly shouted "Go back to Islam" before firing at and killing the victim, the "execution-style" killings of three young Muslims in Chapel Hill, North Carolina, hate vandalism and threats

Nihad Awad

Muhammad Hamed/REUTERS/Alamy Stock Photo

targeting mosques and Islamic schools nationwide, a planned religiously motivated attack on a Muslim community in New York, and the murder of a Muslim teen in Kansas City who was run down by a vehicle painted with anti-Islam slurs.

In one much-publicized incident, armed anti-Islam protesters recently harassed worshipers at an Arizona mosque; several of those present at the rally displayed Nazi-themed symbols.

Racism and Islamophobia are branches of the same poisonous tree: Both rely on stereotypes and misinformation for their creation and continuation; both harm not only those targeted by bigotry, but also the society that allows hate to fester and pits one group against another.

Despite these terrible incidents, there are some clear signs of hope and optimism, particularly in the outpouring of love for the victims of the deadly shooting in Charleston and in the subsequent almost-universal repudiation of the Confederate flag as a symbol of racism and oppression, one to which CAIR [the Council on American-Islamic Relations] added its voice.

We saw a similar outpouring of support for worshipers at the Arizona mosque assaulted by hate-speech, and even witnessed a neighborhood "love-in" for an Iowa Muslim-American whose house was painted with Islamophobic and threatening graffiti.

The American Muslim community will continue to stand with our fellow Americans of all beliefs and backgrounds as we together struggle to achieve true freedom and equality.

As Dr. Martin Luther King said in his 1965 Independence Day sermon delivered at Ebenezer Baptist Church in Atlanta, Georgia, "Never before in the history of the world have so many racial groups and so many national backgrounds assembled together in one nation. And somehow if we can't solve the problem in America the world can't solve the problem, because America is the world in miniature and the world is America writ large."

He added: "We have a great dream. It started way back in 1776, and God grant that America will be true to her dream."

Amen to that.

Source: Awad 2015.

Why Do Hate Crimes Carry Harsher Penalties?

Frequently, one hears of hate crimes being questioned or disputed. After all, the skeptics ask, is not hate involved in every assault or act of vandalism? While many non–hate crimes may be motivated by hatred toward an individual or organization, a hate or bias crime toward a minority is intended to carry a message well beyond the individual victim. When a person is assaulted because he is gay or she is a lesbian, the act is meant to terrorize all gay men and lesbians. Vandalizing a mosque or synagogue is meant to warn all Muslims or Jews that they are not wanted and that their religious faith is considered inferior.

In many respects, today's hate crimes are like the terrorist efforts of the Ku Klux Klan generations ago. Targets may be randomly selected, but the group being terrorized is carefully chosen. In many jurisdictions, having a crime officially classified as a hate crime can increase the punishment. For example, a misdemeanor like vandalism can be increased to a felony. A felony that is a hate crime can carry a greater prison sentence. These sanctions were upheld by the U.S. Supreme Court in the 1993 decision *Mitchell v. Wisconsin*, which recognized that greater harm may be done by hate-motivated crimes (Blazak 2011).

Institutional Discrimination

3.3 **Summarize how institutions discriminate.**

Individuals practice discrimination in one-on-one encounters, and institutions practice discrimination through their daily operations. Indeed, a consensus is growing today that institutional discrimination is more significant than acts committed by prejudiced individuals.

Social scientists are particularly concerned with how patterns of employment, education, criminal justice, housing, health care, and government operations maintain the social significance of race and ethnicity. **Institutional discrimination** is the denial of opportunities and equal rights to individuals and groups that results from the normal operations of a society.

Civil rights activist Stokely Carmichael and political scientist Charles Hamilton are credited with introducing the concept of institutional racism. *Individual discrimination* refers to overt acts of individual Whites against individual Blacks; Carmichael and Hamilton reserved the term *institutional racism* for covert acts committed collectively against an entire group. From this perspective, discrimination can take place without an individual intending to deprive others of privileges and even without the individual being aware that others are being deprived (Ture and Hamilton 1992).

How can discrimination be widespread and unconscious at the same time? A few documented examples of institutional discrimination follow:

1. Standards for assessing credit risks work against African Americans and Hispanics who seek to establish businesses because many lack conventional credit references. Businesses in low-income areas where these groups often reside also have much higher insurance costs.

2. IQ testing favors middle-class children, especially White middle-class children, because of the types of questions included on the test.

3. The entire criminal justice system, from the patrol officer to the judge and jury, is dominated by Whites who find it difficult to understand life in poverty-stricken areas.

4. Hiring practices often require several years' experience at jobs only recently opened to members of subordinate groups.

5. Many jobs automatically eliminate people with felony records or past drug offenses, a practice that disproportionately reduces employment opportunities for people of color.

Institutional discrimination is so systemic that it takes on the pattern of what has been termed "woodwork racism" in that racist outcomes become so widespread that African Americans, Latinos, Asian Pacific Americans, and others endure them as a part of everyday life (Feagin and McKinney 2003).

At the beginning of this chapter, we noted how employers routinely pass over job applicants who are felons. To casual observers, this decision may seem reasonable; however, Black and Latino job applicants are more likely to be passed over than Whites. This is a form of institutional discrimination. Recognizing this problem, the Equal Opportunity Commission ruled in 2012 that while employers may consider criminal records, a policy that excludes all applicants with a conviction could violate employment discrimination laws because of this differential impact. This does not mean employers must hire ex-felons, only that blanket exclusions are to be avoided (Greenhouse 2012).

Despite this positive step, concern is growing over another potential example of institutional discrimination in two areas of voting requirements. First are state laws that bar citizens with past felony convictions from voting. The laws vary from state to state, but some states, including Florida, Iowa, and Virginia, have lifetime bans that are more likely to affect potential African American voters. In fact, in seven states (Alabama, Florida, Kentucky, Mississippi, Tennessee, Virginia, and Wyoming) these laws effectively prevent at least 15 percent of African Americans from voting (Lai and Lee 2016).

Second are laws that require ID to vote, sometimes requiring an officially issued photo ID, ostensibly to prevent voter fraud. However, there is little evidence that people have been impersonating eligible voters at the polls. Figure 3.2 summarizes voter ID requirements in the United States.

Courts have been reluctant to uphold such laws, contending that it is not easy for all eligible voters to obtain such a government-provided ID card. These laws disproportionately disenfranchise members of minority groups, including the elderly, simply because they do not have a driver's license. National surveys have found that 25 percent of African Americans and 16 percent of Latino citizens do not have a valid government-issued photo ID, compared to only 8 percent of White citizens. So, court decisions aside, what we have is another case of institutional discrimination: Through the normal operation of voting regulations, equal rights are more likely to be denied to people of color (Brennan Center 2006, 2013; Dade 2012b).

Figure 3.2 Voter ID Requirements in the United States

NOTE: Data as of June 5, 2017.

SOURCE: Data from National Conference of State Legislatures 2017.

In other situations, even apparently neutral institutional standards can lead to discriminatory effects. African American students at a Midwestern state university protested a policy under which fraternities and sororities that wanted to use campus facilities for a dance were required to post a security deposit to cover possible damage. The Black students complained that this policy had a discriminatory impact on minority student organizations. Campus police countered that the university's policy applied to all student groups interested in using these facilities. However, because almost all White fraternities and sororities at the school had their own houses, which they used for dances, the policy affected only African American and other subordinate groups' organizations.

Institutional discrimination continuously imposes more hindrances on and awards fewer benefits to certain racial and ethnic groups than it does to others. This is the underlying and painful context of American intergroup relations.

Discrimination Today

3.4 Describe the effects of discrimination and the efforts to reduce or eliminate it.

Discrimination continues to be widespread in the United States. It sometimes results from prejudices held by individuals, but more significantly, it is also found in institutional discrimination. We will look first at measuring discrimination in terms of income and then at efforts that are being made to eliminate or at least reduce it.

Discrimination Hits the Wallet

How much discrimination exists? As in measuring prejudice, challenges arise when trying to quantify discrimination. Measuring prejudice is hampered by the difficulties in assessing attitudes and by the need to take many factors into account. It is further limited by the initial challenge of identifying different treatment. A second difficulty of measuring discrimination is assigning a cost to the discrimination.

An important measure of economic well-being for any household is its annual income and the wealth it has to draw upon in cases of emergency. **Income** refers to salaries, wages, and other money received over a specific period of time; **wealth** is a more inclusive term that encompasses all of a person's material assets, including land and other types of property. Wealth is a measure of what a household owns minus what it owes. We first consider income and then look at wealth later in this chapter.

We can make some tentative conclusions about discrimination by examining income and wealth data. Figure 3.3 uses income data to show the vast income disparity between African Americans and Whites and also between men and women. Figure 3.3 encompasses all full-time workers. White men, with a median income of $60,508, earn about one-third more than Black men and almost twice what Hispanic women earn in wages. The "median" income is the number that splits the group in half—so half of all White men earn more than $60,508 annually, and half earn less.

Figure 3.3 Median Income by Race, Ethnicity, and Gender

Income gaps remain significant, with Hispanic and Native American women needing to work two years in order to earn what Asian American and White men earn in one year.

NOTE: Data released in 2016 for income earned in 2015. Median income is from all sources and is limited to year-round, full-time workers at least 25 years old (American Indian data for 16 years or older). Data for White men and women are for non-Hispanics.

SOURCE: American Community Survey 2016a; American Social and Economic Supplement 2016.

Group	Median Income (dollar)
Asian men	$64,622
White men	$60,508
Asian women	$50,304
White women	$45,371
Black men	$42,209
Native American and Alaska Native men	$36,925
Black women	$36,925
Hispanic men	$36,465
Native American and Alaska Native women	$32,121
Hispanic women	$31,810

Yet Asian American men are at the top and edge out White males by $4,000 a year. Why do Asian American men earn so much if race usually serves as a barrier? A significant number of Asian American men with advanced educations have high-earning jobs, which brings up their median income. However, as we will see, given their high levels of schooling, their incomes should be even higher. The economic picture is not entirely positive for Asian Americans, however. Some Asian American groups, such as Laotians and Vietnamese, have high levels of poverty.

Clearly, regardless of race or ethnicity, men outpace women in annual income. The disparity between the incomes of Black women and White men has remained unchanged over the more than 50 years during which such data have been tabulated. It illustrates yet another instance of the greater inequality experienced by minority women.

Are these differences entirely the result of discrimination in employment? No. Individuals within the four groups are not equally prepared to compete for high-paying jobs. Past discrimination is a significant factor in a person's current social position. Taxpayers, predominantly White, were unwilling to subsidize the public education of African Americans and Hispanics at the same levels as White pupils. Even as more money has been invested in schools attended by minority groups, today's schools show the continuing results of this uneven spending pattern from the past.

Table 3.1 Median Income by Race, Ethnicity, and Sex, Holding Education Constant

Even at the very highest levels of schooling, the income gap remains between Whites and Blacks. Education also has little apparent effect on narrowing the income gap between male and female workers (income values in dollars).

	Race or Ethnicity				Sex	
	White Families	Black Families	Asian Families	Hispanic Families	Male	Female
Total	81,531	39,689	91,780	48,359	52,305	41,679
High School						
Nongraduate	36,308	22,211	44,464	34,708	32,143	22,670
Graduate	60,328	36,790	51,687	44,515	41,569	31,249
College						
Associate degree	79,783	53,183	79,269	68,897	52,072	40,186
Bachelor's degree	105,017	81,455	104,884	88,020	71,385	57,681
Master's degree	122,576	92,344	135,972	104,864	86,738	62,379
Professional degree	164,066	127,250	197,355	122,628	131,189	82,473

NOTE: Data released in 2016 for income earned in 2015. Figures are median income from all sources except capital gains. Included are public-assistance payments, dividends, pensions, and unemployment compensation. Incomes are for all workers 25 years of age and older with earnings. High-school graduates include those with GEDs. Data for Whites are for White non-Hispanics. Family data for Black professional degree-holders' families are author's estimate.

SOURCE: Bureau of Census 2016i: Tables FINC01-4, 6, 8, 9, P-24.

Table 3.1 compares the median income of different groups holding education constant, which means that we can compare Blacks and Whites and men and women with approximately the same amount of formal schooling. More education means more income, but the disparity remains. The gap between races does narrow somewhat as education increases. However, both African Americans and women lag behind their more affluent (White, male) counterparts. The contrast remains dramatic: Women with a master's degree have a median income of $62,379, which means they earn about $9,000 *less* than men who complete only a bachelor's degree.

Thinking over the long term, a woman with a bachelor's degree will work full-time three years to earn $173,000. The typical man can work a little more than 29 months, take over seven months off without pay, and still exceed the woman's earnings. Women, regardless of race, pay at every point. They are often hired at lower starting salaries in jobs comparable to those held by men. Salary increases come more slowly. And by their 30s, they rarely recover from even short maternity leaves.

Note what happens to Asian American households. Asian American families often match similarly educated White families in annual income, but typically there are more earners in their household collectively earning that money than in White family households.

This is the picture today, but is it getting better? According to a Census Bureau report, the answer is no. During the early years of the twenty-first century, Blacks were more likely to stay poor than Whites, and those African Americans in the top rung of income were more likely to fall out of that income bracket than their White counterparts among the wealthy. The inequality is dramatic, and the trend is not diminishing (Hisnanick and Giefer 2011).

With education held constant in Table 3.1, can we conclude that the remaining gap is caused by discrimination? Not necessarily. Table 3.1 uses only the amount of schooling, not its quality. Racial minorities are more likely to attend inadequately financed schools. Some efforts have been made to eliminate disparities between school districts, but they have had little success.

How do we explain sex discrimination? Although women usually are not segregated from men in most occupations, educational institutions encourage talented women to enter fields that pay less (nursing or elementary education) than other occupations that require similar amounts of training. Even when women do enter the same occupations as men, the earnings disparity persists. Even controlling for age, a study of census data showed that female physicians and surgeons earned 69 percent of what their male counterparts did. Looking at broad ranges of occupations, researchers in the past few years have attributed between one-quarter and one-third of the wage gap to discrimination rather than to personal choices, skill preparation, and formal schooling (Reskin 2012; Weinberg 2004).

Eliminating Discrimination

Two main agents of social change work to reduce discrimination: (1) voluntary associations organized to solve racial and ethnic problems and (2) the federal government, including the courts. The two are closely related: Most efforts initiated by the government were urged by associations or organizations that represent minority groups. Resistance to social inequality by subordinate groups has been the key to change. Rarely has any government on its own initiative sought to end discrimination based on such criteria as race, ethnicity, and gender.

All racial and ethnic groups of any size are represented by private organizations that are, to some degree, trying to end discrimination. Some groups originated in the first half of the twentieth century, but most have been founded since World War II or have become significant forces in bringing about change only since then. These include church organizations, fraternal social groups, minor political parties, and legal defense funds, as well as more militant organizations operating under the scrutiny of law-enforcement agencies. The purposes, membership, successes, and failures of these resistance organizations dedicated to eliminating discrimination are discussed throughout this book.

The judiciary, charged with interpreting laws and the U.S. Constitution, has a much longer history of involvement in the rights of racial, ethnic, and religious minorities. However, its early decisions protected the rights of the dominant group, as in the 1857 U.S. Supreme Court *Dred Scott* decision, which ruled that slaves remained slaves even when living or traveling in states where slavery was illegal. Not until the 1940s did the Supreme Court revise earlier decisions and begin to grant African Americans the same rights as those held by Whites. The 1954 *Brown v. Board of Education* decision, which stated that "separate but equal" facilities—including schools—were unconstitutional, heralded a new era in which courts began to decide that distinguishing between races in order to segregate was inherently unconstitutional.

The most important legislative effort to eradicate discrimination was the Civil Rights Act of 1964. This act led to the establishment of the Equal Employment

Opportunity Commission (EEOC), which has the power to investigate complaints against employers and to recommend action to the Department of Justice (DOJ). If the DOJ sues and the court finds discrimination, then the court can order appropriate compensation to the injured parties. The original act covered employment practices of all businesses with more than 25 employees and nearly all employment agencies and labor unions. A 1972 amendment broadened the coverage to employers with as few as 15 employees.

In addition to establishing the EEOC, the Civil Rights Act of 1964 prohibited discrimination in public accommodations—hotels, motels, restaurants, gas stations, and amusement parks. Publicly owned facilities such as parks, stadiums, and swimming pools were also prohibited from discriminating. Another important provision forbade discrimination in all federally supported programs and institutions, including hospitals, colleges, and road construction projects.

The Civil Rights Act of 1964 was not perfect. Since 1964, several acts and amendments to the original act have been added to cover the many areas of discrimination it left untouched, such as criminal justice and housing. Even in areas singled out for enforcement, discrimination still occurs. Federal agencies charged with enforcement complain that they are underfunded or are denied wholehearted support by the White House. Also, regardless of how much the EEOC may want to act in a particular case, the person who alleges discrimination has to pursue the complaint over a long time that is marked by lengthy periods of inaction. Despite these efforts, devastating forms of discrimination persist. African Americans, Latinos, and others fall victim to **redlining**, the pattern of discrimination against people trying to buy homes in minority and racially changing neighborhoods. The term comes from the early practice of bankers marking a red line on a map to indicate areas or neighborhoods in which it would not make loans.

In the wake of the U.S. Great Recession that began in 2007, researchers looked at the differential impact of home-loan practices and found that redlining has continued. Controlling for a variety of personal financial factors and home values, the researchers analyzed mortgage records in Baltimore, Maryland, and found that Black neighborhood residents paid 5 to 11 percent more in monthly mortgage payments. In addition, the federal government levied a $22 million fine on Hudson City Savings Bank, the nation's seventh-largest bank, which had purposefully avoided building branches in Black and Latino neighborhoods in Buffalo, Milwaukee, Providence, Rochester, and St. Louis; the bank's goal was to avoid offering home loans to local residents. This was not an isolated case; other banks were also fined. As we shall see when we discuss environmental justice later in this chapter, redlining continues to shape contemporary issues (Rugh, Albright, and Massey 2015; Swarns 2015).

Although civil rights laws often have established rights for other minorities, the Supreme Court made them explicit in two 1987 decisions involving groups other than African Americans. In the first of the two cases, an Iraqi American professor asserted that he had been denied tenure because of his Arab origins; in the second, a Jewish congregation brought suit for damages in response to the defacement of its synagogue with derogatory symbols. The Supreme Court ruled unanimously that, in effect, any member of an ethnic minority might sue under federal prohibitions against discrimination. These decisions paved the way for almost all racial and ethnic groups to invoke the Civil Rights Act of 1964 (Taylor 1987).

A setback in antidiscrimination lawsuits came in the 2007 *Ledbetter v. Goodyear Tire and Rubber Co.* ruling, when the Supreme Court told Lilly Ledbetter, in effect, that she was "too late." Ledbetter had been a supervisor for many years at the Gadsden,

Alabama, Goodyear Tire Rubber plant when she realized that she was being paid $6,500 less per year than the lowest-paid male supervisor. The Court ruled that she must sue within 180 days of the initial discriminatory paycheck even though it had taken years before she even knew of the differential payment. Given the usual secrecy about salaries in workplaces, this ruling made it difficult for victims of pay discrimination to bring their cases to the courts. Two years later, Congress enacted the Lilly Ledbetter Fair Pay Act, which gives victims more time to file a lawsuit.

Nonetheless, proving discrimination continues to be difficult. Many discriminatory practices, such as those that are a part of institutional discrimination, are seldom subject to legal action. The inability of the Civil Rights Act, similar legislation, and court decisions to end discrimination does not result entirely from poor financial and political support, although it does play a role. The number of federal employees assigned to investigate and prosecute bias cases is insufficient. As we see in Research Focus titled "The Sharing Economy—Another Way to Discriminate," new ways of obtaining services online have created new opportunities to discriminate.

Lilly Ledbetter's failed lawsuit showed the difficulty in documenting what seemed to be obvious gender pay discrimination.

Research Focus

The Sharing Economy—Another Way to Discriminate

In the twenty-first century, a new marketplace has blossomed in the United States and other industrial countries—the sharing economy. The **sharing economy** refers to online economic transactions that place buyers and sellers in direct peer-to-peer contact with no change in the ownership of goods and services. Purchases can range from car rides to short-term living or vacation accommodations. While many consumers applaud these services' ease of use and lower prices compared to conventional businesses, this burgeoning business model is not without its problems.

One concern is that old-fashioned discrimination is emerging in these new markets. For example, Airbnb, which allows people to list their homes for rent online, is a vehicle for allowing people to discriminate based on race, gender, religion, or sexual identity. A 2016 study found that requests from guests with distinctively African American names are 16 percent less likely to get accommodations through Airbnb than people with distinctively White names.

A more subtle and disturbing type of bias is reported by minority users of the sharing economy who successfully secure accommodations, but then encounter neighbors who are surprised to see "different people" on the premises and then call security firms or law enforcement, who immediately show up to investigate the renters.

Researchers at MIT, Stanford, and the University of Washington have found that Black people often have to wait longer to get a ride using services such as Uber and Lyft. Uber drivers are also far more likely to cancel rides for Black customers than for White customers. Representatives from both Uber and Lyft have said that their companies have strong nondiscrimination guidelines for their drivers. In fact, they offer a counterargument: Unlike many taxi companies, Uber

(continued)

and Lyft are available to people living in underserved areas that taxis have historically neglected. These areas' residents are now able to access convenient, affordable rides. Yet some drivers still avoid customers whose online profiles indicate they are not White.

In yet another aspect of discrimination in the new online marketplaces, it was revealed that advertisers on Facebook were using "affinities" that users had created either explicitly or through their online browsing habits. These affinities give advertisers the ability to make reasonable assumptions about the Facebook account holder's race or ethnicity. As a result, some advertisers have avoided making real-estate offers and housing opportunities accessible to "undesirable" Facebook members.

How do operators of sharing and social media platforms respond to these bias reports? Typically, they point to company policies that prohibit discrimination and harassment. Yet sometimes the very electronic tools that make these outlets user friendly, such as noting your preferences, may also serve to facilitate bias.

Uber encountered even more criticism when it used a pricing policy that undercut foreign-born taxi drivers who stopped going to international airports as a form of protest when a presidential travel ban from several predominantly Muslim countries was introduced in January 2017. Simultaneously, the Uber CEO was one of the few high-tech CEOs who agreed to meet with President Trump and serve on an economic advisory board. In response, 200,000 customers deleted their Uber accounts. In the wake of these developments, Uber changed its pricing policy, and the CEO resigned from the board, citing a "perception-reality gap" as the reason.

Admittedly, Silicon Valley is vulnerable to accusations of being out of touch with the diversity of the United States because its owners and policymakers are overwhelmingly White or Asian American men. As bias charges came to light, Airbnb and Uber both quickly moved to hire civil rights attorneys as well as diversity specialists to address discrimination in the sharing economy. In response to advertisers' ability to screen out people based on their "affinity," Facebook now requires its advertisers not to engage in discriminatory advertising on its site.

Clearly, as online options continue to multiply and evolve, society will have to remain vigilant that old-fashioned discrimination is not evolving right along with it.

Sources: Angwin and Parris Jr. 2016; Edelman, Luca, and Svirsky 2017; Glusac 2016; Guo 2016; Guynn 2016, 2017; Isaac 2017; Maheshwari and Isaac 2016.

Wealth Inequality: Discrimination's Legacy

Discrimination that has occurred in the past carries into the present and future. African Americans and other minority groups have had less opportunity to accumulate assets such as homes, land, and savings that can insulate them—and later, their children—from economic setbacks.

As noted earlier, *wealth* is a measure of what a household owns minus what it owes. It is a more inclusive term than *income* and encompasses all of a person's material assets, including land, stocks, and other types of property. Wealth allows one to live better; even modest assets provide insurance against the effects of job layoffs, natural disasters, and long-term illness, and they allow individuals to borrow money at much lower interest rates. Wealth allows children to graduate from college with little or no debt. This simple fact reminds us that for many people, wealth is not always related to assets but also can be measured by indebtedness.

Income disparities among groups are even greater when wealth is considered. Households headed by Whites have considerably higher wealth than those headed by Blacks. As Figure 3.4 shows, the median wealth of all White households in 2013 was $141,000, about 13 times that of Black households. The wealth gap between Black

Figure 3.4 Racial and Ethnic Wealth Gap, 1977–2013

By 2013, the typical White household had accumulated about 13 times as much wealth as African American households, and about 10 times as much wealth as Hispanic households.

NOTE: White households are those where both householders are White non-Hispanic or Black non-Hispanic.

SOURCE: Data from Pew Research Center (Kochhar and Fry 2014) analysis of data from the Federal Reserve's Survey of Consumer Finances public-use data.

Median Net Worth of U.S. Households in 2013 Dollars

	Black	Hispanic	White
1977	$10,000	$10,000	$98,700
2013	$11,000	$13,700	$141,000

households and White households has widened since 1983 because Whites as a group have accumulated more assets, while Black households' assets have barely grown. The gap between White and Latino households has followed a similar pattern.

The racial and ethnic differences in median net worth are driven in part by differences in home ownership. White householders have consistently higher rates of home ownership than racial and ethnic minorities. For instance, 72 percent of White householders own their own home, compared with 43 percent of Black householders. Today, 45 percent of Hispanic householders are homeowners, while the Asian American homeownership rate is 49 percent (Pew Research Center 2016).

Environmental Justice

3.5 Explain and discuss environmental justice.

Discrimination takes many forms; it can reach far beyond the labor market. Take the example of Flint, Michigan, a city two-thirds Black or Hispanic. This city of over 100,000 was facing hard times due to the closing of automobile factories; the city budget was stretched beyond its limits. Seeking to save money, the bankrupt city government (now taken over by the state of Michigan) chose in 2014 to get its water from the Flint River, which was cheaper than buying treated water as it had for 50 years from Detroit, which acquired its water from Lake Huron. The new water source was found to cause aging pipes to leach lead at unsafe levels into the water supply, permanently jeopardizing brain development in young children.

It took all too long for Michigan to address the problem and begin distributing bottled water to the entire city. Ironically, at about the same time, the state had approved a tax subsidy for a private beverage company to access a pure water aquifer in the northern part of the state to bottle water for commercial use throughout the Midwest. A state government report observed that decades of institutional discrimination, including redlining, created the social environment that allowed the actions of the past few years to be literally toxic (Eligon 2016; Michigan Civil Rights Commission 2017).

The conflict perspective sees the Flint case as one in which pollution harms minority groups disproportionately. **Environmental justice** refers to efforts to ensure that hazardous substances are controlled so that all communities receive protection, regardless of race or socioeconomic circumstance. After the Environmental Protection Agency (EPA) and other organizations documented discrimination in the location of hazardous waste sites, an executive order was issued in 1994 that requires all federal agencies to ensure that low-income and minority communities have access to better information about their environment and have an opportunity to participate in shaping government policies that affect their communities' health. Initial efforts to implement the policy have met widespread opposition, including criticism from some proponents of economic development who argue that the guidelines unnecessarily delay or altogether block new industrial sites.

A national study of households in 2014 found that most people do not reside near industrial hazards that lead to health problems or impair child development. However, those who do live near toxic sites are much more likely to be African Americans. Race is a key factor here even when controlling for income. Black families are more likely to live near toxic sites than White families with similar incomes. The same national study also found that, over time, Whites are more likely to move away from toxic communities than their Black neighbors (Pais, Crowder, and Downey 2014).

Issues of environmental justice are not limited to metropolitan areas. Another continuing problem is abuse of Native American reservation land. Many American Indian leaders are concerned that tribal lands are too often regarded as toxic waste dumping grounds that go to the highest bidder. However, the economic devastation faced by some tribes in isolated areas has led one tribe in Utah to offer its reservation as a depot for discarded nuclear waste (Jefferies 2007).

As with other aspects of discrimination, experts disagree about environmental issues and their impact on minority groups.

Bankrupt Flint, Michigan, a predominantly Black and Hispanic city of more than 100,000, decided to acquire a cheaper water supply that ended up polluting its residents' drinking water with dangerous levels of lead.

There is controversy within the scientific community over the potential hazards, and there is even some disagreement within the subordinate communities being affected, as some observers question the wisdom of an executive order that may slow economic development in areas that desperately need employment opportunities. Other observers counter that such businesses typically employ only a few unskilled workers and make the environment less livable for those left behind. Despite these different viewpoints, environmental justice is an excellent example of resistance and change in the 1990s that the civil rights workers of the 1950s could not have foreseen.

Affirmative Action

3.6 Explain affirmative action and the legal debate surrounding it.

Affirmative action is the positive effort to recruit subordinate-group members, including women, for jobs, promotions, and educational opportunities. The phrase *affirmative action* first appeared in an executive order issued by President John F. Kennedy in 1961. The order

Affirmative action seeks to diversify the workplace and other organizational settings.

"Oh, you'll love working here. Nobody treats you any differently just because of your age, race, or gender."

called for contractors to "take affirmative action to ensure that applicants are employed, and that employees are treated during employment, without regard to their race, creed, color, or national origin." However, at that time, no enforcement procedures were specified. Six years later, the order was amended to prohibit discrimination on the basis of sex, but affirmative action was still defined vaguely.

Today, affirmative action has become a catchall term for racial-preference programs and goals. It also has become a lightning rod for opposition to any programs that suggest special consideration of women or racial minorities.

Affirmative Action Explained

Affirmative action has been an important tool for reducing institutional discrimination. Whereas earlier efforts were aimed at preventing individual acts of discrimination, federal measures under the "affirmative action" heading have been aimed at procedures that deny equal opportunities, even if they are not intended to be overtly discriminatory.

Affirmative action has been aimed at institutional discrimination in all of the following areas:

- Height and weight requirements that are unnecessarily geared to the physical proportions of White men without regard to the actual characteristics needed to perform the job and that therefore exclude women and some minorities
- Seniority rules, when applied to jobs historically held only by White men, that make more recently hired minorities and women more subject to layoff—the "last hired, first fired" employee—and less eligible for advancement
- Nepotism-based membership policies of some unions that exclude those who are not relatives of members who, because of past employment practices, are usually White
- Restrictive employment leave policies, coupled with prohibitions on part-time work or denials of fringe benefits to part-time workers, that make it difficult for the heads of single-parent families, most of whom are women, to get and keep jobs and also meet their family's needs
- Rules requiring that only English be spoken at the workplace, even when not a business necessity, which result in discriminatory employment practices toward people whose primary language is not English
- Standardized academic tests or criteria geared to the cultural and educational norms of the middle class or White men when these are not relevant predictors of successful job performance
- Preferences shown by law and medical schools in admitting children of wealthy and influential alumni, most of whom are White
- Credit policies of banks and lending institutions that deny mortgages and loans in minority neighborhoods or that deny credit to married women and others who have previously been denied the opportunity to build good credit histories in their own names

Employers also have been cautioned against asking leading questions in interviews, such as "Did you know you would be the first Black to supervise all Whites in that factory?" or "Does your husband mind you working on weekends?" Furthermore, the lack of minority-group or female employees may in itself provide evidence for a case of unlawful exclusion (Commission on Civil Rights 1981; see also Bohmer and Oka 2007).

The Legal Debate

How far can an employer go in encouraging women and minorities to apply for a job before it becomes unlawful discrimination against White men? Since the late 1970s, several bitterly debated cases on this difficult aspect of affirmative action have reached the U.S. Supreme Court. Table 3.2 summarizes the most significant cases.

In the 1978 *Bakke* case (*Regents of the University of California v. Bakke*), by a narrow 5–4 vote, the Supreme Court ordered the medical school of the University of California at Davis to admit Allan Bakke, a qualified White engineer who had originally been denied admission solely on the basis of his race. The justices ruled that the school had violated Bakke's constitutional rights by establishing a fixed quota system for minority students. However, the Court added that it was constitutional for universities to adopt flexible admission programs that use race as one factor in making decisions.

Colleges and universities responded with new policies designed to meet the *Bakke* ruling while broadening opportunities for traditionally underrepresented minority students. The Supreme Court heard arguments in *Fisher v. University of Texas at Austin* arguing that a White woman, Abigail Fisher, missed out on automatic admission under a Texas provision that extended admissions to the top 10 percent of a high school's graduating class. While she was not in the top 10 percent at her school, she contended that non-Whites who did not have comparable academic preparation were admitted and that the top 10 percent provision leaves any further racial consideration unnecessary. In 2016, the Court rejected a lower court's decision challenging this "top 10 percent" admissions policy at the University of Texas at Austin. The ruling did not have any direct impact on any other institution's policies, although other schools probably will re-examine their procedures in light of the *Fisher* decision. Given the long history of legal actions, further challenges to affirmative action can be expected.

So what has happened to minority enrollment in higher education? Because the African American and Latino college-age population is increasing, analysis is difficult. However, in states such as California, Florida, Michigan, and Texas, which have been barred from using race explicitly in admissions, Black and Latino enrollment has dropped. Sometimes schools have approached minority enrollments in a manner similar to that used during the affirmative action period, often by implementing new admissions criteria, but often these non-race-specific criteria have been challenged by the opponents of affirmative action (Hoover 2013).

Has affirmative action truly helped to alleviate employment inequality on the basis of race and gender? This question is difficult to answer, given the complexity of the labor market and the fact that other antidiscrimination measures are in place, but it does appear that affirmative action has had a significant impact in the sectors where it has been applied. Sociologist Barbara Reskin (2012) reviewed available studies looking at workforce composition in terms of race and gender in light of affirmative action

Table 3.2 Key Decisions on Affirmative Action

In a series of split and often very close decisions, the Supreme Court has expressed a variety of reservations regarding affirmative action in specific situations.

Year	Favorable (+) or Unfavorable (−) to Affirmative Action	Case	Vote	Ruling
1971	+	Griggs v. Duke Power Co.	9–0	Private employers must provide a remedy where minorities were denied opportunities, even if unintentional
1978	−	Regents of the University of California v. Bakke	5–4	Prohibited holding a specific number of places for minorities in college admissions
1979	+	United Steelworkers of America v. Weber	5–2	Okay for unions to favor minorities in special training programs
1984	−	Firefighters Local Union No. 1784 (Memphis, TN) v. Stotts	6–1	Seniority means recently hired minorities may be laid off first in staff reductions
1986	+	International Association of Firefighters v. City of Cleveland	6–3	May promote minorities over more-senior Whites
1986	+	New York City v. Sheet Metal	5–4	Approved specific quota of minority workers for union
1987	+	United States v. Paradise	5–4	Endorsed quotas for promotions of state troopers
1987	+	Johnson v. Transportation Agency, Santa Clara, CA	6–3	Approved preference in hiring for minorities and women over better-qualified men and Whites
1989	−	Richmond v. Croson Company	6–3	Ruled a 30 percent set-aside program for minority contractors unconstitutional
1989	−	Martin v. Wilks	5–4	Ruled Whites may bring reverse discrimination claims against Court-approved affirmative action plans
1990	+	Metro Broadcasting v. FCC	5–4	Supported federal programs aimed at increasing minority ownership of broadcast licenses
1995	−	Adarand Constructors Inc. v. Peña	5–4	Benefits based on race are constitutional only if narrowly defined to accomplish a compelling interest
1996	−	Texas v. Hopwood	*	Let stand a lower court decision covering Louisiana, Mississippi, and Texas that race could not be used in college admissions
2003	+	Grutter v. Bollinger	5–4	Race can be a limited factor in admissions at the University of Michigan Law School
2003	−	Gratz v. Bollinger	6–3	Cannot use a strict formula awarding advantage based on race for admissions to the University of Michigan
2009	−	Ricci v. DeStefano	5–4	May not disregard a promotion test because Blacks failed to qualify for advancement
2016	+	Fisher v. University of Texas at Austin	4–3	Rejected a challenge to race-conscious college education programs

*U.S. Court of Appeals Fifth Circuit decision.

policies. She found that gains in minority employment could be attributed to affirmative action policies, both in firms mandated to follow affirmative action guidelines and those that adopted them voluntarily. There is also evidence that some earnings gains can be attributed to affirmative action. Economists M. V. Lee Badgett and Heidi Hartmann (1995), reviewing 26 other research studies, came to similar conclusions: Affirmative action and other federal compliance programs have had a modest impact, but it is difficult to assess their true efficacy, given larger economic changes such as recessions and the rapid increase of women in the paid labor force.

Reverse Discrimination

In addition to academics and researchers, the public—particularly Whites but also some affluent African Americans and Hispanics—have questioned the wisdom of affirmative action. Particularly strident are the charges of **reverse discrimination**: that government actions cause better-qualified White men to be bypassed in favor of women and minority men. *Reverse discrimination* is an emotional term, because it conjures up the notion that somehow women and minorities will subject White men in the United States to the same treatment received by minorities during the past three centuries. Such cases are not unknown, but they are uncommon.

Increasingly, critics of affirmative action call for color-blind policies that would end affirmative action and, they argue, allow all people to be judged fairly. However, would color-blind policies end institutional practices that favor Whites? For example, according to the latest data, 40 percent of applicants who are children of Harvard alumni, who are almost all White, are admitted to the university, compared to 11 percent of nonalumni children.

By contrast, at the competitive California Institute of Technology, which specifically does not use legacy preferences, only 1.5 percent of students are children of alumni. Ironically, studies show that students who are children of alumni are far more likely than either minority students or athletes to run into academic trouble (Kahlenberg 2010; Massey and Mooney 2007; Pincus 2003, 2008).

Supporters of affirmative action contend that as long as businesses rely on informal social networks, personal recommendations, and family ties to make hiring decisions, White men will have a distinct advantage built on generations of being in positions of power. Furthermore, an end to affirmative action would also mean an end to the many programs that give advantages to certain businesses, homeowners, veterans, and farmers. Most of these preference holders are White.

Affirmative action is not just a federal issue. It has also emerged as an increasingly important issue in state and national political campaigns. As noted earlier, in 2003, the Supreme Court reviewed the admission policies at the University of Michigan, which may favor racial minorities (see Table 3.2). In 2006, Michigan citizens voted, by a 58 percent margin, to restrict all their state universities from using affirmative action in their admissions policies.

Generally, at the state and local level, discussions have focused on the use of quotas in hiring practices. Supporters of affirmative action argue that hiring goals establish "floors" for minority inclusion but do not exclude truly qualified candidates from any group. Opponents insist that these "targets" are, in fact, quotas that lead to reverse discrimination (Lewin 2006; Mack 1996). California was a battleground for this controversial issue. The California Civil Rights Initiative (Proposition 209) was placed on the ballot in 1996 as a referendum to amend the state constitution and prohibit any programs that give preference to women and minorities for college admission, employment, promotion, or government contracts. Overall, 54 percent of the voters backed the proposition.

In 2009, the Supreme Court ruled 5–4 in the *Ricci v. DeStefano* case in favor of White firefighters. Many observers felt this outcome recognized reverse racism. In 2003, in New Haven, Connecticut, firefighters took an examination to identify possible candidates for promotions, but no African Americans taking the test qualified for advancement. Rather than select all White (including one Hispanic) firefighters, the city threw out the test results. The qualifying firefighters sued, claiming that they were victims of discrimination, and the Supreme Court eventually concurred.

The Glass Ceiling

3.7 **Explain the glass ceiling in the workplace.**

We have discussed racial and ethnic groups primarily as if they have uniformly failed to keep pace with Whites. Although this general conclusion is accurate, tens of thousands of people of color have matched and even exceeded Whites in terms of income. For example, in 2015, more than 181,000 Black households and over 253,000 Hispanic households earned more than $250,000 (Bureau of the Census 2016i:Table FINC-07). What can we say about financially better-off members of subordinate groups in the United States?

Prejudice does not necessarily end with wealth. Black newspaper columnist De Wayne Wickham (1993) wrote of the subtle racism he had experienced. He heard a White clerk in a supermarket ask a White customer whether she knew the price of an item the computer would not scan; when the problem occurred while the clerk was ringing up Wickham's groceries, she called for a price check. Affluent subordinate-group members routinely report being blocked as they move toward the first-class section aboard airplanes or seek service in upscale stores. Another journalist, Ellis Cose (1993), has called these insults the "soul-destroying slights to affluent minorities" that lead to the "rage of a privileged class."

Discrimination persists for even educated and qualified people from the most privileged family backgrounds. As subordinate-group members are able to compete successfully, they sometimes encounter attitudinal or organizational bias that prevents them from reaching their full potential. They have confronted what has come to be called the **glass ceiling**. This term refers to the barrier that blocks the promotion of qualified workers because of gender or minority-group membership (Figure 3.5). Often, people entering nontraditional areas of employment become marginalized and are made to feel uncomfortable, much like the situation of immigrants who feel like they are part of two cultures, as we discussed in Chapter 1.

There are many reasons for the existence of glass ceilings. It may be that one Black or one woman vice president is regarded as enough, so the second potential minority candidate faces an obstacle to upward movement through the organization. Decision-makers may be concerned that their customers will not trust them if they have too many people of color in top management, or they may worry that a talented woman could become overwhelmed with her duties as a mother and wife and thus perform poorly in a high-level job.

Figure 3.5 Glass Ceilings and Glass Walls

Women and minority men are moving up in corporations, but they encounter glass ceilings that block entry to top positions. In addition, they face glass walls that block lateral moves to areas from which executives are promoted. These barriers contribute to women and minority men not moving into the highest-level decision-making positions in the nation's major corporations.

Concern about women and minorities climbing a broken ladder led to the formation in 1991 of the Glass Ceiling Commission, with the U.S. secretary of labor chairing the 21-member group. Initially, it regarded the following as glass ceiling barriers:

- Lack of management commitment to establishing systems, policies, and practices for achieving workplace diversity and upward mobility
- Pay inequities for work of equal or comparable value
- Sex-, race-, and ethnicity-based stereotyping and harassment
- Unfair recruitment practices
- Lack of family-friendly workplace policies
- "Parent-track" policies that discourage parental leave
- Limited opportunities for advancement to decision-making positions

The significant underrepresentation of women and minority men in managerial positions results in large part from the presence of glass ceilings. Sociologist Max Weber wrote more than a century ago that the privileged class monopolizes the purchase of high-priced consumer goods and wields the power to grant or withhold opportunity from others. To grasp just how White and male the membership of this elite group is, consider the following: 84 percent of the people who serve on the boards of directors of Standard & Poor's listing of the 1,500 largest corporations are men. Among Fortune 500 corporations, just 3 percent of the boards of directors are Hispanic, and 70 percent of the boards did not have a single Latino (Hispanic Association on Corporate Responsibility 2013; Orsagh 2016; Weber 1947).

Catalyst, a nonprofit research organization, conducted interviews in 1992 and again in 2001 with senior and middle managers from larger corporations. The study found that even before glass ceilings are encountered, women and racial and ethnic minorities face **glass walls** that keep them from moving laterally. Specifically, the study found that women tend to be placed in staff or support positions in areas such as public relations and human resources and are often directed away from jobs in core areas such as marketing, production, and sales. Women are assigned to and therefore trapped in jobs that reflect their stereotypical helping nature, and they encounter glass walls that cut off access to jobs that might lead to broader experience and advancement (Bjerk 2008; Catalyst 2001; Lopez 1992).

Researchers have documented a differential impact of the glass ceiling on White males. It appears that men who enter traditionally female occupations are more likely to rise to the top. Male elementary teachers become principals, and male nurses become supervisors. The **glass escalator** refers to the White male advantage experienced in occupations dominated by women. Whereas women may become tokens when they enter traditionally male occupations, men are more likely to be advantaged when they move out of sex-typical jobs. In summary, women and minority men confront a glass ceiling that limits upward mobility and glass walls that reduce their ability to move into fast-track jobs leading to the highest reaches of the corporate executive suite. Meanwhile, White men who choose to enter female-dominated occupations are often rewarded with promotions and positions of responsibility coveted by their fellow female workers (Budig 2002; Cognard-Black 2004).

Figure 3.6 summarizes the spectrum of intergroup relations discussed in this chapter.

Figure 3.6 Spectrum of Intergroup Relations: Discrimination

EXPULSION — SEGREGATION — ASSIMILATION
INCREASINGLY UNACCEPTABLE ← → MORE TOLERABLE

EXTERMINATION or genocide | **SECESSION** or partitioning | **FUSION** or amalgamation or melting pot | **PLURALISM** or multiculturalism

- Hate Crimes
- Roma from France
- Redlining
- Glass Ceilings
- Environmental Justice
- Roma Schoolchildren in Czech Republic
- Federal Government Reservation System for Native Americans
- Civil Rights Act of 1964

Conclusion

What is it like to experience discrimination over and over again? Not just an occasional slight or a possible instance of discrimination, but constantly being treated differently because of your race, ethnicity, or gender? W. E. B. Du Bois (1903:9) wrote in his classic *The Souls of Black Folks*, "To be a poor man is hard, but to be a poor race in a land of dollars is the very bottom of hardships." Of course, not all members of racial and ethnic minorities, much less all women, are poor, but virtually all can recall instances where they were treated as second-class citizens, not necessarily by White men, but even by members of their own group or by other women.

Discrimination takes its toll, and people can be discriminated against in the informal economy or when looking for a job on the Internet. Even members of minority groups who are not today overtly discriminated against continue to fall victim to past discrimination.

From the conflict perspective, it is not surprising to find the widespread presence of an underclass. Derrick Bell (1994), an African American law professor, has made the sobering assertion that "racism is permanent." He contends that the attitudes of dominant Whites prevail, and society is willing to advance programs on behalf of subordinate groups only when they coincide with White needs.

The surveys presented in Chapter 2 show gradual acceptance of the earliest efforts to eliminate discrimination, but that support is failing as color-blind racism takes hold, especially as it relates to affirmative action. Indeed, concerns about alleged reverse discrimination are as likely to be voiced as concerns about racial or gender discrimination against Whites and men.

Institutional discrimination remains a formidable challenge in the United States. Attempts to reduce discrimination by attacking institutional discrimination have met with staunch resistance. Partly as a result of this outcry from some of the public, especially White Americans, the federal government gradually de-emphasized its affirmative action efforts, beginning in the 1980s and continuing into the twenty-first century. Most of the material in this chapter has been about racial groups, especially Black Americans and White Americans. It would be easy to see intergroup hostility as a racial phenomenon, but that would be incorrect. Throughout the history of the United States, relations between some White groups have also been characterized by resentment and violence. The next two chapters examine the ongoing legacy of immigration and the nature and relations of White ethnic groups.

Summary of Learning Objectives

3.1 Distinguish between relative and absolute deprivation.

1. Discrimination is likely to result in a feeling of relative deprivation, not necessarily absolute deprivation.

3.2 Define hate crimes.

2. A hate crime occurs when offenders are motivated to choose a victim because of some characteristic, such as race, ethnicity, religion, sexual orientation,

or disability. Hate crimes are caused by hostility that culminates in a criminal offense.

3.3 Summarize how institutions discriminate.

3. Institutional discrimination results from the normal operations of a society.
4. Discrimination in hiring has been documented through job-testing experiments.

3.4 Describe the effects of discrimination and the efforts to reduce or eliminate it.

5. Inequality continues to be apparent in the analysis of annual incomes (controlling for the amount of education attained) and wealth.
6. The Civil Rights Act of 1964 is a key piece of legislation seeking to reduce or eliminate discrimination. Presidential executive orders, legislative acts, and judicial decisions have all played a part in reducing discrimination.

3.5 Explain and discuss environmental justice.

7. Environmental justice refers to the efforts to ensure that hazardous substances are controlled so that all communities receive protection regardless of race or socioeconomic circumstance.

3.6 Explain affirmative action and the legal debate surrounding it.

8. For over 60 years, affirmative action as a remedy to inequality has been a hotly contested issue, with its critics contending that it amounts to reverse discrimination.

3.7 Explain the glass ceiling in the workplace.

9. Upwardly mobile professional women and minority men may encounter a glass ceiling and be thwarted in their professional efforts by glass walls.

Key Terms

absolute deprivation, *page 70*
affirmative action, *page 85*
discrimination, *page 69*
environmental justice, *page 84*
glass ceiling, *page 90*
glass escalator, *page 92*
glass walls, *page 92*
hate crime, *page 71*
income, *page 76*
institutional discrimination, *page 74*
redlining, *page 80*
relative deprivation, *page 70*
reverse discrimination, *page 89*
sharing economy, *page 81*
wealth, *page 76*

Review Questions

1. Why might people feel disadvantaged even though their incomes are rising and their housing circumstances have improved?
2. How do hate crimes differ from other types of felony crimes?
3. Why does institutional discrimination sometimes seem less objectionable than individual discrimination?
4. How do national income data point to discrimination?
5. What is the wealth disparity among racial and ethnic groups, and what is the trend in this disparity?
6. Explain how the concept of environmental justice relates to understanding racial and ethnic groups.

7. Why does affirmative action remain controversial even though inequality persists?
8. Define and provide an example of reverse discrimination.
9. Distinguish among glass ceilings, glass walls, and glass escalators. How do they differ from more obvious forms of employment discrimination?

Critical Thinking

1. What are the purposes of hate crimes? Do you think they serve those purposes?
2. Discrimination can take many forms. Select a case of discrimination that you think almost everyone would agree is wrong. Then describe another incident in which the alleged discrimination was subtler. Who is likely to condemn and who is likely to overlook such situations?
3. Discuss the social implications of wealth disparity between racial and ethnic groups on social mobility.
4. Resistance is a continuing theme of intergroup race relations. Discrimination implies the oppression of a group, but how can discrimination also unify the oppressed group to resist such unequal treatment? How can acceptance or integration weaken the sense of solidarity within a group?
5. Voluntary associations such as the National Association for the Advancement of Colored People (NAACP) and government units such as the courts have been important vehicles for bringing about a measure of social justice. In what ways can the private sector—corporations and businesses—also work to end discrimination?

Chapter 4
Immigration

Learning Objectives

4.1 Summarize the general patterns of immigration to the United States.

4.2 Describe how restrictionist sentiment has increased in the past 100 years.

4.3 Identify the concerns about immigration policy today.

4.4 Discuss the scope of and issues related to illegal immigration.

4.5 Outline the process of naturalization.

4.6 Explain the connection between globalization and immigration.

4.7 Describe the United States' policies toward refugees.

The 2016 presidential campaign saw candidates addressing immigration policy in vastly different ways. Some proudly posed next to immigrant workers who had revitalized long-shuttered businesses, while others trekked to the U.S.–Mexico border to make the case for increased surveillance and even the building of a wall between the two countries.

Well before that campaign season, immigration had profoundly shaped the United States, and it continues to do so today. For example, in South Orange, New Jersey, a small group of Haitian immigrants can be found every day in the public library, where they study together in their quest to become nurses. When, in 1996, the city became a stop on a direct commuter line into Manhattan, many immigrant households relocated from New York City to take advantage of the more affordable housing in the New Jersey suburbs. Now nearly a third of the library's patrons speak a language other than English at home. Over three-quarters of the public school students are immigrants, mostly illegal, or the children of illegal immigrants.

Also consider rural Garden City, Kansas, a city of 30,000 that coincidentally has a replica of the Statue of Liberty donated by the Boy Scouts in 1950. At the time the statue was donated, Garden City had virtually no foreign-born residents. Today, three-quarters of the public schools' students are immigrants or the children of immigrants. The overseas residents were first attracted to Garden City by new jobs at a beef processing plant, and the economic expansion that followed was fueled by the availability of workers. Eventually, the unemployment rate dropped well below the national average. Today, Garden City residents include immigrants from Burma (Myanmar), Laos, Somalia, and Vietnam, as well as Latin American countries. The relative calm of Garden City was marred when the FBI uncovered a plot by three men from neighboring communities to bomb a housing complex that is home to many Somali Americans. The city's police chief responded that the plot was not just an attack on a specific group but also an attack on "our community."

Garden City, Kansas, a rural community of 30,000, has attracted immigrants from many countries and built a replica of the Statue of Liberty outside the county court house.

Clarkston, Georgia, outside of Atlanta, is not an immigrant destination but rather a refugee haven. The town has accepted and helped to resettle more than 60,000 refugees since 1983. At that time, Clarkston embraced a short-lived federal refugee-resettlement program because more of its housing was becoming vacant as residents moved to more affluent communities. Four out of five refugee families became self-sufficient with six months of arriving. However, challenges do exist, especially in educating the refugee children and bringing them up to state educational norms. Now home to 150 nationality groups, Clarkston has come to rely on refugees as a source of economic progress.

American communities (large and small) across the continent are home to immigrants and refugees. While criticism continues about many aspects of immigration policy, which we will consider in this chapter, 53 percent of the public in 2017 indicated they were satisfied with the level of immigration into the United States, and another 5 percent favored more immigrants (Aust 2016; Gates 2017; Gomez 2014; Jonsson 2016a; Toppo and Overberg 2014).

The world is now a global network. The core and periphery countries, described in world systems theory (see Chapter 1), link not only commercial goods but also families and workers across political borders. Social forces that cause people to emigrate are complex. Scholars of immigration often point to *push factors* and *pull factors*. For example, economic difficulties, religious or ethnic persecution, and political unrest may *push* individuals from their homelands. The *pull* factors may be perceptions of a better life in another country or a desire to reunite families or join a community of fellow nationals already established abroad. Immigration into the United States, in particular, has been facilitated by cheap ocean transportation and by other countries' removal of restrictions on emigration.

A potent factor contributing to immigration anywhere in the world is chain immigration. **Chain immigration** refers to a process by which an immigrant sponsors several other immigrants who, upon their arrival, may sponsor still more immigrants. Laws that favor would-be immigrants who already have relatives or someone who can vouch for them financially in the receiving country may facilitate this sponsorship. But probably the most important aspect of chain immigration is that immigrants anticipate knowing someone who can help them adjust to their new surroundings and find a new job, a place to live, and even the kinds of foods that are familiar to them.

Patterns of Immigration to the United States

4.1 Summarize the general patterns of immigration to the United States.

Immigration to the United States has three unmistakable patterns: (1) the number of immigrants has fluctuated dramatically over time, largely because of government policy changes; (2) settlement has not been uniform across the country but centered in certain regions and cities; and (3) the immigrants' countries of origin have changed over time. First, we look at the historical picture of immigrant numbers.

Vast numbers of immigrants have come to the United States. Figure 4.1 indicates the high but fluctuating number of immigrants who arrived during every decade from the 1820s through the beginning of the twenty-first century. The United States received the largest number of legal immigrants during the first decade of the 2000s; that number likely will be surpassed in the second decade of the 2000s. However, the country's population was much smaller in the period from 1900 through 1910, so the numerical impact was even greater then.

Immigrants to the United States have not always received a friendly reception. Open bloodshed, restrictive laws, and the eventual return of almost one-third of immigrants and their children to their home countries attest to some Americans' uneasy feelings toward strangers who want to settle among them. Generally, surveys show immigrants perceiving some ambivalence, and occasionally outright intolerance, from some native-born Americans they encounter.

Before considering the sweep of past immigration policies, let us consider today's immigrant population. About 14 percent of the nation's people are foreign-born—the highest level since the 1920s. As recently as 1979, this proportion was just 4.7 percent. By global comparisons, the foreign-born population in the United States is large but not unusual. Whereas most industrial countries have a foreign-born population of around 6–11 percent, Canada's foreign-born population is 20 percent, and Australia's is 28 percent (Porter 2015).

Figure 4.1 Legal Immigration to the United States, 1820–2020

Through the 1950s, immigration to the United States was largely from Europe and Canada. However, since the 1960s, immigration has largely been from Asia and Latin America.

SOURCE: Office of Immigration Statistics 2016 and author's estimates for projection out to 2020.

As noted earlier, immigrants have not settled evenly across the nation. As Figure 4.2 shows, four states—California, New York, Florida, and New Jersey—account for 45 percent of the nation's total foreign-born population but less than 28 percent of the nation's total overall population.

The source regions of immigrants have changed. First, settlers came from Europe, then Latin America, and now, increasingly, Asia. Europeans were the dominant immigrant group through the 1950s. The majority of today's 41.7 million foreign-born people are from Latin America rather than Europe. Primarily, they are from Central America and, more specifically, Mexico (although Mexico is sometimes considered a part of North America). By contrast, Europeans, who dominated the early settlement of the United States, now account for fewer than one in seven of the foreign-born today. The changing patterns of immigration have continued into the twenty-first century. Beginning in 2010, the annual immigration from Asia exceeded the level of annual immigration from Latin America for the first time.

The Early Immigrants

Settlers, the first immigrants to the Western Hemisphere, soon followed the European explorers of North America. The Spanish founded St. Augustine, Florida, in 1565, and the English founded Jamestown, Virginia, in 1607. Protestants from England

Figure 4.2 Foreign-Born Population in the United States

SOURCE: Data from American Community Survey 2016a: R0501.

Percent
- 20.0 or higher
- 15.0 to 19.9
- 10.00 to 14.9
- 5.0 to 9.9
- Less than 5.0

U.S. percent: 12.9

emerged from the colonial period as the dominant force numerically, politically, and socially. The English accounted for 60 percent of the 3 million White Americans in 1790. Although exact statistics are lacking for the early years of the United States, the English were soon outnumbered by other nationalities— particularly Scotch-Irish and Germans—as their numbers swelled. However, the English colonists maintained their dominant position.

Throughout American history, immigration policy has been politically controversial. The U.S. Declaration of Independence criticized the policies of King George III of England for obstructing immigration to the colonies. Toward the end of the nineteenth century, the American republic itself was criticized for enacting immigration restrictions. In the beginning, however, the country encouraged immigration. Legislation initially fixed the residence requirement for naturalization at five years, although briefly, under the Alien Act of 1798, it was 14 years, and so-called dangerous people could be expelled. Other than this brief period of harshness, immigration was unregulated through most of the 1800s, and naturalization was easily available. Until 1870, naturalization was limited to "free white persons" (Calavita 2007).

Although some people hold the mistaken belief that concern about immigration is a relatively new phenomenon, some people also assume that immigrants to the United States rarely reconsider their decision to come to a new country. Analysis of available records, beginning in the early 1900s, suggests that about 35 percent of all immigrants to the United States eventually migrate back to their home country. The proportion varies, with the figures for some countries being much higher, but the overall pattern is clear: About one in three immigrants to this nation eventually choose to return home (Wyman 1993).

The relative absence of federal legislation from 1790 to 1881 does not mean that all new arrivals were welcomed. **Xenophobia** (the fear or hatred of strangers or foreigners) led naturally to **nativism** (beliefs and policies favoring native-born citizens over immigrants). Although the term *nativism* has largely been used to describe nineteenth-century sentiments, anti-immigration views and organized movements have continued into the twenty-first century. Political scientist Samuel P. Huntington (1993, 1996) articulated the continuing immigration as a "clash of civilizations" that could be remedied only by significantly reducing legal immigration, in addition to closing the borders to illegal arrivals. His view, which enjoys support, is that the fundamental world conflicts of the new century are cultural rather than ideological or even economic (Citrin et al. 2007; Schaefer 2008b).

The most dramatic outbreak of nativism in the nineteenth century was aimed at the Chinese.

The Anti-Chinese Movement

Before 1851, official records show that only 46 Chinese had immigrated to the United States. Over the next 30 years, more than 200,000 Chinese came to this country, lured by the discovery of gold and the opening of job opportunities in the West. Overcrowding, drought, and warfare in China also encouraged them to take a chance in the United States. Another important factor was improved oceanic transportation; it was cheaper to travel from Hong Kong to San Francisco than from Chicago to San Francisco. The frontier communities of the West, particularly in California, looked on the Chinese as a valuable resource to fill manual jobs. As early as 1854, so many Chinese wanted to emigrate that ships had difficulty handling the volume.

In the 1860s, railroad work provided the greatest demand for Chinese labor until the Union Pacific and Central Pacific railroads were joined at Promontory Summit, Utah, in 1869. Union Pacific relied primarily on Irish laborers, but 90 percent of Central Pacific's labor force was Chinese because Whites generally refused to do the backbreaking work over the Western terrain.

Chinese workers, such as these pictured in 1844, played a major role in building railroads in the West.

With the dangerous railroad work largely completed, people began to rethink the wisdom of encouraging Chinese to immigrate to do the work no one else would do. Reflecting their xenophobia, White settlers found the Chinese immigrants, their customs, and religion difficult to understand. Indeed, few people tried to understand these immigrants from Asia. Although they'd had no firsthand contact with Chinese Americans, Easterners and legislators soon jumped on the anti-Chinese bandwagon as they read sensationalized accounts of the new arrivals' lifestyles.

Even before the Chinese immigrated, stereotypes of them and their customs were prevalent. American traders returning from China, European diplomats, and Protestant missionaries consistently emphasized the exotic and sinister aspects of life in China. **Sinophobes**, people who fear anything associated with China, subscribed to the racist theory developed during the slavery controversy that non-Europeans were subhuman. Americans also were becoming more conscious of biological inheritance and disease, so it was not hard to conjure up fears of alien genes and germs. The only real challenge the anti-Chinese movement faced was convincing people that the negative consequences of unrestricted Chinese immigration outweighed any possible economic gain. Earlier, racial prejudice was subordinated to industrial dependence on Chinese labor for the work that Whites shunned, but acceptance of the Chinese was short-lived. The fear of the "yellow peril" overwhelmed any desire to know more about Asian peoples and their customs (Takaki 1998).

Employers were glad to pay the Chinese low wages, but non-Chinese laborers began directing their resentment against the Chinese rather than against their compatriots' willingness to exploit the Chinese. Only a generation earlier, the same concerns were expressed about the Irish, but with the Chinese, the hostility reached new heights because of another factor.

Although many arguments were voiced, racial fears motivated the anti-Chinese movement. Race was the critical issue. The labor-market fears were largely unfounded, and most advocates of restrictions knew that. There was no possibility of the Chinese immigrating in numbers that would match those of Europeans at that time, so it is difficult to find any explanation other than racism for their fears (Winant 1994).

From the sociological perspective of conflict theory, we can explain how the Chinese immigrants were welcomed only when their labor was necessary to fuel growth in the United States. When that labor was no longer necessary, the welcome mat for the immigrants was withdrawn. Furthermore, as conflict theorists point out, restrictions were not applied evenly: Americans focused on a specific nationality (the Chinese) to reduce the number of foreign workers in the nation. Because decision-making at that time rested in the hands of the descendants of European immigrants, the steps taken were most likely to be directed against the least powerful: immigrants from China, who, unlike Europeans seeking entry, had few allies among legislators and other policymakers.

In 1882, Congress enacted the Chinese Exclusion Act, which outlawed Chinese immigration for ten years. It also explicitly denied naturalization rights to the Chinese in the United States; that is, they were not allowed to become citizens. There was little debate in Congress, and discussion concentrated on how to best handle suspending Chinese immigration. No allowance was made for wives and children to be reunited with their husbands and fathers in the United States. Only brief visits of Chinese government officials, teachers, tourists, and merchants were exempted.

In 1892, Congress extended the Exclusion Act for another ten years and added that Chinese laborers had to obtain certificates of residence within a year or face deportation. After the turn of the century, the Exclusion Act was extended again. In 2012, Congress unanimously passed a resolution apologizing for the passage of the Chinese Exclusion Act. This marked only the fourth official apology in the past 25 years—the other three were for slavery, the internment of Japanese Americans during World War II, and mistreatment of native Hawaiians and the overthrow of their rule of the islands (Nahm 2012).

Restrictionist Sentiment Increases

4.2 **Describe how restrictionist sentiment has increased in the past 100 years.**

As Congress closed the door to Chinese immigration, the debate on restricting immigration turned in new directions. Prodded by growing anti-Japanese feelings, the United States entered into the so-called gentlemen's agreement, which was completed in 1908. Japan agreed to halt further immigration to the United States, and the United States agreed to end discrimination against the Japanese who had already arrived. The immigration ended, but anti-Japanese feelings continued. Americans were growing uneasy that the "new immigrants" would overwhelm the culture established by the "old immigrants." The earlier immigrants, if not Anglo-Saxon, were from similar groups such as the Scandinavians, the Swiss, and the French Huguenots. These people were more experienced in democratic political practices and had a greater affinity with the dominant Anglo-Saxon culture. By the end of the nineteenth century, however, more and more immigrants were neither English-speaking nor Protestant and came from dramatically different cultures.

The National Origin System

Beginning in 1921, a series of measures was enacted that marked a new era in American immigration policy. Whatever the legal language, the measures were drawn up to block the growing immigration from southern Europe (from Italy and Greece, for example) and also to block all Asian immigrants by establishing a zero quota for them.

To understand the effect of the national origin system on immigration, it is necessary to clarify the quota system. Quotas were deliberately weighted to favor immigration from northern Europe. Because of the ethnic composition

Many of the late 19th century and early 20th century immigrants to the United States were Jews seeking the opportunity to work at the jobs they wanted and to practice their faith, both of which were often restricted in their country of origin. Shown here are Jewish shoppers, many of them immigrants, crowding Orchard Street in New York City in 1923.

of the United States in 1920, the quotas placed severe restrictions on immigration from the rest of Europe and from other parts of the world. Immigration from the Western Hemisphere (i.e., Canada, Mexico, Central and South America, and the Caribbean) continued unrestricted. The quota for each nation was set at 3 percent of the number of people descended from each nationality recorded in the 1920 census. Once the statistical manipulations were completed, almost 70 percent of the quota for the Eastern Hemisphere went to just three countries: Great Britain, Ireland, and Germany.

Although it was not opened until 1892, New York Harbor's Ellis Island—the country's first federal immigration facility—quickly became the symbol of all migrant streams to the United States. By the time it closed in late 1954, it had processed 17 million immigrants. Today, their descendants number over 100 million Americans.

The absurdities of the system soon became obvious, but it was nevertheless continued. British immigration had fallen sharply, so most of its quota of 65,000 went unfilled. However, the openings could not be transferred, even though countries such as Italy (with a quota of only 6,000) had 200,000 people who wanted to immigrate to the United States. However one rationalizes the purpose behind the act, the result was obvious: Any English person, regardless of skill and whether related to anyone already in the United States, could enter the country more easily than, say, a Greek doctor whose children were American citizens. The quota for Greece was 305, with the backlog of people wanting to come to the United States reaching 100,000.

By the end of the 1920s, annual immigration had dropped to one-fourth of its pre–World War I level. The worldwide economic depression of the 1930s decreased immigration still further. A brief upsurge in immigration just before World War II reflected the flight of Europeans from the oppression of expanding Nazi Germany. The war virtually ended transatlantic immigration. The era of the great European migration to the United States had been legislated out of existence.

The Immigration and Nationality Act

The national origin system was abandoned with the passage of the 1965 Immigration and Nationality Act (also called the Hart-Cellar Act), signed into law by President Lyndon B. Johnson at the foot of the Statue of Liberty. The primary goals of the act were to reunite families and to protect the American labor market. The act also initiated restrictions on immigration from Latin America. After the act, immigration increased by one-third, but the act's influence was primarily on the composition rather than the size of immigration. The sources of immigrants

Figure 4.3 Legal Immigrants Admitted to the United States by Region of Last Residence, 1820–2015

SOURCE: Office of Immigration Statistics 2016.

1820–1860
- Europe 90%
- Other 8%
- Canada 2%

1861–1900
- Europe 90%
- Canada 7%
- Other 1%
- Asia 2%

1901–1940
- Europe 79%
- Canada 10%
- Latin America 6%
- Asia 4%
- Other 1%

1941–1980
- Europe 34%
- Latin America 34%
- Asia 19%
- Canada 10%
- Other 3%

1981–2015
- Latin America 49%
- Asia 34%
- Europe 12%
- Other 3%
- Canada 2%

now included Italy, Greece, Portugal, Mexico, the Philippines, the West Indies, and South America.

The lasting effect is apparent when we compare the changing sources of immigration over the past 200 years, as shown in Figure 4.3. The most recent period shows that Asian Pacific and Latin American immigrants combined to account for 83 percent of the people who were permitted entry. This contrasts sharply with early immigration (1820–1940), which was dominated by arrivals from Europe.

The nature of immigration laws is exceedingly complex and is subjected to frequent, often minor, adjustments. From 2005 to 2015, between 990,000 and 1,270,000 people were legally admitted to the United States each year. In 2015, people were admitted for the following reasons:

- Relatives of citizens   55%
- Relatives of legal residents   10%
- Employment-based   14%
- Refugees/people seeking political asylum   14%
- Diversity (lottery among applications from nations historically sending few immigrants)   4%
- Other   3%

Overall, two-thirds of immigrants come to join their families, one-seventh because of skills needed in the United States, and another one-seventh because of special refugee status. However, it would be a mistake to think family reunions are easy to accomplish. Because there are limits on how many people can enter legally each year for any one country, backlogs exist for such nations as China, India, Mexico, and the Philippines. So, for example, as of 2016, there was a 23-year backlog for adult children from the Philippines to join their American citizen parents. Similarly, there was a 21-year backlog for the Mexican married children of American citizens to join their parents (Aptekar 2016; Office of Immigration Statistics 2016: Table 6).

Contemporary Social Concerns

4.3 Identify the concerns about immigration policy today.

Although current U.S. immigration policies are less restrictive than those of other nations, they are the subject of great debate. Table 4.1 summarizes the benefits and concerns regarding immigration to the United States. We now consider six continuing criticisms relating to U.S. immigration policy: the brain drain, population growth, mixed-status families, English-language acquisition, economic impact, and illegal immigration. All six, but particularly illegal immigration, have provoked

Table 4.1 Immigration Benefits and Concerns

Potential Benefits	Areas of Concern
Provide needed skills	Drain needed resources from home country
Pay taxes	Send money home
May come with substantial capital to start business	Less-skilled immigrants compete with already disadvantaged residents
Maintain growth of consumer market	Population growth
Diversify the population	Language differences
Maintain ties with countries throughout the world	May include people with destructive tendencies, such as terrorists and other criminals
Offset relatively low birth rate among U.S.-born nationals	Illegal immigration

heated debates on the national level and continuing efforts to resolve them with new policies.

The Brain Drain

How often have you identified your science or mathematics teacher or your physician as someone who was not born in the United States? This nation has clearly benefited from attracting human resources from throughout the world, but this phenomenon has had negative effects on the immigrants' nations of origin.

Brain drain is the immigration to the United States of skilled workers, professionals, and technicians who are desperately needed by their home countries. In the mid-twentieth century, many scientists and other professionals from industrial nations, principally Germany and Great Britain, came to the United States. More recently, the brain drain has pulled emigrants from developing nations, including India, Pakistan, the Philippines, and several African nations. They are eligible for H-1B visas that qualify them for permanent work permits.

The H-1B visa program began in 1990. Currently, 65,000 foreigners with at a least a bachelor's degree and a specialized skill receive the H-1B visa. Another 20,000 such visas go to foreign nationals with advanced degrees from U.S. universities. In these cases, people come to the United States on a student visa, secure a degree (say, in engineering), and then may apply for the H-1B.

More than one out of four physicians (27 percent) in the United States is foreign-born and plays a critical role in serving areas with too few doctors. Thousands of doctors have sought to enter the United States, pulled by the economic opportunity. Persons born in India, the Philippines, and China account for the largest groups of foreign-born physicians. The pay differential is so great that, beginning in 2004, when foreign physicians were no longer favored with entry to the United States, physicians in the Philippines retrained as nurses so that they could immigrate to the United States where, employed as nurses, they would make four times what they would earn as doctors in the Philippines. By 2010, one-third of the foreign-born workers employed as registered nurses were born in the Philippines (McCabe 2012; *New York Times* 2005).

Many foreign students say they plan to return home. Fortunately for the United States, many do not, instead continuing to make their talents available in the United States. One study showed that the majority of foreign students receiving their doctorates in the sciences and engineering remained here four years later. Critics note, however, that this foreign supply means that the United States overlooks its own minority scholars. Currently, for every African American and Latino student who receives a doctorate, a foreign citizen receives the same degree in the United States. More encouragement must be given to African Americans and Latinos to enter high-tech career paths.

Conflict theorists see the current brain drain as yet another symptom of the unequal distribution of world resources. In their view, it is ironic that the United States gives foreign aid to improve the technical resources of African and Asian countries while maintaining an immigration policy that encourages professionals in such nations to migrate to our shores. These countries have unacceptable public-health conditions and need native scientists, educators, technicians, and other professionals. In addition, by relying on foreign talent, the United States is not encouraging native members of subordinate groups to enter these desirable fields of employment (Collier 2013).

The H-1B visa program became a part of the controversy over efforts to institute new immigration policies in 2017, which even included a travel ban from certain predominantly Muslim countries. Most heads of tech firms, generally known for being silent on political controversies, condemned these efforts, or at the very least said they did not support measures that either directly or indirectly reduced the flow of desired workers and their relatives and friends. Also relevant is the fact that many successful start-up tech firms were founded or are operated by recent immigrants (Sorkin 2017).

Population Growth

The United States, like a few other industrialized nations, continues to accept large numbers of permanent immigrants and refugees. Although such immigration has increased since the passage of the 1965 Immigration and Nationality Act, the nation's birth rate has decreased. Consequently, the contribution of immigration to population growth has become more significant. As citizen "baby boomers" (Americans born during the post–World War II baby boom) age, the country has increasingly depended on the younger population fueled by immigration.

Immigration, legal and illegal, accounted for 55 percent of the nation's growth from 1965 to 2015. Looking further ahead, consider the following estimates:

- 2055 U.S. population with NO future immigration 338 million
- 2055 U.S. population with immigration continuing at current levels 441 million

These projections compare to a population of 325 million in 2017.

To some observers, the United States is already overpopulated. Environmentalists have weighed in on the immigration issue, questioning immigration's possible negative impact on the nation's natural resources. We consider that aspect of the immigration debate later in this chapter. Thus far, the majority of environmentalists have indicated a desire to keep a neutral position rather than enter the politically charged immigration debate (Lopez, Passel, and Rohal 2015).

The patterns of uneven settlement by immigrants in the United States are expected to continue, so future immigrants' impact on population growth will be felt much more in certain areas, for example, in California and New York rather than in Wyoming or West Virginia. Although immigration and population growth may be viewed as national concerns, their impact is localized in certain areas, such as Southern California and large urban centers nationwide.

Mixed-Status Families

Little is simple when it comes to immigration. This is particularly true regarding the challenge of the estimated 9 million people living in mixed-status families. **Mixed status** refers to families in which one or more members are citizens and one or more are noncitizens. This situation becomes especially problematic when the noncitizens are illegal or undocumented immigrants.

The problem of mixed status emerges on two levels. On the macro level, when policy debates are made about issues that seem clear to many people—such as whether illegal immigrants should be allowed to attend state colleges or whether illegal immigrants should be immediately deported—the complicating factor of mixed-status families quickly emerges. On the micro level, the daily toll on members of mixed-status households is considerable. Often, the legal resident or even the U.S. citizen in a household finds daily life limited for fear of revealing the undocumented status of a parent, brother, sister, son, or daughter.

About three-quarters of illegal immigrants' children were born in the United States and thus are citizens. This means that perhaps half of all adult illegal immigrants have a citizen in their immediate family. This proportion has grown in recent years. Therefore, some of the issues facing illegal immigrants, whom we discuss later, also affect the citizens in their families; these citizens avoid calling attention to themselves for fear of revealing their mother or father's illegal status. Immigration issues aside, one can only begin to imagine the additional pressure this fear places on families beyond the usual stresses of balancing work and home, school, and children moving through adolescence to adulthood (Gonzales 2011; Gonzalez 2009; Passel and Cohn 2009; Pew Hispanic Center 2011b).

Imagine that you are a U.S. citizen, born here, and that you are unable to prevent both of your parents from being deported. Such was the case for Diane Guerrero, who is better known for her work in television than for her volunteer work with the Immigrant Legal Resource Center, a nonprofit group that advances immigrants' rights. In the Speaking Out box, "My Parents Were Deported," she recounts her family's situation.

A sensitive aspect of mixed-status households is the young people who are in the United States illegally but came here at such a young age that they have no experience in their "home nation," often not understanding the language and culture of the nation to which they could potentially be deported. One solution suggested for children over 15 years old is the DREAM Act: Development, Relief, and Education for Alien Minors. This act would offer a path to legal resident status for high-school graduates despite being in the country illegally. During his administration, President Barack Obama issued an executive order sparing the 750,000 "Dreamers" from deportation; however, executive orders can be reversed by the next administration. At his final press conference as president, Obama (2017) noted the threat to U.S. core values of any attempt to "round up kids ... and send them someplace else when they love this country." The issues facing mixed-status families continue to remain a challenge to policymakers.

Language Barriers

For many people in the United States, the most visible signs of immigration are non-English speakers, businesses with foreign-language storefronts, and even familiar stores assuring potential customers that their employees speak Spanish, Polish, Chinese, or another foreign language. Non-English speakers cluster in certain states,

Speaking Out

My Parents Were Deported

Diane Guerrero

In *Orange Is the New Black*, I play Maritza Ramos, a tough Latina from the 'hood. In *Jane the Virgin*, I play Lina, Jane's best friend and a funny know-it-all who is quick to offer advice.

I love both parts, but they're fiction. My real story is this: I am the citizen daughter of immigrant parents who were deported when I was 14. My older brother was also deported.

My parents came here from Colombia during a time of great instability there. Escaping a dire economic situation at home, they moved to New Jersey, where they had friends and family, seeking a better life, and then moved to Boston after I was born.

Throughout my childhood I watched my parents try to become legal but to no avail. They lost their money to people they believed to be attorneys, but who ultimately never helped. That meant my childhood was haunted by the fear that they would be deported. If I didn't see anyone when I walked in the door after school, I panicked.

And then one day, my fears were realized. I came home from school to an empty house. Lights were on and dinner had been started, but my family wasn't there. Neighbors broke the news that my parents had been taken away by immigration officers, and just like that, my stable family life was over.

Not a single person at any level of government took any note of me. No one checked to see if I had a place to live or food to eat, and at 14, I found myself basically on my own.

Diane Guerrero

Robin Platzer/Twin Images/ZUMA Press/Newscom

While awaiting deportation proceedings, my parents remained in detention near Boston, so I could visit them. They would have liked to fight deportation, but without a lawyer and in an immigration system that rarely gives judges the discretion to allow families to stay together, they never had a chance. Finally, they agreed for me to continue my education at Boston Arts Academy, a performing arts high school, and the parents of friends graciously took me in.

Insecure about being a nuisance and losing my invitation to stay, I worked a variety of jobs in retail and at coffee shops all through high school. And though I was surrounded by people who cared about me, part of me ached with every accomplishment, because my parents weren't there to share my joy.

My family and I worked hard to keep our relationships strong, but too-short phone calls and the annual summer visits I made to Colombia didn't suffice. They missed many important events in my life, including my singing recitals—they watched my senior recital on a tape I sent them instead of from the audience. And they missed my prom, my college application process, and my graduations from high school and college.

My story is all too common. Every day, children who are U.S. citizens are separated from their families as a result of immigration policies that need fixing.

I consider myself lucky because things turned out better for me than for most, including some of my own family members. When my brother was deported, his daughter was just a toddler. She still had her mother, but in a single-parent household, she faced a lot of challenges. My niece made the wrong friends and bad choices. Today, she is serving time in jail, living the reality that I act out on screen. I don't believe her life would have turned out this way if her father and my parents had been here to guide and support her.

I realize the issues are complicated. But it's not just in the interest of immigrants to fix the system: It's in the interest of all Americans. Children who grow up separated from their families often end up in foster care, or worse, in the juvenile justice system, despite having parents who love them and would like to be able to care for them.

I don't believe it reflects our values as a country to separate children and parents in this way. Nor does it reflect our values to hold people in detention without access to good legal representation or a fair shot in a court of law. . . . Keeping families together is a core American value.

Congress needs to provide a permanent, fair legislative solution, but in the meantime families are being destroyed every day, and the president should do everything in his power to provide the broadest relief possible now. Not one more family should be separated by deportation.

Source: Guererro, Diane, Op-Ed, "'Orange is the New Black' actress: My parents were deported." Los Angeles Times. November 15, 2014. Used with permission.

---

but bilingualism attracts nationwide passions. The release in 2006 of "Nuestro Himno," the Spanish-language version of "The Star-Spangled Banner," led to a strong reaction, with 69 percent of people saying it was appropriate to be sung only in English. Yet at least one congressman who decried the Spanish version sang the anthem himself in English with incorrect lyrics (Carroll 2006; Koch 2006).

About 21 percent of the population speaks a language other than English at home, as Figure 4.4 shows. Indeed, 39 different languages are spoken at home by at least 90,000 residents. Spanish accounts for 62 percent of the foreign-language speakers at

Figure 4.4 Ten Languages Most Frequently Spoken at Home, Other Than English and Spanish, 2013

Of 291 million people over five years of age, 231 million only speak English at home, 38 million speak Spanish, and about 22 million speak some other language.

SOURCE: Data for 2009–2013 in Bureau of the Census 2015a.

Language	Millions
Italian	0.7
French Creole	0.7
Russian	0.9
Arabic	0.9
German	1.0
Korean	1.1
French	1.3
Vietnamese	1.4
Tagalog	1.6
Chinese	2.9

home. As of 2013, about half of the 61 million people speaking a foreign language at home spoke English less than "very well." Since 1980, the largest growth has been in speakers of Spanish, Chinese, Korean, Vietnamese, Tagalog (the language of the Philippines), Russian, and Farsi (the language of Iran). The largest decreases have all been in European-based languages such as Italian, Greek, German, Yiddish, and Polish (Ryan 2013).

Until the past 40 years, a conscious effort was made to devalue Spanish and other languages and to discourage the use of foreign languages in schools. In the case of Spanish, this practice was built on a pattern of segregating Hispanic schoolchildren from Anglos. In the recent past in the Southwest, Mexican Americans were assigned to Mexican schools to keep Anglo schools all White. These Mexican schools, created through explicit school segregation resulting from residential segregation, were substantially underfunded compared with the Anglo public schools. Legal action against such schools dates back to 1945, but it was not until 1970 that the U.S. Supreme Court ruled, in *Cisneros v. Corpus Christi Independent School District*, that segregation of Mexican Americans was unconstitutional. Appeals delayed implementation of that decision, and not until September 1975 was the plan forcibly overturned in Corpus Christi, Texas (Commission on Civil Rights 1976).

Is it essential that English be the sole language of instruction in schools in the United States? **Bilingualism** is the use of two or more languages in places of work or educational facilities, and it accords each language equal legitimacy. Thus, a program of **bilingual education** may instruct children in their native language (for example, Spanish) while gradually introducing them to the language of the dominant society (English). If such a program also is bicultural, it will teach children about the culture of both linguistic groups. Bilingual education allows students to learn academic material in their own language while they learn a second language. Proponents believe that, ideally, bilingual education programs should also allow English-speaking pupils to become bilingual, but generally these programs are directed only at making non-English speakers proficient in more than one language.

Do bilingual programs help children learn English? It is difficult to reach firm conclusions on the effectiveness of bilingual programs in general because they vary so widely in their approach. The programs differ in the length of the transition to English and how long they allow students to remain in bilingual classrooms. A major study analyzed more than three decades of research, combining 17 different studies, and found that bilingual education programs produce higher levels of student achievement in reading. The most successful are paired bilingual programs—those offering ongoing instruction in a native language and English at different times of the day (Callahan and Gándara 2014; Slavin and Cheung 2003; Soltero 2008).

Attacks on bilingualism in voting and education have taken several forms and have even broadened to question the appropriateness of U.S. residents using any language other than English. Federal policy has become more restrictive. Local schools have been given more authority to determine appropriate methods of instruction; they also have been forced to provide more of their own funding for bilingual education. Adding to the difficulty is that increasingly, school districts outside the central city in suburbs and rural agricultural areas face the challenge of serving non-English-speaking schoolchildren.

In the United States, as of 2017, 32 states have made English their official language. Repeated efforts have been made to introduce a constitutional amendment declaring English as the nation's official language. Even such an action would not completely outlaw bilingual or multilingual government services. It would, however, require that such services be called for specifically, as in the Voting Rights Act of 1965, which requires voting information to be available in multiple languages (U.S. English 2017).

The Economic Impact

There is much public and scholarly debate about the economic effects of immigration, both legal and illegal. Varied, conflicting conclusions have resulted from research ranging from case studies of Korean immigrants' dominance among New York City greengrocers to mobility studies charting the progress of all immigrants and their children. The confusion results in part from the different methods of analysis. For example, the studies do not always include political refugees, who generally are less prepared than other refugees to become assimilated. Sometimes, the research focuses only on economic effects, such as whether people are employed or are on welfare; in other cases, it also considers cultural factors, such as knowledge of English.

Perhaps the most significant factor in determining the economic impact of immigration is whether a study examines the national impact of immigration or only its effects on a local area. Overall, we can conclude from the research that immigrants adapt well and are assets to the national economy. In some local areas, heavy immigration may drain a community's resources. However, it can also revitalize a local economy. Marginally employed workers, most of whom are either themselves immigrants or are African Americans, often experience a negative impact as a result of new arrivals. With or without immigration, competition for low-paying jobs in the United States is high, and those who gain the most from this competition are the employers and the consumers who want to keep wages and prices down (Peri 2014).

The impact of immigration on African Americans deserves special attention. Given that African Americans are a large minority and many continue to be in the underclass, many people, including some Blacks themselves, perceive immigrants as advancing at the expense of the African American community. There is evidence that in the very lowest paid jobs—for example, workers in chicken-processing plants—wages have dropped with the availability of unskilled immigrants to perform them, and Blacks have left these jobs for good. Many of these African Americans do not necessarily move to better or even equivalent jobs. This pattern is repeated in other relatively low-paying, undesirable employment sectors, so Blacks are not alone in being affected; but, given the lack of other job opportunities, the impact on Blacks is longer lasting (Peri 2014).

About 70 percent of illegal immigrant workers pay taxes of one type or another. Many of them do not file to receive refunds or benefits to which they are entitled. For example, the Social Security Administration estimates that nearly 2 million illegal immigrants annually contribute $10 billion into the retirement trust fund and only receive about $1 billion in benefits. This is a net $9 billion cash flow into Social Security, which is a positive effect on this significant federal government program. Supporters of immigration reform also point to increased tax revenue and even more net financial benefits to all local governments if illegal immigrants move toward legal residency (Campbell 2016; Bruinius 2017).

Table 4.2 Immigrant Adaptation to the United States

Less Encouraging Signs	Positive Signs
• Although immigrants have lower divorce rates and are less likely to form single-parent households than natives, their rates equal or exceed these rates by the second generation.	• Immigrant families and, more broadly, noncitizen households are more likely to be on public assistance, but their time on public assistance is shorter and they receive fewer benefits than other groups. This generalization is true even when considering special restrictions that may apply to noncitizens.
• Children in immigrant families tend to be healthier than U.S.-born children, but the advantage declines.	• Second-generation immigrants (i.e., children of immigrants) are overall doing as well as or better than White non-Hispanic natives in educational attainment, labor-force participation, wages, and household income.
• Immigrant children attend schools that are disproportionately attended by other poor children and students with limited English proficiency, so they are ethnically, economically, and linguistically isolated.	• Immigrants overwhelmingly (65 percent) continue to see learning English as an ethical obligation of all immigrants.

Social science studies generally contradict many of the negative stereotypes about the economic impact of immigration. A variety of recent studies found that immigrants are a net economic gain for the population in times of economic boom as well as in periods of recession. But despite national gains, in some areas and for some groups, immigration may be an economic burden or create unwanted competition for jobs (Kochhar 2006).

What about the immigrants themselves? Considering contemporary immigrants as a group, we can draw the following conclusions, summarized in Table 4.2. They represent a mix of successes and challenges to adaptation. These positive trends diverge among specific immigrant groups, with Asian immigrants doing better than European immigrants, who do better than Latino immigrants (Capps, Leighton, and Fix 2002; Farkas 2003; Myers, Pitkin, and Park 2004; Zimmerman 2008).

One economic aspect of immigration that has received increasing attention is the role of **remittances**, the monies that immigrants send back to their countries of origin. The amounts are significant and measure in the hundreds of millions of dollars flowing from the United States to other countries, where they provide substantial support for families and even venture capital for new businesses. Although some observers express concern over this outflow of money, others counter that it probably represents a small price to pay for the human capital that the United States is able to use in the form of the immigrants themselves.

Immigrants in the United States send about $56 billion to their countries of origin annually, and worldwide remittances bring about $582 billion to all the world's countries, easily surpassing all other forms of foreign aid. This cash inflow is integral to the economies of many nations, but it can also fluctuate dramatically during times of economic stress. With the Great Recession beginning in 2008, it was clear that low-skilled immigrants (legal or illegal) took the hardest hit, and as a result, remittances immediately declined (Connor 2016; World Bank Group 2016).

Illegal Immigration

4.4 **Discuss the scope of and issues related to illegal immigration.**

The most bitterly debated aspect of U.S. immigration policy has been the control of illegal or undocumented immigrants. These immigrants and their families usually come to the United States in search of higher-paying jobs than their home countries can provide. While some people contend there are differences in the terms *illegal, undocumented,* and *unauthorized,* we use the terms interchangeably to refer to people who entered the country without the proper documents, as well as people who entered legally as students or tourists but then remained illegally.

Because by definition illegal immigrants are in the country illegally, the exact number of these undocumented or unauthorized workers is subject to estimates and disputes. Based on the best available information in early 2017, about 11.3 million illegal or unauthorized immigrants live in the United States. This compares with about 3.5 million in 1990 and a peak of 12.2 million in 2007. With employment opportunities drying up during the Great Recession beginning in 2008, significantly fewer people tried to enter illegally, and many unauthorized immigrants returned to their countries (Krogstad 2016).

The public has tied illegal immigrants—and even legal immigrants—to almost every social problem in the nation. They are the scapegoats for unemployment; they are labeled "drug runners" and, especially since September 11, 2001, "terrorists." Arrest, detention, and deportation of illegal immigrants has greatly increased. Their vital economic and cultural contributions to the United States are generally overlooked, as they have been for more than 100 years. Considering illegal immigration from the immigrant's perspective, the possibility of apprehension and punishment does not pose a significant deterrent. However, the decision to enter the country illegally is affected by their assessment of the employment possibilities in the home country and the dangers of border crossing.

Illegal immigration poses significant costs for *aliens*—that is, foreign-born noncitizens—and for other citizens. Civil rights advocates have expressed concern that the procedures used to apprehend and deport people are discriminatory and deprive many aliens of their legal rights. American citizens of Hispanic or Asian origin, some of whom were born in the United States, may be greeted with prejudice and distrust, as if their names automatically imply that they are in the country illegally. In 2017, immigration officials held up the re-entry into the United States of Muhammad Ali, Jr., son of the famous boxer and a U.S.-born citizen. The officials felt he had a suspicious-sounding name, and Ali, Jr., told them he was Muslim when they asked about his religion. Furthermore, citizens and legal residents of the United States may be unable to find work because employers wrongly believe that their documents are forged.

Congress approved the Immigration Reform and Control Act of 1986 (IRCA) after debating it for nearly a decade. The act marked a historic change in immigration policy compared with earlier laws, which are summarized in Table 4.3. Amnesty was granted to 2.7 million illegal immigrants who could document that they had established long-term residency in the United States. Under the IRCA, hiring illegal aliens became illegal, and employers became subject to fines and even prison sentences. Annually, about 400,000 people are deported—increasingly at the border; these people are typically not guilty of any offense other than illegal

Table 4.3 Major Immigration Policies

Policy	Target Group	Impact
Chinese Exclusion Act, 1882	Chinese	Effectively ended all Chinese immigration for more than 60 years
National origin system, 1921	Southern Europeans	Reduced overall immigration and significantly reduced likely immigration from Greece and Italy
Immigration and Nationality Act, 1965 (Hart-Cellar Act)	Western Hemisphere and the less skilled	Facilitated entry of skilled workers and relatives of U.S. residents
Immigration Reform and Control Act, 1986 (IRCA)	Illegal immigrants	Modest reduction of illegal immigration

entry. Farther from the border, deportation has been more limited to those committing crimes, but what constitutes a serious enough crime has been subject to change and periodic review (Thompson and Cohen 2014; Bruinius 2017).

Many illegal immigrants continue to live in fear and in hiding, subject to even more severe harassment and discrimination than before. From a conflict perspective, these immigrants, who are primarily poor and Hispanic or Asian, are firmly lodged at the bottom of the nation's social and economic hierarchies. However, from a functionalist perspective, employers, by paying low wages, are able to produce goods and services that are profitable for industry and more affordable to consumers. Despite the poor working conditions often experienced by illegal immigrants, they continue to come because it is still in their best economic interest to work here in disadvantaged positions rather than to seek wage labor unsuccessfully in their home countries.

As the nation became polarized over illegal immigration, some cities decided to become **sanctuary cities** where local law-enforcement officers do not actively hand over illegal immigrants to federal enforcement agents. The "cities" are sometimes entire counties or metropolitan areas, and they include Los Angeles, Denver, Dallas, Chicago, New Orleans, New York City, and Boston. Some border states have even become "sanctuary states." They include New Mexico, California, and North Dakota.

Typically, an illegal immigrant may be arrested for an offense unrelated to citizenship, such as a driving offense, and authorities move forward with disciplining the person based on the offense. However, in sanctuary areas, no further action is taken on the person's illegal status, nor is it brought directly to the attention of federal authorities. Courts have generally ruled that cooperation with federal immigration authorities is voluntary (Cameron 2017).

Illegal aliens or undocumented workers are not necessarily transient. One estimate indicates that 66 percent have been here for at least ten years. Many have established homes, families, and networks with relatives and friends in the United States whose legal status might differ from theirs. These are the mixed-status households noted earlier. For the most part, their lives are not much different from those of legal residents, except when they seek services that require documentation proving citizenship status (Krogstad 2016).

The public often thinks in terms of controlling illegal immigration through greater surveillance at the border. After the terrorist attacks of September 11, 2001, greater control of border traffic took on a new sense of urgency, even though almost all of the hijackers had entered the United States legally. It also is very difficult to secure the vast boundaries that mark the United States on land and sea. The cost of the federal government's attempt to police the nation's borders and locate illegal immigrants is sizable.

Numerous civil rights groups and migrant advocacy organizations have expressed alarm regarding people who cross into the United States illegally and perish in the attempt. We will revisit this aspect of immigration in Chapter 9.

So what is the future of immigration reform? It is unlikely to be resolved in any satisfying way because the issues are complex and are wrapped up in economic interests, humanitarian concerns, party politics, constitutional rights, and even foreign policy. Alongside immigration policy is the question of how the nation should accommodate people escaping political and religious persecution.

Border security continues to be a hot-button topic, with "Build a wall" the rallying cry for advocates of increased security.

Naturalization: The Path to Citizenship

4.5 Outline the process of naturalization.

In **naturalization**, citizenship is conferred on a foreign-born person. The process for achieving citizenship has been outlined by Congress. Naturalization extends to foreigners the same benefits given to native-born U.S. citizens. Naturalized citizens, however, cannot serve as the U.S. president.

Until the 1970s, most people who were naturalized had been born in Europe. Reflecting changing patterns of immigration, Asia and Latin America are now the largest sources of new citizens. In fact, the number of naturalized citizens from Mexico has come close to matching those from all of Europe. In recent years, the number of new citizens going through the naturalization process has been close to 1 million a year (Baker 2009).

To become a naturalized U.S. citizen, a person must meet the following general conditions:

- be 18 years of age;
- have continually resided in the United States for at least five years (three years for the spouses of U.S. citizens);
- have good moral character as determined by the absence of conviction for selected criminal offenses;
- be able to read, write, speak, and understand words of ordinary usage in the English language; and
- pass a test in U.S. government and history administered orally in English.

Table 4.4 So You Want to Be a Citizen?

Try these sample questions from the naturalization test (answers below).

1. What do the stripes on the flag represent?
2. How many amendments are there to the Constitution?
3. Who is the chief justice of the Supreme Court?
4. Who was president during World War I?
5. What do we call the first 10 amendments to the Constitution?
6. What are two rights in the Declaration of Independence?
7. Name one right or freedom from the First Amendment.
8. When was the Constitution written?

Answers:
(1) The first 13 states; (2) 27; (3) John Roberts; (4) Woodrow Wilson; (5) Bill of Rights; (6) life, liberty, and the pursuit of happiness; (7) the rights are freedom of speech, religion, assembly, and press, and freedom to petition the government; (8) 1787.

SOURCE: Department of Homeland Security 2017.

Table 4.4 lists some of the questions that immigrants must answer on the citizenship test. This is a sample of the actual questions used; those seeking citizenship must get six out of ten correct to pass. If a person fails, he or she can immediately retake the test with different questions. After failing a second time, typically the person must wait 90 days to retake the test. As of 2013, the fee for applying for citizenship is $725, compared with $95 in 1998.

Although we often picture the United States as having a very insular, nativistic attitude toward foreigners living here, the country has a rather liberal policy toward people maintaining citizenship in their countries of origin. Although most countries do not allow people to maintain dual (or even multiple) citizenships, the United States does not forbid it. Dual citizenship is most common when a person goes through naturalization after already being a citizen of another country or is a U.S.-born citizen and goes through the process of becoming a citizen of another country—for example, after marrying a foreigner (Department of State 2013).

The continuing debate about immigration reform often includes calls for some type of "amnesty" or pathway to citizenship for illegal immigrants. Proposals vary, but requirements usually include proof of long-term residence in the United States, absence of criminal activity, and willingness to accept a waiting period before actual citizenship can occur. Critics of such proposals question the wisdom of "rewarding illegals" but also argue that legal residency for illegal immigrants makes it more likely that their relatives will also apply for legal residency. Current policy, as earlier noted, has created long waiting periods for those abroad trying to join their relatives, but surveys also show that, as in 1986 when some type of amnesty was offered, not all qualified illegal immigrants will seek legal status. For example, in recent years only 46 percent of Hispanic immigrants eligible to naturalize have chosen to become citizens, compared with 71 percent of non-Hispanic immigrants. Difficulties with the English language and the costs of application serve as barriers to the path to citizenship (Lopez and Gonzalez-Barrera 2013).

Being born in the United States of immigrant parents or going through the naturalization process does not mean that ties to different cultural practices end. In the Research Focus feature, we consider one cultural practice of some Asian Americans and recent arrivals from Africa that is not a part of U.S. mainstream culture: arranged marriages.

Research Focus

Arranged Marriages in America

In some cultures, the proverbial question is not "Does he or she love me?" but rather "Whom do my parents want me to marry?" An **arranged marriage** occurs when others (often the parents) choose a person's marital partner. Typically, in arranged marriages, the two people in the couple do not even know each other, much less have any mutual romantic interest.

The idea of arranged marriages seems strange to most youth growing up in the U.S. culture that romanticizes finding Mr. or Ms. Right. In an arranged marriage, the bride and groom start off on neutral ground, with no expectations of each other. Understanding develops between them as the relationship matures. The couple selected is assumed to be compatible because they are chosen from very similar social, economic, and cultural backgrounds.

Historically, arranged marriages are not unusual and even today are common in many parts of Asia and Africa. In cultures where arranged marriage is common, young people tend to be socialized to expect and look forward to such unions.

But what happens in cultures that send very different messages? For example, immigrants from India, Pakistan, Bangladesh, and Nigeria may desire that their children enter an arranged union, but their children are growing up in a culture where many of their schoolmates are obsessed with dating as a prelude to marriage and endlessly discuss the latest episodes of *The Bachelor* and *The Bachelorette*.

Are arranged marriages in the United States successful? Several studies (based on small samples) have attempted to answer this question and have come to widely different conclusions. Such studies have reached widely different conclusions. Some studies have found that arranged marriages result in higher marital satisfaction, while other studies find lower marital satisfaction or no difference from love-based marriages.

Studies of young people (in countries such as Canada and the United States) whose parents still cling to the tradition of arranging their children's marriages document the challenges of arranged marriages. Many young people do still embrace their parents' tradition. As one first-year female Princeton student of Asian Indian ancestry put it, "In a lot of ways, it's easier. I don't have pressure to look for a boyfriend" (Herschthal 2004). Young people like her will look to their parents and other relatives to finalize a mate or accept a match with a partner who has been selected in their parents' home country.

In some cases, arranged marriages have been modified to *assisted marriages* in which parents identify a limited number of possible mates based on "biodata" that screen for caste, family background, and geography. Children get final veto power but rarely head out on their own when seeking a mate. Young men and women may date on their own, but when it comes to marrying, they limit themselves to a very narrow field of eligibles brought to them by their parents.

The combination of arranged and assisted marriages has meant that Asian Indian immigrants have the highest rates of ethnic endogamy (in-group marriage) of any major immigrant group in the United States—about 92 percent in-group marriage, with the majority of Indian American couples including spouses who were both raised in the United States.

Sources: Bellafante 2005; Chakravorty, Kapur, and Singh 2017; Johnson and Bachan 2013; Regan, Lakhanpal, and Anguiano 2012.

The Global Economy and Immigration

4.6 **Explain the connection between globalization and immigration.**

Immigration is defined by political boundaries that bring the movement of people crossing borders to the attention of government authorities. Within the borders of the United States, people may move their residence, but they are not immigrating. For residents in the member nations of the European Union, free movement of people within the union is also protected.

Yet, increasingly, people recognize the need to think beyond national borders and national identity. As noted in Chapter 1, **globalization** is the worldwide integration of government policies, cultures, social movements, and financial markets through trade, movement of people, and the exchange of ideas. In this era of globalization, immigrants are less likely to think of themselves as residents of only one country. For generations, immigrants have used foreign-language newspapers to keep up to date with events in their home countries. Today, cable channels carry news and variety programs from their home countries, and the Internet offers immediate access to the homeland and kinfolk thousands of miles away.

Although it helps in bringing the world together, globalization has also highlighted the dramatic economic inequalities between nations. Today, people in North America, Europe, and Japan consume 32 times more resources than the billions of people in developing nations. Thanks to tourism, media, and other aspects of globalization, the people of less-affluent countries are aware of such affluent lifestyles and, of course, often aspire to enjoy them (Diamond 2003).

Transnationals are immigrants who sustain multiple social relationships that link their societies of origin and settlement. Immigrants from the Dominican Republic, for example, not only identify themselves with Americans but also maintain very close ties to their Caribbean homeland. They return for visits, send remittances, and host extended stays of relatives and friends. Back in the Dominican Republic, villages reflect these close ties, as shown in billboards promoting special long-distance services to the United States and by the presence of household appliances sent by relatives. The volume of remittances worldwide is easily the most reliable source of foreign money going to poor countries, far outstripping government-sponsored foreign-aid programs.

The presence of transnationals in a country is an example of pluralism. Because transnationals move back and forth, it is not unusual for different generations of the same family to find themselves residing in different countries at any given moment. The recognition that many immigrants sustain multiple relationships, including homeland connections as transnationals, serves to amend the assimilationist view, which appears to gloss over this aspect of immigrants' daily lives in the their new homes (Waldinger 2015).

The growing number of transnationals, as well as immigration in general, directly reflects the world systems analysis we considered in Chapter 1. Transnationals are not new, but the ability to communicate and transfer resources makes the immigration experience today different from that of the nineteenth (and most of the twentieth) century. The sharp contrast between the industrial "have" nations and the developing "have-not" nations only encourages movement across borders. The industrial "haves" gain benefits from such movement even when they seem to discourage it.

The back-and-forth movement also serves to increase globalization and helps to create informal social networks between people who seek a better life and those already enjoying increased prosperity.

The transnationals themselves maintain a multithreaded relationship between friends and relatives in the United Sates, their home country, and perhaps other countries where relatives and friends have resettled. Besides the economic impact of remittances described earlier, scholars are increasingly giving attention to "social remittances" that include ideas, social norms, and practices (religious and secular) throughout this global social network (Levitt and Jaworsky 2007).

Refugees

4.7 Describe the United States' policies toward refugees.

Refugees are people who live outside their country of citizenship for fear of political or religious persecution. Approximately 20 million refugees exist worldwide, enough to populate an entire "nation." That nation of refugees would be larger than the Netherlands or Guatemala. The United States has touted itself as a haven for political refugees. However, political refugees have not always received an unqualified welcome.

Policies

The United States resettles between 50,000 and 73,000 refugees annually. Following 9/11, resettlement procedures have become much more cumbersome, and it is much more difficult for foreigners to acquire refugee status and gain entry to the United States. Most refugees receive that designation overseas by the United Nations (UN) and go through medical screening, retinal screening, DNA sampling, and background checks. Other refugees are approved without UN referral because they are close relatives of those already successfully resettled. In either situation, those headed to the United States go through additional security screening undertaken by the Department of State and the Department of Homeland Security.

The United States, insulated by distance from wars and famines overseas, has been able to be selective about which and how many refugees are welcomed. From the arrival of refugees uprooted by World War II through the 1980s, the United States allowed three groups of refugees to enter in numbers greater than regulations would ordinarily permit: Hungarians, Cubans, and Southeast Asians.

Refugees are granted the right to enter a country while they are still residing abroad. **Asylees** are foreigners who have already entered the United States and seek protection because of persecution or a well-founded fear of persecution in their home country. This persecution may be based on the individual's race, religion, nationality, membership in a particular social group, or political opinion. Asylees are eligible to adjust to lawful permanent resident status after one year of continuous presence in the United States. Asylum is granted to about 10,000 people annually.

Because asylees, by definition, are already here, they are either granted legal entry or returned to their home country. The practice of deporting people who are fleeing poverty has been the subject of criticism. The United States has a long tradition of facilitating the arrival of people leaving Communist nations, including, until 2017, people seeking asylum from Cuba. Mexicans who are refugees from poverty and Haitians running from despotic rule are not similarly welcomed. The plight of Haitians is of particular concern.

Haitians began fleeing their country, often on small boats, in the 1980s. The U.S. Coast Guard intercepted many Haitians at sea, saving some of these boat people from death in their rickety and overcrowded wooden vessels. The Haitians said they feared detentions, torture, and execution if they remained in Haiti. Yet at the time the government viewed most Haitian exiles as economic migrants rather than as political refugees, and thus opposed granting them asylum and permission to enter the United States. Once apprehended, the Haitians were returned to Haiti. In 1993, the U.S. Supreme Court, by an 8–1 vote, upheld the government's right to intercept Haitian refugees at sea and return them to their homeland without asylum hearings.

The devastating 2010 earthquake in Haiti made the government reconsider this policy. At the time, tens of thousands of Haitians in the United States were subject to deportation. A moratorium on deportation was imposed, only to be lifted in 2016 over the objection of social service agencies and members of the Haitian American community. Despite continuing obstacles, the Haitian American community exhibits pride in those who have succeeded. In fact, the initial earthquake refugees tended to come from the Haitian middle class or higher. Some even expressed annoyance at the quality of the public schools their children attended in America compared to the private ones in Haiti (Buchanan, Albert, and Beaulieu 2010; Semple 2016; Winerip 2011).

Concerns About the Refugee Program

Public concerns about admitting refugees have been noted at both extremes. On one side are those who lobby vigorously in favor of allowing more refugees to enter from a particular country that has been especially hard hit by some type of crisis. On the other side are those who feel we do too much already for noncitizens or who believe that U.S. national security is threatened by allowing people to migrate to the United States from the world's trouble spots.

The U.S. government is officially committed to accepting refugees from other nations—but how many and from where is always subject change. Table 4.5 lists the major sources of refugees. Changing political situations and changing policy priorities here and abroad can alter this mix. Because of unrest in the Middle East and

Table 4.5 Top Sources of Refugees, 2005 and 2015

2005		2015	
1. Somalia	10,405	Burma (Myanmar)	18,356
2. Laos	8,517	Iraq	12,676
3. Cuba	6,361	Somalia	8,858
4. Russia	5,982	Dem. Rep. of Congo	7,876
5. Liberia	4,289	Bhutan	5,775
Total of All Countries:	53,813		69,920

SOURCE: Jefferys 2006:2; Mossaad 2016:3.

North Africa, the United States accepted, in just a four-month period from October 2016 through January 2017, over 4,000 refugees each from Iraq, Syria, and Somalia (Department of State 2017).

According to the United Nations treaty on refugees, which the U.S. government ratified in 1968, countries are obliged to refrain from forcibly returning people to territories where their lives or liberty might be endangered. However, it is not always clear whether a person is fleeing for his or her personal safety or to escape poverty. Although people in the latter category deserve humane treatment, they do not meet the official definition of refugees and are subject to deportation.

To place the U.S. refugee program in perspective, while in absolute number we may seem to accept large numbers, the United States ranks 47th among 170 countries in terms of wealth and 75th in terms of population. Many other much smaller and poorer nations have received much larger numbers of refugees, with Lebanon, Pakistan, and Turkey hosting more than 1 million refugees each (Martin and Yankay 2013; United Nations High Commission on Refugees 2015, 2016).

While the nation may rethink its refugee policy, people generally view refugees as genuinely deserving of assistance. We might help them by:

- Steering money and goods to individual refugees through crowdfunding sites online
- Donating money directly to refugee and resettlement agencies
- Donating money directly to local organizations working with refugees
- Volunteering time to assist refugees through tutoring, accompanying them to get driver's licenses, and so forth
- Hosting a dinner or serving as an escort for a shopping trip
- Directly sponsoring a refugee family for their first year (This option is not available in the United States but is available to people in Canada and other nations.)
- Advocating at the national or local level for an appropriate refugee policy

These suggestions address the refugee needs in the United States, but most refugee households spend many months or even years in overseas resettlement camps, which offer yet another area of possible assistance (Bernard 2015, 2017; Lieber 2017).

Refugee status has also been generated by environmental factors. Famine, typhoons, rising sea levels, expanding deserts, chronic water shortages, and earthquakes lead to cross-border migration. **Environmental refugees** are people forced to leave their communities because of natural disasters or the effects of climate change and global warming. Overwhelmingly, this forced environmental migration is by vulnerable poor people to developing countries ill suited to accept the arrivals. Despite the exception granted temporarily to Haitian environmental refugees, the United States has no ongoing policy of granting entry to those displaced by environmental factors (Hunter, Luna, and Norton 2015).

In 2017, following through on campaign promises, President Donald Trump cited national security concerns when he issued an executive order instituting an indefinite ban on Syrian refugees and a 120-day ban on refugees from the rest of the world. The administration also indicated that once immigration resumed, the number of refugees allowed into the country would be cut in half from the levels shown in Table 4.5. At the

Figure 4.5 Spectrum of Intergroup Relations: Immigration

EXPULSION	SEGREGATION	ASSIMILATION
INCREASINGLY UNACCEPTABLE		MORE TOLERABLE

EXTERMINATION or genocide
- Alien Act of 1798
- Chinese Exclusion Act
- Refugees (From native country)
- Asylees (From native country)
- Environmental refugees

SECESSION or partitioning

FUSION or amalgamation or melting pot
- Xenophobia
- Nativism
- Occupational segregation

PLURALISM or multiculturalism
- Birthright Citizenship
- Naturalization
- Impact on Health
- Bilingualism
- Transnationals
- Chain Immigration
- Sanctuary city
- Remittances

time, most people in national surveys indicated opposition to these steps, but a significant minority, about one-third, approved of President Trump's actions. In a matter of days, courts overruled the bans, but the expectation of a significant reduction in the approval process for new refugees looms (Newport 2017).

Figure 4.5 shows the spectrum of intergroup relations with respect to the concepts discussed in this chapter.

Conclusion

The immigrant presence in the United States can often be heard on the streets and in the workplace as people speak in different languages. Witness the debates of policymakers or among school board members. These debates are not new. The United States has, throughout its history, seen intense debate over the nation's policies that bring immigrants and refugees to the country. In a sense, this debate reflects the deep value conflicts in the U.S. culture and parallels the "American dilemma" identified by Swedish social economist Gunnar Myrdal (1944). One strand of our culture—epitomized by the words "Give us your tired, your poor, your huddled masses" on the Statue of Liberty—has emphasized egalitarian principles and a desire to help people in their time of need.

At the same time, however, hostility to potential immigrants and refugees—the Chinese in the 1880s, European Jews in the 1930s and 1940s, Mexicans and Muslims today—reflects not only racial, ethnic, and religious prejudice but also a desire to maintain the dominant culture of the in-group by keeping out those viewed as outsiders. The conflict between these cultural values is central to the American dilemma of the twenty-first century.

The current debate about immigration is highly charged and emotional. Some people see it in economic terms, while others see the new arrivals as a challenge to the very culture of our society. For many, the general perception is that immigration presents a problem rather than a promise for the future.

Today's concern about immigrants follows generations of people coming to settle in the United States. This immigration in the past produced a very diverse country in terms of both nationality and religion, even before the immigration of the past 60 years. Therefore, the majority of Americans today are not descended from the English, and Protestants account for fewer than half of all worshipers. This diversity of religious and ethnic groups is examined in Chapter 5.

Summary of Learning Objectives

4.1 Summarize the general patterns of immigration to the United States.

1. Immigration to the United States has changed over time from unrestricted to restricted, with the primary sending nations now in Latin America and Asia rather than in Europe.
2. Immigration began being regulated by the United States in the nineteenth century; the first significant restriction was the Chinese Exclusion Act in 1882.

4.2 Describe how restrictionist sentiment has increased in the past 100 years.

3. Beginning in 1921, the national origins system favored northern and western European immigrants. Not until 1965 were quotas by nation largely lifted.

4.3 Identify the concerns about immigration policy today.

4. The issues affecting immigration policy today include the brain drain, population growth, mixed-status households, English-language acquisition, and economic impact, as well as debates over illegal immigration.

4.4 Discuss the scope of and issues related to illegal immigration.

5. Often more of a concern than legal immigration has been the continuing presence of a large number of illegal immigrants. It is estimated that about 11.1 million illegal immigrants live in the United States.

4.5 Outline the process of naturalization.

6. Naturalization is a complex process that is still pursued by those abroad as well as by unauthorized immigrants.

4.6 Explain the connection between globalization and immigration.

7. The worldwide integration of societies has been facilitated by transnationals who sustain multiple social relationships across borders.

4.7 Describe the United States' policies toward refugees.

8. Refugees present a special challenge to policymakers, who must balance humanitarian values against an unwillingness to accept all those who are fleeing poverty and political unrest.

Key Terms

arranged marriage, *page 119*
asylees, *page 121*
bilingual education, *page 112*
bilingualism, *page 112*
brain drain, *page 107*
chain immigration, *page 98*

environmental refugees, *page 123*
globalization, *page 120*
mixed status, *page 109*
nativism, *page 101*
naturalization, *page 117*

refugees, *page 121*
remittances, *page 114*
sanctuary city, *page 116*
sinophobes, *page 102*
transnationals, *page 120*
xenophobia, *page 101*

Review Questions

1. How would you describe the general patterns of immigration to the United States over the past two centuries?
2. What were the social and economic issues when public opinion mounted against Chinese immigration to the United States in the nineteenth century?
3. How did restrictionist immigration policies develop in the twentieth century?
4. What are the contemporary social concerns about legal immigration today? Briefly describe each.
5. What are the main issues surrounding illegal immigration?
6. How can one become a naturalized citizen in the United States?
7. How is globalization furthered by immigration?
8. What principles appear to guide U.S. refugee policy?

Critical Thinking

1. What are the functions and dysfunctions of immigration?
2. Ultimately, what do you think is the major concern people have about contemporary immigration to the United States: the numbers of immigrants, their legal status, or their nationality and religion?
3. What challenge does the presence of people in the United States speaking languages other than English present for them? For schools? For the workplace? For you?
4. What is your family's immigrant root story? Consider how your ancestors arrived in the United States and also how other immigrant groups have shaped your family's past.

Chapter 5
Ethnicity, Whiteness, and Religion

Learning Objectives

5.1 Understand what is meant by ethnicity, including Whiteness.

5.2 Describe the German American experience.

5.3 Identify the major periods of Irish American immigration.

5.4 Explain the Italian American experience.

5.5 Describe the Polish American immigration story.

5.6 Define and explain religious pluralism.

5.7 Understand court rulings on religion.

The changing nature of ethnicity in America's cities was underscored when the 2010 census showed not a single Italian-born person living in New York City's Little Italy. While some people of Italian descent resided there, one was much more likely to find Chinese-born people than people of any other nationality.

Once China and the United States established diplomatic relations in 1868, Chinese were allowed to legally immigrate to the United States. Most settled in California, but some made their way to New York City and settled around Mott Street just south of Canal Street. Italians began immigrating in large numbers around the same time, settling in several areas, including along Mulberry Street, one street over from Mott but north of Canal. For 150 years, Italian and Chinese Americans lived in adjoining densely populated neighborhoods.

By 1940, both Little Italy and Chinatown were tourist destinations. A decade later, few Italians immigrated, and those already in Little Italy began to move out. Over the following decades, the Chinese community and its Chinatown expanded, and by 1980, the Chinese population in New York's Chinatown had surpassed that of San Francisco.

The character of Little Italy (see photo to the left) changed. In 1950, half of the residents were Italian American, with 20 percent of them born in Italy. By 2000, the neighborhood was only 6 percent Italian American, with very few born in Italy. By 2010, the proportion of Italian Americans had edged down to 5 percent, with not a single Italian-born resident. While the area along Mulberry Street remains a powerful symbol to ethnic Italians, today it is defined not as a place to live but by two elements. One is food, as represented by 50 or so restaurants and cafés, as well as an occasional bakery. The other is religion.

Going to church? The Zion English Lutheran Church established in 1801 became in 1853 the Church of the Transfiguration, as the Catholic Church took over the facility to serve the poor Irish. By 1891, it served the Italian neighborhood, but a couple of generations later, Chinese Catholics began to attend, and now its congregation is almost entirely Chinese. Masses are offered in English, Mandarin, and Cantonese.

Looking for the Chinese American Planning Council? Its offices are in Little Italy. Looking for the Museum of Chinese in America? Little Italy. By 2010, the 38-block area of Little Italy and Chinatown were listed as a single historic district on the National Register of Historic Places. So is it "Arrivederci, Little Italy"?

Not yet. Near the Church of the Transfiguration, the annual 11-day festival of San Gennaro takes over several blocks and honors the patron saint of Naples—the point of origin for many of the early Italian immigrants. The festival's climactic parade runs on both Mott Street and Mulberry Street, where most of the residents are Chinese. Some of these Chinese are Catholic, but others follow the Protestant, Buddhist, or Daoist faiths.

Yes, the Italian Americans express concern over the visible Chinese American presence, but often they work with their ethnic neighbors to maintain an Italian presence. What really worries the Italians and even the much more numerous Chinese Americans about losing their ethnic neighborhood and religious institutions is the encroachment of boutiques, fancy little restaurants prepared to pay higher rents, and the dreaded arrival of a Starbucks. There is no negotiating the maintenance of ethnic ties with these agents of social change, so the Italian and Chinese Americans work together. For example, the two groups organized the annual Marco Polo Day, which honors the explorer from Venice who journeyed in the thirteenth century through Central Asia to China (Guest 2003; Krase 2006; National Park Service 2009; Roberts 2011; Tonelli 2004; Two Bridges 2017).

Ethnicity, Whiteness, and Religion   **129**

It's May—are you ready for the National Day of Prayer? Congress formalized this observance in 1952. While 89 percent of people in the United States believe there is a God who answers prayers, the increasing diversity of believers makes even the practice of praying increasingly contentious. Some more ecumenical prayers (those with no reference to Jesus Christ, for example, or even to a supreme being) affront many. Specific Biblical, Talmudic, or Qur'anic references have limited appeal across a nation tolerant of so many faiths. So are we too religious or not religious enough (Newport 2016)?

One person's religious or ethnic experience is unlikely to be identical to the next person's; it is this type of diversity that we consider in this chapter. Also, with this diversity we consider how one goes about "fitting in" to a new society. First we will consider the social canvas against which this diversity is painted—Whiteness.

Unpacking Ethnicity

5.1 Understand what is meant by ethnicity, including Whiteness.

Race and ethnicity are discussed all the time in everyday speech, but, as we have seen, they are exceedingly complex terms. Race is socially constructed, as we learned in Chapter 1. Sometimes we seem to define race in a clear-cut manner. A descendant of a Pilgrim is White, for example. But sometimes race is more ambiguous: Children of an African American and Vietnamese American union are biracial, mixed, or whatever they come to be seen as by others. Our recognition that race is socially constructed has sparked a renewed interest in what it means to be White in the United States.

It has also generated interest in what we mean by *ethnicity*. Can we really see "European Americans" as a distinct, identifiable group? Probably not, but we do have ways to differentiate one group from another, often by using nationality terms like "German Americans" (even though Germany as we know it dates back only to about the 1830s). Two aspects of the White race and their ethnic divisions are useful to consider: the historical creation of Whiteness and how contemporary White people may reflect this identity.

Studying Whiteness

When English immigrants established themselves as the political founders of the United States, they also came to define what it meant to be White. Other groups that today are regarded as White—such as Irish, Germans, Norwegians, or Swedes—were not always considered White in the eyes of the English. Differences in language and religious worship, as well as past allegiance to a European king other than the English monarch, meant these groups were seen not so much as Whites in the Western Hemisphere but more as nationals of their home country who happened to reside in North America.

With all the attention that is given to race and ethnicity, little thought is typically given to what it means to be White and the privileges it carries in everyday life.

The old distrust in Europe, where, for example, the English viewed the Irish as socially and culturally inferior, continued on this side of the Atlantic Ocean. Writing from England, Karl Marx reported that the average English worker looked down on the Irish the way poor Whites in the U.S. South looked down on Black people (Ignatiev 1994, 1995; Roediger 1994).

As European immigrants and their descendants assimilated to the English and distanced themselves from other oppressed groups such as American Indians and African Americans, they came to be viewed as White rather than as part of a particular "alien" culture. Writer Noel Ignatiev (1994:84), contrasting being White with being Polish, argues, "Whiteness is nothing but an expression of race privilege." This strong statement argues that being White, as opposed to being Black or Asian, is characterized by being a member of the dominant group. Although it may often be invisible, Whiteness is aggressively embraced and defended (Giroux 1997).

In general, White people do not think of themselves as a race or have a conscious racial identity. A White racial identity emerges only when filling out a form asking for self-designation of race or when Whites are culturally or socially surrounded by people who are not White.

However, "Whiteness" is sometimes viewed negatively. One study examined teachers at a predominantly Latino and Black school with a White minority student population. Teachers viewed White students (who would seem to be "privileged") more negatively than poor minority students if the White students came from a lower-class background ("trailer trash") (Morris 2005).

Many immigrants who were not "White on arrival" had to "become White" in a process long forgotten by today's White Americans. The long-documented transparent racial divide that engulfed the South during slavery let us ignore how Whiteness was constructed.

Therefore, contemporary White Americans give little thought to "being White." Consequently, there is little interest in studying "Whiteness" or "being White" except that being White is "not being Black." Unlike non-Whites, who are much more likely to take orders from Whites and who see Whites as leading figures in the mass media, Whites are in the position of not being reminded of their Whiteness.

Unlike racial minorities, Whites usually downplay the importance of their racial identity, although they are willing to receive the advantages that come from being White. Advocating a "color-blind" or "race-neutral" outlook permits the privilege of Whiteness to prevail (Bonilla-Silva 2002; Feagin and Cobas 2008; Yancey 2003).

New scholarly interest seeks to study Whiteness, but not from the vantage point of a White supremacist. Rather, focusing on White people as a race or on what it means to be White today goes beyond any definition that implies superiority over non-Whites. It also is recognized that "being White" is not the same experience for all Whites, any more than "being Asian American" or "being Black" is the same for all Asian Americans or all Blacks. Ignatiev observes that studying Whiteness is a necessary stage in the desired "abolition of whiteness"—just as, in Marxist analysis, class-consciousness is a necessary stage in the desired abolition of class. By confronting and understanding Whiteness, society grasps the all-encompassing power held by the socially constructed White race (Lewis 2004; McKinney 2003; Roediger 2006).

White privilege, introduced in Chapter 2, refers to the rights granted as a benefit or favor of being White and can be an element of Whiteness. Although some Whites consciously minimize the exercise of this privilege, it is difficult to ignore White privilege when a White person is more likely than not to see national leaders, celebrities, and role models who also are White. For every Barack Obama and Jesse Jackson, there are hundreds of movers and shakers who are White. For example, many White people champion the cause of the HBCUs (historically Black colleges and universities), conveniently ignoring that those schools exist because of thousands of HWCUs (historically White colleges and universities) (Bonilla-Silva 2012).

Being White may mean you experience privilege, but it does not necessarily mean that White people are comfortable in "owning" this privilege. In 2017, the public high school in the affluent town of Westport, Connecticut (which is over 90 percent White) asked its students to reflect on the role of White privilege in their lives. The students were largely fine with this assignment of a 1,000-word essay; for example, one senior felt the discussion was important "because on a daily basis, we really aren't exposed to much diversity within our town." Yet the community as a whole was less comfortable with the topic, even though Westport could generally be viewed as liberal, having just voted by a factor of 2–1 for Hillary Clinton over Donald Trump. Some residents indicated their belief that "[saying there is] white privilege was just as racist as saying there is black privilege." Others felt that having the high school discuss the topic would suggest to outsiders that Westport was throwing up "barricades" to others. In short: Whiteness is a sensitive topic.

The people of Westport may not have been comforted when the 2017 winning essay, "The Colors of Privilege," was announced. In his essay, a fifteen-year-old African American sophomore wrote about his experience of moving to Westport from New York City with his family six years earlier. He recounted a series of slights he had experienced. For example, at track practice, some of his White friends were discussing the challenge of getting into their preferred college. Out of nowhere, one said, "Chet, you don't have this problem because you're black." The essayist recalled being stunned and mumbling something instead of firing back, "Your parents are third-generation Princeton and your father runs a hedge fund and yet you think my ride is free?" The second-prize winner, a White student, wrote of recognizing White privilege when seeing how his adopted brother from Ethiopia was treated (Brennan 2017; Melia 2017; Victor 2017).

When race is articulated or emphasized for Whites, it is more likely to be seen as threatening to Whites than as allowing them to embrace their own race or national roots with pride. Behavioral economists Michael Norton and Samuel Sommers (2011) found that Whites view race as a zero-sum game—that is, decreases in bias against African Americans over the past 60 years are associated with increases in what they perceive as bias against Whites. While Norton and Sommers see anti-Black bias as more prevalent today than anti-White feeling in society, their analysis shows that, in the minds of the White respondents, the two biases are coming closer together. In contrast, Black respondents in the study also saw a marked decline in anti-Black bias during the same period but perceived only a modest increase in anti-White feelings. While Norton and Sommers' research deals only with perception of reality, it does suggest that race, and not just that of non-Whites, influences one's perception of society.

Rediscovering Ethnicity

Robert Park (1950:205), a prominent early sociologist, wrote in 1913, "A Pole, Lithuanian, or Norwegian cannot be distinguished, in the second generation, from an American, born of native parents." At one time, sociologists saw the end of ethnicity as nearly a foregone conclusion. W. Lloyd Warner and Leo Srole (1945) wrote in their often-cited *Yankee City* series that the future of ethnic groups seemed to be limited in the United States and that they would be quickly absorbed. Oscar Handlin's *The Uprooted* (1951) told of the destruction of immigrant values and their replacement by American culture. Although Handlin was among the pioneers in investigating ethnicity, assimilation was the dominant theme in his work.

Many writers have shown an almost fervent hope that ethnicity will vanish. For some time, sociologists treated the persistence of ethnicity as dysfunctional because it meant continuing old values that interfered with the allegedly superior new values. For example, holding onto one's language delayed entry into the larger labor market and the upward social mobility it afforded. Ethnicity was expected to disappear, not only because of assimilation but also because aspirations to higher social class and status demanded that it vanish. It was assumed that one could not be ethnic and middle class, much less affluent.

BLENDED IDENTITY Racial identity and ethnic identity are important aspects of the immigrant experience. **Blended identity** is a self-image and worldview that combines religious faith, a cultural background based on nationality, and the status of being a resident of the United States. We have already considered how *blended identity* functions among other ethnic groups, but how might this identity change over time for Arab Americans? An Arab immigrant to the United States does not necessarily go through a process of shedding one identity for another (assimilation). Immigrants and even their children and future generations may hold onto multiple identities.

Consider the example of a Pakistani American. As Figure 5.1 shows, Muslims often find their daily activities defined by their faith, their nationality, and their status as Americans. Younger Muslims especially can move freely among the different identities. In Chicago, Muslim college students perform hip-hop in Arabic with lyrics like "La ilaha ila Allah" ("There is no God but Allah"). In Fremont, California, high-school Muslim girls and some of their non-Muslim girlfriends hold an alternative prom, decked out in silken gowns, dancing to both 50 Cent and Arabic music, and dining on lasagna but pausing at sunset to face Mecca (one of Islam's holiest sites, located in Saudi Arabia) and pray.

Figure 5.1 Blended Identity of Muslim Americans

MUSLIM
- Faith
- Family
- Moral code
- Qur'anic schools

PAKISTANI
- Politics
- Kinfolk
- Remittances
- Imported books/videos

AMERICAN
- Voting
- Occupation
- Community
- Mass media
- Public schools

Being an ethnic American or, in this case, Arab American does not mean that you do not see yourself as American. Indeed, 94 percent of Arab Americans who are citizens describe themselves as very or quite proud to be American, compared to 98 percent of the general population.

Interestingly, younger Arab Americans seem more willing to use the label "Arab American." Researchers wonder if the post–9/11 world has given being Arab and/or Muslim American new meaning. Will younger people, as they become adults, embrace "Arab American" in a sense of unity or seek to distance themselves from it due to fear of being marginalized by society?

THE PRINCIPLE OF THIRD-GENERATION INTEREST Historian Marcus Hansen's (1952) **principle of third-generation interest** was an early exception to the assimilationist approach to White ethnic groups. Simply stated, Hansen maintained that in the third generation—the grandchildren of the original immigrants—ethnic interest and awareness would increase. According to Hansen, "What the son wishes to forget, the grandson wishes to remember."

Hansen's principle has been tested several times since it was first put forth. John Goering (1971), in interviewing Irish and Italian Catholics, found that ethnicity was more important to members of the third generation than to the immigrants themselves. Similarly, Mary Waters (1990)—in her interviews with White ethnics living in suburban areas of San Jose, California, and Philadelphia, Pennsylvania—observed that many grandchildren wanted to study their ancestors' language, even though it would be a foreign language to them. They also expressed interest in learning more of their ethnic group's history and a desire to visit their homeland. However, it would be incorrect to assume that White ethnics are expressing or even aware of their ethnicity in very dramatic ways. Old European ethnicity is becoming more and more invisible except in largely ceremonial ways (explored later in this chapter) (Gans 2014).

Like Whites of European descent, many members of third and successive generations of Asian and Latin American immigrants are showing renewed interest in their native languages. The very languages they avoided or even scorned themselves as children, they now want to learn as young adults. "Heritage language" programs have become increasingly common. Even when the descendants may easily communicate in their native language in everyday life, they often lack the language tools necessary for more sophisticated vocabulary or to read their grandparents' language easily (Nawa 2011).

THE ETHNIC PARADOX While many nearly assimilated Whites are rediscovering their ethnicity (i.e., the principle of third-generation interest), others are at least publicly acknowledging their ethnicity from time to time (i.e., symbolic ethnicity, discussed below). Yet research confirms that preserving elements of one's ethnicity may advance economic success and further societal acceptance.

The term **ethnic paradox** refers to the maintenance of one's ethnic ties in a manner that can assist with assimilation into the larger society. Immigrant youth and adults who maintain their ethnicity tend to have more success as indicated by health measures, educational attainment, and lower incidence of behavioral problems such as delinquency and truancy.

Researchers typically measure ethnic maintenance by facility in the mother language (not just conversational or "street" use) and living with others of the same ethnic background. These clear ethnic ties are not an automatic recipe for success. For example, residing with co-ethnics can lead to exploitation in neighborhoods where people steer those of their own ethnicity into dead-end, poor-paying, and even unhealthy working conditions. Yet for many ethnics, enclaves offer a refuge, sort of a halfway house, between two different cultures. Language maintenance is often critical to being literate and comfortable with English (Desmond and Kubrin 2009).

In the Speaking Out feature, sociologist Tomás Jiménez from Stanford University considers the role of new arrivals in shaping the U.S. national identity and how immigrants manage life in a new society.

SYMBOLIC ETHNICITY Observers comment on both the evidence of assimilation and the signs of ethnic identity that support a pluralistic view of society. How can both exist simultaneously?

Speaking Out

The Next Americans

Tomás Jiménez

How immigrants and their descendants see themselves will change over time, and they will simultaneously transform many aspects of what it means to be an American. This is undoubtedly an uncomfortable process, fraught with tension between newcomers and established Americans that can occasionally become explosive. But the real issue is whether the United States can provide opportunities for upward mobility so that immigrants can, in turn, fortify what is most essential to our nation's identity.

History is instructive on whether immigrants will create a messy patchwork of ethnicities in the United States. About a century ago, a tide of southern and eastern European immigrants arriving on our shores raised fears similar to those we hear today. Then, as now, Americans worried that the newcomers were destroying American identity. Many were certain that Catholic immigrants would help the pope rule the United States from Rome, and that immigrants from southern Europe would contaminate the American gene pool.

None of this came to pass, of course. The pope has no political say in American affairs, the United States is still a capitalist democracy, and there is nothing wrong with the American gene pool. The fact that these fears never materialized is often cited as proof that European-origin immigrants and their descendants successfully assimilated into an American societal monolith.

However, as sociologists Richard Alba and Victor Nee point out, much of the American identity, as we know it today, was shaped by previous waves of immigrants. For instance, they note that the Christian tradition of the Christmas tree and the leisure Sunday made their way into the American mainstream because German immigrants and their descendants brought these traditions with them. Where religion was concerned, Protestantism was the clear marker of the nonsecular mainstream. But because of the assimilation of millions of Jews and Catholics, we today commonly refer to an American "Judeo-Christian tradition," a far more encompassing notion of American religious identity than the one envisioned in the past....

Even in Los Angeles County, where 36 percent of the population is foreign-born and more than half speak a language other than English at home, English is not losing out in the long run. According to a recent study by social scientists Rubén Rumbaut, Douglas Massey, and Frank Bean, published in the *Population and Development Review*, the use of non-English languages virtually disappears among nearly all U.S.-born children of immigrants in the country. Spanish shows more staying power among the U.S.-born children and grandchildren of Mexican immigrants, which is not surprising given that the size of the Spanish-speaking population provides near-ubiquitous access to the language. But the survival of Spanish among U.S.-born descendants of Mexican immigrants does not come at the expense of their ability to speak English and, more strikingly, English overwhelms Spanish-language use among the grandchildren of these immigrants.

An equally telling sign of how much immigrants and their children are becoming "American" is how different they have become from those in their ethnic homelands. Virtually all of today's immigrants stay connected to their countries of origin. They send money to family members who remain behind. Relatively inexpensive air, rail, and bus travel and the availability of cheap telecommunication and e-mail enable them to stay in constant contact, and dual citizenship allows their political voices to be heard from abroad. These enduring ties might lead to the conclusion that continuity between here and there threatens loyalty to the Stars and Stripes.

But ask any immigrant or their children about a recent visit to their country of origin, and they are likely to tell you how American they felt. The family and friends they visit quickly recognize the prodigal children's tastes for American styles, their American accents, and their declining cultural familiarity with life in the ethnic homeland—all telltale signs that they've Americanized. As sociologist David Fitzgerald puts it, their assimilation into American society entails a good deal of "dissimilation" from the countries the immigrants left behind.

American identity is absorbing something quite significant from immigrants and being changed by them. Language, food, entertainment, and holiday traditions are palpable aspects of American culture on which immigrants today, as in the past, are leaving their mark. Our everyday lexicon is sprinkled with Spanish words. We are now just as likely to grab a burrito as a burger. Hip-hop is tinged with South Asian rhythms. And Chinese New Year and Cinco de Mayo are taking their places alongside St. Patrick's Day as widely celebrated American ethnic holidays.

Source: Jiménez, Tomás R. 2007. The Next Americans. *Los Angeles Times* (May 27): M1, M7. Used with permission.

First, the visible evidence of **symbolic ethnicity** might lead us to exaggerate the persistence of ethnic ties among White Americans. According to sociologist Herbert Gans (1979, 2014), ethnicity today increasingly involves symbols of ethnicity, such as eating ethnic food, acknowledging ceremonial holidays such as St. Patrick's Day, and supporting specific political issues or issues confronting the old country. One example was the push in 1998 by Irish Americans to convince state legislatures to make it compulsory that public schools teach about the Irish potato famine—a significant factor in Irish immigration to the United States. This symbolic ethnicity may be more visible, but it does not interfere with what people do, read, or say, or even whom they befriend or marry. By one analysis, only an estimated 7 percent of White non-Hispanics self-express a significant sense of ethnicity (Scully 2012; Torkelson and Hartmann 2010).

The ethnicity of the twenty-first century, as embraced by English-speaking Whites, is largely symbolic. It does not include active involvement in ethnic activities or participation in ethnic-related organizations. In fact, sizable proportions of White ethnics have gained large-scale entry into almost all clubs, cliques, and fraternal groups. Such acceptance is a key indicator of assimilation. Ethnicity has become increasingly peripheral to the lives of the ethnic groups' members. Although today's White ethnics may not relinquish their ethnic identity entirely, other identities become more important.

Second, the ethnicity that exists may be more a result of living in the United States than of importing practices from the past or the old country. Many so-called ethnic foods or celebrations, for example, began in the United States. The persistence of ethnic consciousness, then, may not depend on foreign birth, a distinctive language, and a unique way of life. Instead, it may reflect the experiences in the United States of a unique group that developed a cultural tradition distinct from that of the mainstream. For example, in Poland, the *szlachta*, or landed gentry, rarely mixed socially with the peasant class. In the United States, however, even with those associations still fresh, *szlachta* and peasants interacted together in social organizations as they settled in concentrated communities segregated physically and socially from other communities (Lopata 1994; Winter 2008).

Third, maintaining ethnicity can be a critical step toward successful assimilation. This ethnic paradox facilitates full entry into the dominant culture. The ethnic community may give its members not only a useful financial boost but also the psychological strength and positive self-esteem that will allow them to compete effectively in a larger society. Thus, we may witness people participating actively in their ethnic enclave while trying to cross the bridge into the wider community (Lal 1995).

Therefore, ethnicity provides continuity with the past in the form of an effective or emotional tie. The significance of this sense of belonging cannot be emphasized enough. Whether reinforced by distinctive behavior or by what Milton Gordon (1964) called a sense of *peoplehood*, ethnicity is an effective, functional source of cohesion. Proximity to fellow ethnics is not necessary for a person to maintain social cohesion and in-group identity. Fraternal organizations or sports-related groups can preserve associations between ethnics who are separated geographically. Members of ethnic groups may even maintain feelings of in-group solidarity after leaving ethnic communities in the central cities for the suburban fringe.

We will now consider four of the many White ethnic groups—German, Irish, Italian, and Polish Americans—that have expressed and to different degrees continue to express their ethnic identity in the United States today.

The German Americans

5.2 Describe the German American experience.

Germany is the largest single source of ancestry of people in the United States today, even exceeding the continents of Africa or Asia. Yet except in a few big-city neighborhood enclaves, the explicit presence of German culture seems largely relegated to bratwurst, pretzels, and Kris Kringle.

Settlement Patterns

In the late 1700s, the newly formed United States experienced the arrival of a number of religious dissenters (including the Amish) from Germany who were attracted by the proclamation of religious freedom as well as prospects for economic advancement. At the time of the American Revolution, immigrants from Germany accounted for about one in eight White residents. German colonial subjects split their loyalty between the revolutionaries and the British, but they were united in their optimistic view of the opportunities the New World would present.

Although Pennsylvania was the center of early settlements, German Americans, like virtually all other Europeans, moved west (to Ohio, Michigan, and beyond), where land was abundant. In many isolated communities, they established churches and parochial schools, and, in some instances, ethnic enclaves that sometimes spoke of creating "New Germanys."

Beginning in the 1830s through 1890, Germans represented at least one-quarter of the immigrants, ensuring their destiny in the settlement of the United States (Figure 5.2).

Figure 5.2 Immigration from Germany, Ireland, Italy, and Poland

Note: Immigration after 1925 from Northern Ireland is not included. No separate data are included for Poland from 1900 to 1920.

SOURCE: Data from Office of Immigration Statistics 2009: Table 2.

Their major urban presence was in Milwaukee, Chicago, Cleveland, Detroit, and Cincinnati.

Early in the history of America, German immigrant cultural influence was apparent. Although the new United States never voted on making German the national language, publications of the proceedings of the Continental Congress were published in German and English. Yet even in those early years, the fear of foreigners—that is, non-Anglos—prevented Germans from ever getting equal footing with the English.

German Americans, then representing about 10 percent of the population, established bilingual programs in many public schools, but the rise of Germany as a military foe in the twentieth century ended that movement (Harzig 2008; Nelsen 1973).

German Americans in the Twenty-First Century

In 1901, the German-American National Alliance (Deutsche-Amerikanischer National-Bund) was founded to speak for all Germans in the United States—especially urban Protestant middle-class German Americans. As time passed, it sought to commemorate Germans' contributions to the nation's development but also sought to block prohibition against alcohol. With the rise of German military power, many German Americans argued for U.S. neutrality. But these efforts ended quickly, and the organization disbanded after the United States declared war on Germany in 1917.

With World War I and especially the rise of the Nazi era and the war years of the 1930s and 1940s, most German Americans sought to distance themselves from the politics in their homeland. There were anti-German incidents of harassment and intimidation. About 11,000 German Americans (out of 5 million) were interned. Internment refers to World War II-era confinement, within the United States, of people of certain nationalities who by virtue of their national origin were regarded as less trustworthy. However, the scope of German internment did not come close to the internment experienced by Japanese Americans. By comparison, many more German Americans enlisted in the military and played important roles in the war effort (including President Dwight Eisenhower, whose ancestors immigrated to Pennsylvania from Germany in 1741).

Overall, German Americans made the group transition into core society. Indeed, Horace Kallen, who popularized the term *pluralism*, held up German Americans as a success in finding a place in the United States. With the end of wartime tensions, German Americans moved from having multiple identities that included being somewhat marginalized as "Germans" to an identity of "American" and, less explicitly, White (Casey 2015; Russell 2015).

Anti-German sentiment spread in the United States during World War I, escalating dramatically after the United States entered the war in April 1917. A wave of verbal and physical attacks on German Americans was accompanied by a campaign to repress German culture. In this photograph from 1917, a group of children stand in front of an anti-German sign posted in Chicago. As the sign suggests, some people in the United States questioned the loyalty of their German American neighbors.

By the latter half of the twentieth century, the animosity toward Germany seemed a part of the distant past. Germany and its people became stalwart friends of the United States, as reflected in statements made by President John F. Kennedy in Berlin in 1963 and President Ronald Reagan in 1987. Both spoke of the U.S. commitment to uniting Germany, and presidential candidate Barack Obama in 2008 spoke in Berlin of a united Europe. When Indian Prime Minister Narendra Modi visited in the United States in 2016, the Indian American community was visibly overjoyed, but when German Chancellor Angela Merkel paid President Donald Trump a state visit in 2017, German America hardly paid notice.

In the past ten years, immigration from Germany, a country of 82 million, has fluctuated between 6,000 and 10,000 annually. The steady immigration for decades placed Germany in the 2000 census as the tenth-largest source of foreign-born residents today, with more than 700,000 (only about 170,000 behind Cuba and Korea). Yet the broad dispersion of these immigrants and their bilingual capability means the numbers are insufficient to create (or re-create) a German cultural presence. Rather, today's German American community is characterized by postwar and historical ties that have long since overshadowed the lingering bitterness of World Wars I and II (Harzig 2008; Office of Immigration Statistics 2016).

Famous German Americans include industrialist John D. Rockefeller, General John Pershing, baseball players Babe Ruth and Lou Gehrig, celebrity Paris Hilton, and actors Sandra Bullock and Katherine Heigl.

The Irish Americans

5.3 Identify the major periods of Irish American immigration.

The Irish presence in the United States stretches back to the 1600s and reflects a diversity based on time of entry, settlement area, and religion. Irish Americans have been visible both in a positive way in terms of playing a central role in American life and in a negative way at certain historical periods, being victimized as so many other immigrant groups have been.

Irish Immigration

The Roman Catholics among the early Irish immigrants were a diverse group. Some were members of the privileged classes seeking even greater prosperity. Protestant settlers of all national backgrounds, including those coming from Ireland, were united in their hatred of Catholicism. In most of the colonies, Catholics could not practice their faith openly and either struggled inwardly or converted to Anglicanism (or both). Other Roman Catholics and some Protestants came from Europe as an alternative to prison or after signing articles of indenture and arriving bound to labor for periods of three to five years, and sometimes as long as seven years (Meagher 2005).

The American Revolution (1765–1783) temporarily stopped the flow of immigration, but deteriorating economic conditions in Ireland soon spurred even greater movement to North America. British officials, by making passage to the newly formed republic of the United States expensive, diverted many immigrants to British North America (Canada). Yet the number of Irish immigrants to the United States remained significant and, although still primarily Protestant, drew from a broader spectrum of Ireland both economically and geographically.

Many people mistakenly overlook this early immigration and begin with Irish immigration during the Great Famine (1845–1852). Yet the Irish were the largest group after the English among immigrants during the colonial period. The historical emphasis on the famine immigrants is understandable, given the role that the famine played in Ireland and its impetus for the massive transfer of population from Ireland to the United States.

In 1845, a fungus wiped out the potato crop of Ireland, as well as that of much of western Europe and even coastal America. Potatoes were central to the lives of the Irish, and the devastating starvation did not begin to recede until 1851. Mortality was high, especially among the poor and in the more agricultural areas of the island. To escape starvation and death, some 2 million Irish fled, mostly to England, but then many continued on to the United States. From 1841 through 1890, more than 3.2 million Irish arrived in the United States (Figure 5.1).

These new immigrants fleeing the old country were much more likely to consist of families rather than single men. The arrival of entire households and extended kinship networks increased significantly the rapid formation of Irish social organizations in the United States. This large influx of immigrants led to the creation of ethnic neighborhoods like those described at the beginning of this chapter, complete with parochial schools and parish churches serving as focal points. Fraternal organizations such as the Ancient Order of Hibernians, corner saloons, local political organizations, and Irish nationalist groups seeking the ouster of Britain from Ireland rounded out neighborhood social life in the United States.

Even in the best of times, the lives of the famine Irish would have been challenging in the United States, but they arrived at a very difficult time. Nativist—that is, anti-Catholic and anti-immigrant—movements were already emerging and being embraced by politicians. Antagonism was not limited to harsh words. From 1834 to 1854, mob violence against Catholics across the country led to death, the burning of a Boston convent, the destruction of a Catholic church and the homes of Catholics, and the use of Marines and state militia to bring peace to American cities as far west as St. Louis.

In retrospect, the reception given to the Irish is not difficult to understand. Many immigrated after the potato crop failure and famine in Ireland. They fled not so much to a better life as from almost certain death. The Irish Catholics brought with them a celibate clergy, who struck the New England aristocracy as strange and reawakened old religious hatreds. The Irish were worse than Blacks, according to the dominant Whites, because unlike the slaves and even the freed Blacks, who "knew their place," the Irish did not suffer their mistreatment in silence. Employers balanced minorities by judiciously mixing immigrant groups to prevent unified action by the laborers. For the most part, nativist efforts only led the foreign-born to emphasize their ties to Europe.

Mostly of peasant backgrounds, the arriving Irish were ill prepared to compete successfully for jobs in the city. Their children found it much easier to improve their occupational status over that of their fathers, and they experienced upward mobility in their own lifetimes (Miller 2014:268–270).

Becoming White

Ireland had a long antislavery tradition, including practices that prohibited Irish trade in English slaves. Some 60,000 Irish signed an address in 1841, petitioning Irish Americans to join the abolitionist movement in the United States. Many Irish Americans already opposed to slavery applauded the appeal, but they were soon drowned out by fellow immigrants who denounced or questioned the petition's authenticity.

The Irish immigrants, subjected to derision and menial jobs, sought to separate themselves from the even lower classes, particularly Black Americans and especially slaves. It was not altogether clear that the Irish were considered "White" during the antebellum (pre–Civil War) period. Irish character was rigidly cast in negative racial typology. Although the shared experiences of oppression could have led Irish Americans to ally with Black Americans, they grasped for Whiteness at the margins of their lives in the United States. Direct competition was not common between the two groups. For example, in 1855, Irish immigrants made up 87 percent of New York City's unskilled laborers, whereas free Blacks accounted for only 3 percent (Greeley 1981; Ignatiev 1995; Roediger 1994).

As Irish immigration continued in the latter part of the nineteenth century until Irish independence in 1921, Irish Americans began to see themselves favorably in comparison to the initial waves of Italian, Polish, and Slovak Roman Catholic immigrants.

Irish Americans began to assume more leadership positions in politics and labor unions. Loyalty to the church still played a major role. By 1910, the priesthood was the professional occupation of choice for second-generation Irish American men. Irish women were more likely than their German and English immigrant counterparts to become schoolteachers. In time, Irish Americans' occupational profiles diversified, and they began to experience slow advancement and gradually were welcomed into the White working class as their identity as "White" overcame any status as "immigrant."

For many Irish Americans, a St. Patrick's Day parade is the most visible expression of Irish symbolic ethnicity during the entire year.

With mobility came social class distinctions within Irish America. The immigrants and their children who began to move into the more affluent urban areas were derogatorily referred to as the "lace-curtain Irish." Meanwhile, the lower-class Irish immigrants they left behind were referred to as the "shanty Irish." But as immigration from Ireland slowed and upward mobility quickened, fewer and fewer Irish qualified as the poor cousins of their predecessors. Furthermore, Irish Americans came to play a leadership role in the Roman Catholic Church in the United States. The Irish dominance persisted long after other ethnic groups swelled the ranks of the faithful (Fallows 1979; Lee and Bean 2007; Lee and Casey 2006).

The Contemporary Picture

By 2015, 32.7 million people identified themselves as having Irish ancestry—second only to German ancestry and more than five times the current population of Ireland itself. Massachusetts has the largest concentration of Irish Americans, with 24 percent of the state indicating Irish ancestry.

Irish immigration today is relatively slight, accounting for perhaps one out of 1,000 legal arrivals until 2010, when it climbed to 2,800 because of tough economic times in Ireland. About 122,000 people in the United States today were born in Ireland. Today's Irish American typically enjoys the symbolic ethnicity of food, dance, and music. Gaelic language instruction is limited to fewer than 30 colleges. Visibility as a collective ethnic group is greatest with the annual St. Patrick's Day celebrations, when everyone seems to be Irish, or with the occasional fervent nationalism aimed at curtailing Great Britain's role in Northern Ireland, which is part of the United Kingdom rather than part of the Republic of Ireland. Yet some stereotypes remain concerning excessive drinking, despite available data indicating that alcoholism rates are no higher and are sometimes lower among people of Irish ancestry compared to descendants of other European immigrant groups (Bureau of the Census 2011b; Chazan and Tomson 2011).

St. Patrick's Day celebrations offer an example of how ethnic identity evolves over time. The Feast of St. Patrick has a long history, but public celebrations with parties, concerts, and parades originated in the United States and were then exported to Ireland in the latter part of the twentieth century. Even today, the large Irish American population often defines what authentic Irish is globally. For example, participants in Irish step dancing in the United States have developed such clout in international competitions that they have come to define many aspects of cultural expression, much to the consternation of the Irish in Ireland (Bureau of the Census 2009b; Hassrick 2007).

Well-known Irish Americans can be found in all arenas of American society, including celebrity chef Bobby Flay, songwriter and musician Kurt Cobain, comedian Conan O'Brien, and author Frank McCourt, as well as the political dynasties of the Kennedys in Massachusetts and the Daleys in Chicago. Reflecting growing rates of intermarriage, Irish America also includes singer Mariah Carey (her mother is Irish, her father African American and Venezuelan). Furthermore, on an official state visit to Ireland during his presidency, Barack Obama made a side trip to the village of Moneygall. President Obama's great-great-grandfather Falmouth Kearney, a shoemaker's son, left Moneygall for the United States in 1850.

The Irish were the first immigrant group to encounter prolonged organized resistance. However, strengthened by continued immigration, facility with the English language, strong community and family networks, and familiarity with representative politics, Irish Americans became an integral part of the United States.

The Italian Americans

5.4 Explain the Italian American experience.

Although each European country's immigration to the United States has its own social history, the case of Italians, though not typical of every nationality, offers insight into the White ethnic experience. Italians immigrated even during the colonial period, coming from a highly differentiated homeland, because Italian states were not unified as one nation and escaped foreign domination until 1848.

Early Immigration

Italian Americans played prominent roles during the American Revolution and the early days of the republic. Mass immigration began in the 1880s, peaking in the first 20 years of the twentieth century, when Italians accounted for one-fourth of European immigration (see Figure 5.1).

Italian immigration was concentrated not only in time but also by geography. The majority of the immigrants were landless peasants from rural southern Italy, the Mezzogiorno. Although many people in the United States assume that Italians are a nationality with a single culture, this is not true either culturally or economically. The Italian people recognize multiple geographic divisions within Italy reflecting sharp cultural distinctions. Immigrants brought these divisions with them to the New World.

Many Italians, especially in the early years of mass immigration in the nineteenth century, received their jobs through an ethnic labor contractor, the *padrone*. Similar arrangements have been used by Asian, Hispanic, and Greek immigrants, where the labor contractors, most often immigrants, have mastered sufficient English to mediate for their compatriots. Exploitation was common within the padrone system through kickbacks, provision of inadequate housing, and withholding of wages. By World War I,

90 percent of Italian girls and 99 percent of Italian boys in New York City were leaving school at age 14 to work, but by that time, Italian Americans were sufficiently fluent in English to seek out work on their own, and the padrone system disappeared. Still, by comparison to the Irish, the Italians in the United States were slower to accept formal schooling as essential to success (Sassler 2006).

Along with manual labor, the Catholic Church was a very important part of Italian Americans' lives at that time. Yet they found little comfort in a Catholic Church dominated by an earlier immigrant group: the Irish. The traditions were different; weekly church attendance for Italian Americans was overshadowed by the religious aspects of the *feste* (or festivals) held throughout the year in honor of saints (the Irish viewed the *feste* as practically a form of paganism). These initial adjustment problems were overcome with the establishment of ethnic parishes, a pattern repeated by other non-Irish immigrant groups. Thus, parishes would be staffed by Italian priests, sometimes imported for that purpose. Although the hierarchy of the church adjusted more slowly, Italian Americans were increasingly able to feel at home in their local parish church. Today, more than 70 percent of Italian Americans identify themselves as Roman Catholics (Luconi 2001).

Over the first few generations in the United States, Italian Americans rose up through the social classes largely by acquiring skills in low-skilled occupations rather than acquiring advanced degrees and entering professions. Eventually they began to achieve success in wine and fruit growing and became entrepreneurs of retail outlets in the urban Northeast and Midwest (Llosa 2013).

Constructing Identity

As assimilation proceeded, Italian Americans began to construct a social identity as a nationality group rather than viewing themselves in terms of their native village or province. As Figure 5.3 shows, over time, Italian Americans shed old identities for new ones. As immigration from Italy declined, the descendants' ties became more nationalistic. (This move from local or regional to national identity was followed by the same pattern among

Figure 5.3 Constructing Social Identity Among Italian Immigrants

Over time, Italian Americans moved from seeing themselves in terms of their provincial or village identity to their national identity, at which point they successfully became indistinguishable from other Whites.

Town or provincial identities such as
  Calabrians
  Genoese
  Milanese
  Neapolitans
  Pugliesi
  Romans
  Sicilians
  Tuscans
→ Italian Americans → White Americans

Irish and Greek Americans.) In general, early Italian immigrants were not treated well. For example, in turn-of-the-century New Orleans, Italian Americans established special ties with the Black community because both groups were marginalized in Southern society. Gradually, Italian Americans became White and enjoyed all the privileges that came with it. Today, it would be inconceivable to imagine that Italian Americans of New Orleans would reach out to the African American community as their natural allies on social and political issues (Guglielmo and Salerno 2003; Luconi 2001; Steinberg 2007:126).

A controversial aspect of the Italian American experience involves organized crime, as typified by Al Capone (1899–1947). Arriving in the United States poor and uneducated, Italians lived in decaying, crime-ridden neighborhoods. For a small segment of these immigrants, crime was a significant means of upward social mobility. In effect, entering and leading criminal activity was one aspect of assimilation, though not a positive one. Complaints linking ethnicity and crime actually began in colonial times with talk about the criminally inclined Irish and Germans, and they continue with contemporary stereotyping of groups such as Colombian drug dealers and Vietnamese street gangs. The image of Italians as criminals has persisted from Prohibition-era gangsters to the view of Mob families today. It is not at all surprising that Italian Americans have organized groups to counter such negative images.

The fact that Italians often are characterized as criminal, even in the mass media, is an example of **respectable bigotry** toward White ethnics. The persistence of linking Italians, or any other minority group, with crime probably is attributable to attempts to explain a problem by citing a single cause: the presence of perceived undesirables. Many Italian Americans still see their image tied to old stereotypes. A 2001 survey of Italian American teenagers found that 39 percent felt the media presented their ethnic group as criminal or gang members and 34 percent as restaurant workers (Girardelli 2004; IAAMS 2009; National Italian American Foundation 2006; Parrillo 2008).

The immigration of Italians was slowed by the national origins system, described in Chapter 4. As Italian Americans settled permanently, the mutual aid societies that had grown up in the 1920s to provide basic social services began to dissolve. More slowly, Italian Americans came to value education as a means of upward mobility. Even becoming more educated did not ward off prejudice, however. In 1930, for example, President Herbert Hoover rebuked Fiorello La Guardia, then an Italian American member of Congress from New York City, stating that "the Italians are predominantly our murderers and bootleggers" and recommending that La Guardia "go back to where you belong" because "like a lot of other foreign spawn, you do not appreciate this country which supports you and tolerates you" (Baltzell 1964:30).

Although U.S. troops, including 500,000 Italian Americans, battled Italy during World War II, some hatred and sporadic violence emerged against Italian Americans and their property. However, these hate crimes were not limited to actions against individuals. The federal government confined Italian Americans in specific areas of California by virtue of their ethnicity alone, and 10,000 were relocated from coastal areas. In addition, 1,800 Italian Americans who were citizens of Italy were placed in an internment camp in Montana. The internees were eventually freed on Columbus Day 1942 as President Roosevelt lobbied the Italian American community to gain full support for the impending land invasion of Italy (Department of Justice 2001; Fox 1990).

In the Research Focus, we consider how social scientists examine the economic experience of these early Italian immigrants and their children and compare it to the Mexican experience today.

Research Focus

Immigrants: Yesterday and Today

Anyone thinking about the future of today's immigrants might reflect back on the experiences of those who came a century ago. It is widely agreed that, despite difficult times and often harsh treatment by those already here, the immigrants of the late nineteenth and early twentieth century ultimately fared well. Certainly their descendants are doing well today. So can we generalize from this experience to today's immigrants?

Sociologist Joel Perlmann and other scholars have considered the experience of immigrants from southern, central, and eastern Europe who were predominantly low-skilled workers. A significant number of these workers were Italian and Poles. Based on his analysis and that of other sociologists, we find that these early immigrant workers earned typically only between 60 and 88 percent of the wages earned by nonimmigrant Whites in the same occupations.

Contrary to a commonly held belief, these immigrants did not end up in well-paying jobs in manufacturing that led them into the middle class in their own lifetimes. Rather, they remained firmly working class until after World War II. Upward mobility occurred across generations typically, not within the lifetimes of the arriving Italian, Polish, and other southern, central, and eastern European immigrants. In other words, economic parity took about three or four generations, not a decade (as some writers have romantically portrayed it).

With these data as a backdrop, Perlmann looked at contemporary Mexican immigrants. In many ways the deck is stacked against this current immigrant group, which is by far the largest. Unlike their European counterparts of a century ago, many arrivals from Mexico (about 55 percent) labor as illegal immigrants, which obviously curtails the opportunities available to them and their family members. Today's second-generation Mexicans in the United States are lagging further behind in education compared to the general population than was the comparable generation of the turn-of-the century European immigrants.

The education gap among today's Latinos does not facilitate upward mobility. This situation is particularly challenging given the much greater importance that formal schooling has today for economic success compared to a century ago.

Language acquisition does not appear to be an issue, even given the large concentrations of Spanish-speaking neighborhoods that might seem to work against Hispanics becoming fluent English speakers. Although 23 percent of Hispanic immigrants as a group speak English very well, the percentage of these immigrants who are fluent in English rises to 88 percent among their U.S.-born children and then to 94 percent in the third generation.

It is early to make firm direct comparisons because second-generation Mexican Americans are just coming of age, which means they have less labor-force experience and are just beginning to create their own families. Although the complete entry of today's immigrants into the economy is likely to occur, comparisons to White ethnics suggests that it may take Mexican immigrants longer by at least an additional generation.

Sources: Bean and Stevens 2003; Camarota 2007a; Dickson 2006; Hakimzadeh and Cohn 2007; Katz, Stern, and Fader 2007; Perlmann 2005; Portes 2006; Portes and Rumbaut 2006.

The Contemporary Picture

In politics, Italian Americans have been more successful, at least at the local level, where family and community ties can translate into votes. However, political success did not come easily because many Italian immigrants anticipated returning to their homeland and did not always take neighborhood politics seriously. It was even more difficult for Italian Americans to break into national politics.

Not until 1962 was an Italian American named to a cabinet-level position. Geraldine Ferraro's nomination as the Democratic vice presidential candidate in 1984 was as much an achievement for Italian Americans as it was for women. The opposition to the nomination of Judge Samuel Alito to the Supreme Court in 2006 struck many as bordering on anti–Italian American. Numerous critics used the phrase "Judge Scalito" in obvious reference to the sitting Italian American on the Court, Justice Antonin Scalia (Cornacchia and Nelson 1992).

While as a group, Italian Americans are firmly a part of middle America, they frequently continue to be associated with crime. In 2009, three New Jersey mayors were indicted for corruption, and not all of them were Italian. At the core of the scandal were five Syrian American rabbis, yet newspapers quickly dubbed the situation "New Jersey's 'Italian' Problem." MTV's 2009–2012 successful reality show *Jersey Shore,* which seemed to focus on drinking, hot tubbing, and brawling stars, did not help. Stereotypes and labeling do not go away, and truth is no antidote (McGurn 2009).

There is no lack of famous Italian Americans. They include athlete Joe DiMaggio, politician Rudolph Giuliani, film director Francis Ford Coppola, singers Lady Gaga and Madonna, writer Mario Puzo, actor Leonardo DiCaprio, chef Rachael Ray, and auto racing legend Mario Andretti.

Today, Italian Americans are the seventh-largest immigrant group in the United States. Just how ethnically conscious is the Italian American community? Although the number is declining, 700,000 Americans speak Italian at home; only ten languages are spoken more frequently at home: Spanish, Chinese, Tagalog (Philippines), Vietnamese, Korean, Russian, German, Arabic, Russian, and French Creole. For most of the 17-plus million Italian Americans, however, the language tie to their culture is absent, and, depending on their degree of assimilation, only traces of symbolic ethnicity may remain. As we saw in the chapter opener describing Little Italy in New York City, Italian ethnic enclaves throughout North America are more and more limited to a cluster of Italian restaurants and bakeries. In a later section, we look at the role that language plays for many immigrants and their children (Ryan 2013:3).

The Polish Americans

5.5 Describe the Polish American immigration story.

Immigrants from Poland have had experiences similar to those of the Irish and Italians. They had to overcome economic problems and personal hardships just to make the journey. Once in the United States, they found themselves often assigned to the jobs many citizens had not wanted to do. They had to adjust to a new language and a familiar yet different culture. And always, they were looking back to the family members left behind who either wanted to join them in the United States or never wanted them to leave Poland in the first place.

Like other arrivals, many Poles sought improvement in their lives, a migration that was known as Za Chlebem (For Bread). The Poles who came were, at different times, more likely than many other European immigrants to see themselves as forced immigrants and were often described by, and themselves adopted, the terminology directly reflecting their social roles—exiles, refugees, displaced persons, or émigrés. The primary force for this exodus was Poland's changing political status through most of the nineteenth and twentieth centuries, which was as turbulent as the lives of the new arrivals.

Early Immigration

Polish immigrants were among the settlers at Jamestown, Virginia, in 1608, to help develop the colony's timber industry, but it was the Poles who came later in that century who made a lasting mark. The successful exploits of Polish immigrants such as cavalry officer Casimir Pulaski and military engineer Thaddeus Kosciuszko are still commemorated today in communities with large Polish American populations. As Figure 5.1 shows, it was not until the 1890s that Polish immigration was significant in comparison to some other European arrivals. It is difficult to document the size of this immigration exactly because at various historical periods Poland or parts of the country became part of Austria-Hungary, Germany (Prussia), and the Soviet Union, so that the migrants were not officially coming from a nation called "Poland."

Many of the Polish immigrants had to adjust not only to a new culture but also to a more urban way of life. Sociologists William I. Thomas and Florian Znaniecki, in their classic study *The Polish Peasant in Europe and America* ([1918] 1996), traced the path from rural Poland to urban America. Many of the peasants did not necessarily come directly to the United States but first traveled through other European countries. This pattern is not unique and reminds us that, even today, many immigrants have crossed several countries, sometimes establishing themselves for a period of time before finally settling in the United States (Abbott and Egloff 2008).

Like the Germans, Italians, and Irish, Poles arrived at the large port cities of the East Coast but, unlike the other immigrant groups, they were more likely to settle in cities further inland or work in mines in Pennsylvania. In such areas, they would join kinfolk or acquaintances through the process of chain migration (described in Chapter 4).

The Poles' choice of coal mining as an occupation reflects the continuing tendency of immigrants to work in jobs avoided by most U.S. citizens because they paid little, were dangerous, or both. For example, in September 1897, a group of miners in Lattimer, Pennsylvania, marched to demand safer working conditions and an end to special taxes placed only on foreign-born workers. In the ensuing confrontation with local officials, police officers shot at the protesters, killing 19 people, most of whom were Polish; the others were Lithuanians and Slovaks (Duszak 1997).

Polonia

With growing numbers of Polish immigrants, the emergence of Polonia (meaning Polish communities outside of Poland) became more common in cities throughout the Midwest. Male immigrants who came alone often took shelter through a system of inexpensive boarding houses called *tryzmanie bortnków* (brother keeping), which allowed the new arrival to save money and send it back to Poland to support his family. These funds eventually provided the financial means necessary to bring family members over, adding to the size of Polonia in cities such as Buffalo, Cleveland, Detroit,

Milwaukee, Pittsburgh, and, above all, Chicago, where the population of Poles was second only to that in Warsaw, Poland.

Religion has played an important role among Polish immigrants and their descendants. Most of the Polish immigrants who came to the United States before World War I were Roman Catholic. They quickly established their own parishes where new arrivals could feel welcome. Although religious services at that time were in Latin, as they had been in Poland, the many service organizations around the parish, in addition to the Catholic schools, kept the immigrants steeped in the Polish language and the latest happenings back home. Jewish Poles began immigrating during the first part of the twentieth century to escape the growing hostility they felt in Europe, which culminated in the Holocaust. Their numbers swelled greatly until movement from Poland stopped with the invasion of Poland by Germany in 1939; Polish immigration resumed after the war.

Although the Jewish–Catholic distinction may be the most obvious distinguishing factor among Polish Americans, there are other divisions as well. Regional subgroups such as the Kashubes, the Górali, and the Mazurians have often carried great significance with the Polish American community. Some Poles emigrated from areas where German was the language of origin.

As with other immigrant groups, Polish Americans could make use of a rich structure of voluntary self-help associations that were already well established by the 1890s. However, not all organizations smoothly cut across different generations of Polish immigrants. For example, the Poles who came immediately after World War II as political refugees fleeing Soviet domination were quite different in their outlook than the descendants of the economic refugees from the turn of the century. These kinds of tensions in an immigrant community are not unusual, even if they go unnoticed by the casual observer who lumps all immigrants of the same nationality together (Jaroszyn'ska-Kirchmann 2004).

Like many other newcomers, Poles were stigmatized as outsiders and also stereotyped as simple and uncultured—the typical biased view of working-class White ethnics. Their struggles in manual occupations placed them in direct competition with other White ethnics and African Americans, which occasionally led to labor disputes and longer-term tense and emotional rivalries. "Polish jokes" continue to have a remarkable shelf life in casual conversation well into the twenty-first century. Jewish Poles suffer the added indignities of anti-Semitism (Dolan and Stotsky 1997).

The Contemporary Picture

Today, the number of Polish Americans in the United States is nearly 10 million. Although this number may not seem significant in a country of more than 300 million, we need to recall that today Poland itself has a population of only about 39 million. Polish Americans are a central part of the global Polish community, which has also included Lech Walesa, the Solidarity movement leader who confronted the Soviet Union in the 1980s, and Karol Józef Wojtyla, who became Pope John Paul II in 1978.

Polish American actress Scarlett Johansson reflects the multiple ethnic roots of many Americans today. Though Johansson was born in New York City, her father is a Danish immigrant, and her mother is a U.S.-born Jew whose parents came from Poland and Belarus, then part of the former Soviet Union. She reports celebrating both Hanukkah and Christmas and holds both American and Danish citizenship.

Many Polish Americans have retained little of their rich cultural traditions and may barely acknowledge even symbolic ethnicity. Data released in 2013 show about 600,000 whose primary language is Polish—a decline from over 800,000 in 1980. For those still immersed in Polonia, their lives revolve around many of the same religious and social institutions that were the center of Polonia a century ago. For example, 54 Roman Catholic churches in the metropolitan Chicago area still offer Polish-language masses. Although in many of these parishes there may be only one service in Polish serving a declining number of worshippers, a few traditional "Polish" churches still have Polish-speaking priests in residence. Even with the decline in Polish-language service, the Roman Catholic Church actively recruits Polish seminarians, although now English-language training is often emphasized.

In the latter part of the twentieth century, some of the voluntary associations relocated or built satellite centers to serve the outlying Polish American populations. To sustain their activities financially, these social organizations also reached out of the central cities in order to tap into the financial resources of suburban Poles. Increasingly, people of Polish descent also have now made their way into the same social networks populated by German, Irish, Italian, and other ethnic Americans (Bukowczyk 2007; Erdmans 1998, 2006; Lopata 1994; Mocha 1998; Polzin 1973; Shin and Kominski 2010; Stone 2006).

Except for immigrants who fled persecution in their homelands, immigration typically has back-and-forth movement. In the early years of the twenty-first century, there was an identifiable movement of Polish Americans from Polonia to Poland, especially as economic opportunity improved in the home country. One estimate of returnees places it at 50,000 from 2004, when Poland entered the European Union, to 2009. This number is significant in absolute terms but is relatively small given the size of the Polish American community (Fihel and Grabowska-Lusinska 2014; Mastony 2013).

Among the many Polish Americans well known or remembered today are home designer Martha (Kostyra) Stewart, comedian Jack Benny (Benjamin Kubelsky), guitarist Richie Sambora of the rock group Bon Jovi, *Wheel of Fortune* host Pat Sajak, baseball star Stan Musial, football star Mike Ditka, novelist Joseph Conrad (Józef Korzeniowski), singer Bobby Vinton (Stanley Ventula, Jr.), polio vaccine pioneer Albert Sabin, and motion picture director Stanley Kubrick.

Religious Pluralism

5.6 Define and explain religious pluralism.

Religion plays a fundamental role in society and affects even those who do not practice or even believe in organized religion. **Religion** refers to a unified system of sacred beliefs and practices that encompass elements beyond everyday life that inspire awe, respect, and even fear (Durkheim [1912] 2001).

In popular speech, the term *pluralism* has often been used in the United States to refer explicitly to religion. Although certain faiths are more prominent than others, the United States has a history of greater religious tolerance than most other nations. Today, religious bodies number more than 1,500 in the United States and range from the more than 68 million members of the Roman Catholic Church to sects with fewer than 1,000 adherents. In every region of the country, religion is being expressed in

Religious diversity characterizes the United States and includes many non-Christian faiths, including Sikhism—a religion that dates from sixteenth-century India and rejects the idea that any single faith has a monopoly on the truth. Here the faithful gather for a Sikh Day parade in New York City.

greater variety, whether it be the Latinization of Catholicism and some Christian faiths, the de-Europeanizing of some established Protestant faiths (as with Asian Americans), or the de-Christianizing of the overall religious landscape with Muslims, Buddhists, Hindus, Sikhs, and others. Much of the growth in U.S. religious pluralism is fueled by immigration. For example, the fast-growing Muslim population is 63 percent immigrant (Lipka 2016; Roof 2007).

How do we view the United States in terms of religion? Increasingly, the United States has a non-Christian presence. In 1900, an estimated 96 percent of the nation was Christian; slightly more than 1 percent was nonreligious, and approximately 3 percent held other faiths. In 2014, it was estimated that the nation was 68 percent Christian and another 37 percent are affiliated with non-Christian faiths. The United States has a long Jewish tradition, and Muslims number close to 5 million. A smaller but also growing number of people adhere to such Eastern faiths as Hinduism, Buddhism, Confucianism, and Taoism. Scholars of religious practices have documented the rise of people moving away formal church organizations but note that spirituality remains high and that those who attend services are more devout (McCauley 2015; Pew Research Center 2015a).

Sociologists use the word **denomination** for a large, organized religion that is not linked officially with the state or government. By far, the largest denomination in the United States is Catholicism; yet at least 24 other Christian religious denominations have 1 million or more members (Table 5.1).

At least four non-Christian religious groups in the United States have numbers that are comparable to any of these large denominations: Jews, Muslims, Buddhists, and Hindus. In the United States, each of these denominations numbers more than 1 million members. Within each of these groups are branches or sects that distinguish themselves from one another. For example, the Jewish faith embraces several factions—Orthodox, Conservative, Reconstructionist, and Reform—that are similar in their roots but marked by sharp distinctions. Some Muslims are Sunni and others are Shia. Further divisions are present within these groups, just as among Protestants and, in turn, among Baptists.

The United States has long been described as a Judeo-Christian nation, but with interest in other faiths and continuing immigration. This description, perhaps not accurate to begin with, is certainly not accurate now, partially as a result of the large increase in the number of Muslim Americans.

Islam in the United States has a long history stretching from Muslim Africans who came as slaves into the Muslim community of the present day, which includes

Table 5.1 Christian Churches with More Than a Million Members

Denomination Name	Inclusive Membership
Roman Catholic Church	68,503,456
Southern Baptist Convention	16,160,088
United Methodist Church	7,774,931
Church of Jesus Christ of Latter-Day Saints	6,058,907
Church of God in Christ	5,499,875
National Baptist Convention, U.S.A., Inc.	5,000,000
Evangelical Lutheran Church in America	4,542,868
National Baptist Convention of America, Inc.	3,500,000
Assemblies of God	2,914,669
Presbyterian Church (U.S.A.)	2,770,730
African Methodist Episcopal Church	2,500,000
National Missionary Baptist Convention of America	2,500,000
Lutheran Church—Missouri Synod (LCMS)	2,312,111
Episcopal Church	2,006,343
Churches of Christ	1,639,495
Greek Orthodox Archdiocese of America	1,500,000
Pentecostal Assemblies of the World, Inc.	1,500,000
African Methodist Episcopal Zion Church	1,400,000
American Baptist Churches in the U.S.A.	1,310,505
Jehovah's Witnesses	1,162,686
United Church of Christ	1,080,199
Church of God (Cleveland, TN)	1,076,254
Christian Churches and Churches of Christ	1,071,616
Seventh-Day Adventist Church	1,043,606
Progressive National Baptist Convention, Inc.	1,010,000

Note: Most recent data as of 2017.

SOURCE: Eileen Lindner (ed.) 2012. *Yearbook of American and Canadian Churches 2011*, Table 2, p. 12. Nashville, TN: Abingdon Press. Reprinted by permission of the National Council of Churches, 2011 Yearbook of American & Canadian Churches.

immigrants and native-born Americans. President Obama, whose father was a practicing Muslim who lived for years in Indonesia (the country with the largest Muslim population), never sought to hide his roots. However, reflecting the prejudices of many toward non-Christians, Obama stressed his Christian upbringing throughout his presidential campaigns. Indeed, a national survey showed that 55 percent believe the U.S. Constitution establishes the country as a "Christian nation" (Cose 2008; Thomas 2007).

Many faiths have played critical roles in resisting racism and in trying to bring together the nation in the name of racial and ethnic harmony. Broadly defined, faiths represent a variety of ethnic and racial groups. Figure 5.4 considers the interaction of White, Black, and Hispanic races with religions. Muslims, Pentecostals, and Jehovah's Witnesses are much

Figure 5.4 Racial and Ethnic Makeup of Selected Religions in the United States

Note: "Other" includes self-identified mixed races. Evangelical includes Baptist, Lutheran (Missouri and Wisconsin Synods), and Pentecostal, among others. Mainline Protestant includes Methodist, Lutheran (ELCA), Presbyterian, Episcopal, and United Church of Christ, among others, but excludes historically Black churches. Based on a national survey of 35,556 adults conducted in August 2007.

SOURCE: Data from Pew Forum on Religion and Public Life 2008a:120.

Roman Catholics: White 65%, Hispanic 29%, 2%, 2%, 2%

Jehovah's Witnesses: White 48%, Black 22%, Hispanic 24%, Other 5%

Muslims: White 37%, Black 24%, Other 15%, Asian 20%, Hispanic 4%

Buddhists: White 53%, Asian 32%, Other 5%, Hispanic 6%, Black 4%

Evangelical: White 81%, Asian 6%, Black 2%, Other 4%, Hispanic 7%

Mainline Protestant: White 91%, Black 3%, Other 2%, Asian 1%, Hispanic 3%

Jewish: White 95%, Hispanic 3%, Black 1%, Other 2%

Legend: White, Hispanic, Other, Black, Asian

more diverse than Presbyterians or Lutherans. Religion plays an even more central role for Blacks and Latinos than it does for Whites. A national survey indicated that 65 percent of African Americans and 51 percent of Latinos attend a religious service every week, compared to 44 percent of White non-Hispanics (Winseman 2004).

It would be a mistake to focus only on older religious organizations when considering religion's role in society. Local churches that developed into national faiths in the 1990s, such as Calvary Chapel, Vineyard, and Hope Chapel, have a following among Pentecostal believers, who embrace a more charismatic form of worship devoid of traditional ornamentation, with pastors and congregations alike favoring informal attire. New faiths develop with increasing rapidity in what can only be called a very competitive market for individual religious faith. In addition, many people, with or without religious affiliation, become fascinated with spiritual concepts such as angels or become a part of loose-knit fellowships. Religion in the United States is an ever-changing social phenomenon. Other nonmainstream faiths emerge in new arenas, as evidenced by the successful campaign of Mitt Romney, a Mormon, to win the Republican nomination for president in 2012 or the visible role of celebrities promoting the Church of Scientology (Schaefer and Zellner 2015).

Perhaps not surprisingly, adherents to religious faiths vary dramatically in how they see themselves aligned with the Republican and Democratic political parties, as Table 5.2 shows. While religious faiths typically do not explicitly endorse a party or even specific candidates, they often take positions on social issues that align more with either Republican and Democratic positions.

Despite the sharp divide in political party support, divisive conflicts along religious lines are muted in the United States compared with those in, say, the Middle East. Although not entirely absent, conflicts about religion in the United States seem to be overshadowed by civil religion. **Civil religion** is the religious dimension in the United States that merges public life with sacred beliefs. It also reflects the idea that no single faith is privileged over all others. Indeed, it even encompasses the views of nonbelievers regarding the human condition.

Sociologist Robert Bellah (1967) borrowed the phrase *civil religion* from eighteenth-century French philosopher Jean-Jacques Rousseau to describe a significant phenomenon in the contemporary United States. Civil religion exists alongside established religious faiths, and it embodies a belief system that incorporates all religions but is not associated specifically with any single religion. It is the type of faith to which presidents refer in inaugural speeches and to which American Legion posts and Girl Scout troops swear allegiance. In 1954, Congress added the phrase *under God* to the Pledge of Allegiance as a legislative recognition of religion's

A rabbi blesses a young girl at her bat mitzvah in the temple. Jewish children often celebrate a coming-of-age ceremony. According to Jewish law, when Jewish children reach the age of maturity (12 years for girls, 13 years for boys), they become responsible for their actions. At this point, a boy is said to become bar mitzvah; a girl is said to become bat mitzvah.

Table 5.2 Religious Faiths and Politics

Arranged in descending levels of support for the Republican Party

	Republican/Lean Republican	Democrat/Lean Democratic
Mormon	70	19
Evangelical	69	18
United Methodist Church	54	35
Baptist	44	43
Presbyterian	44	47
Roman Catholic	37	44
Jewish	26	64
Muslim	17	62
Buddhist	16	69
Hindu	13	61
African Methodist Episcopal Church	4	92

Notes: Data for 2014. Other possible responses were Independent, Other, No preference, No lean.
SOURCE: Data from Pew Research Center 2015a:188–190.

significance. Elected officials in the United States, beginning with Ronald Reagan, often conclude even their most straightforward speeches with "God bless the United States of America," which in effect evokes the civil religion of the nation.

Functionalists see civil religion as reinforcing central American values that may be more patriotic than sacred in nature. After major societal upheavals or tragedies, from the 1995 Oklahoma City bombing to the 2001 terrorist attacks and beyond, the mass media often show church services with clergy praying and asking for national healing.

In the following sections, we explore the diversity among the major Christian groups in the United States, such as Roman Catholics and Protestants, as well as how Islam has emerged as a significant religious force in the United States and can no longer be regarded as a marginal faith in terms of the number of followers (Gorski 2010).

Diversity Among Roman Catholics

Social scientists have persistently tended to ignore the diversity within the Roman Catholic Church in the United States. Recent research has not supported the conclusion that Roman Catholics are melding into a single group, following the traditions of the American Irish Catholic model, or even that parishioners are attending English-language churches. Religious behavior has been different for each ethnic group within the Roman Catholic Church. The Irish and French Canadians left societies that were highly competitive both culturally and socially. Their religious involvement in the United States is more relaxed than it was in Ireland and Quebec. However, the influence of life in the United States has increased German and Polish involvement in the Roman Catholic Church, whereas Italians have remained largely inactive. Variations by ethnic background continue to emerge in studies of contemporary religious involvement in the Roman Catholic Church (Eckstrom 2001).

The "ethnic empowerment" of the Roman Catholic Church by European immigration has declined not only as a result of the lower numbers of immigrants from European countries, but also by the next generation losing interest in Catholicism. Move than one in three of the U.S.-born White ethnics have left the Catholic Church since the 1970s (Hout 2016).

So, where does the Roman Catholic Church look for new members? Since the mid-1970s, the Roman Catholic Church in America has received a significant number of new members in immigrants from the Philippines, Southeast Asia, and particularly Latin America. Although these new members have been a stabilizing force offsetting the loss of White ethnics, they have also presented challenges to a church that for generations was dominated by Irish, Italian, and Polish parishes. Perhaps the most prominent subgroup in the Roman Catholic Church is Latinos, who now account for one-third of all Roman Catholic parishioners. Clearly, immigrants are seen as a significant part of the Catholic Church's future in the United States. More than 150 immigration-oriented programs are mounted by the Catholic Church nationwide. Often a program for a patron saint or national feast begins with two national anthems sung—that of the participant's native country and "The Star-Spangled Banner" (Dolan 2013; Goodstein and Steinhauer 2010; Navarro-Rivera, Kosmin, and Keysar 2010).

The Roman Catholic Church, despite its ethnic diversity, has been a powerful force in reducing the ethnic ties of its members, making it a significant assimilating force. The irony here is that so many nineteenth-century Americans heaped abuse on U.S. Catholics for allegedly being un-American and having a dual allegiance. The history of the Catholic Church in the United States may be portrayed as a struggle within the membership between the Americanizers and the anti-Americanizers, with the former ultimately winning. Unlike the various Protestant churches that accommodated immigrants of a single nationality, the Roman Catholic Church had to Americanize a variety of linguistic and ethnic groups. The Catholic Church may have been the most potent assimilating force after the public school system. Comparing the assimilationist goal of the Catholic Church and the current diversity in it leads us to conclude that ethnic diversity has continued in the Roman Catholic Church despite, not because of, this religious institution.

Diversity Among Protestants

Protestantism, like Catholicism, often is portrayed as a monolithic entity. Little attention is given to the doctrinal and attitudinal differences that sharply divide the various denominations in both laity and clergy. However, several studies document the diversity. Unfortunately, many opinion polls and surveys are content to learn only whether a respondent is a Catholic, a Protestant, or a Jew. Digging deeper, Stark and Glock (1968) found sharp differences in religious attitudes within Protestant churches. For example, 99 percent of Southern Baptists had no doubt that Jesus was the divine son of God, as contrasted to only 40 percent of Congregationalists. We can identify four "generic theological camps":

1. *Liberals:* United Church of Christ (Congregationalists) and Episcopalians
2. *Moderates:* Disciples of Christ, Methodists, and Presbyterians
3. *Conservatives:* American Lutherans and American Baptists
4. *Fundamentalists:* Missouri Synod Lutherans, Southern Baptists, and Assembly of God

Roman Catholics generally hold religious beliefs similar to those of conservative Protestants, except on essentially Catholic issues such as papal infallibility (the pope's authority in all decisions regarding faith and morals). Whether or not there are four distinct camps is not important: The point is that the familiar practice of contrasting Roman Catholics and Protestants is clearly not productive. Some differences between Roman Catholics and Protestants are inconsequential compared with the differences between Protestant sects.

Secular criteria as well as doctrinal issues may distinguish religious faiths. Research has consistently shown that denominations can be arranged in a hierarchy based on social class. As Figure 5.5 reveals, members of certain faiths, such as Episcopalians, Jews, and Presbyterians, have a higher proportion of affluent members. Members of other faiths, including Baptists, tend to be poorer. Of course, all Protestant groups draw members from each social stratum. Nonetheless, the social significance of these class differences is that religion becomes a mechanism for signaling social mobility. A person who is moving up in wealth and power may seek out a faith associated with a higher social ranking. Figure 5.6 shows similar contrasts in formal schooling.

Protestant faiths have been diversifying, and many of their members have been leaving them for churches that follow strict codes of behavior or fundamentalist interpretations of biblical teachings. This trend is reflected in the gradual decline of the five mainline churches: Baptist, Episcopalian, Lutheran, Methodist, and Presbyterian. As with the Roman Catholic Church, many Protestant faiths have seen their numbers helped by immigrants. Among the countries outside the United States with large Christian populations are China, Mexico, the Philippines, and Nigeria, which are all significant sources of immigrants to the United States (Brown 2015; Davis, Smith, and Marsden 2007).

Although Protestants may seem to define the civil religion and the accepted dominant orientation, some Christian faiths feel that they, too, experience the discrimination usually associated with non-Christians such as Jews and Muslims. For example,

---

Figure 5.5 Income and Denominations

Denominations attract different income groups. All groups have both affluent and poor members, yet some denominations have a higher proportion of members with high incomes, while others are comparatively poor.

SOURCE: Based on interviews with a representative sample of 35,000 adults reproduced in the *Pew Forum on Religion and Public Life* 2008b:78–79, 84–85.

Denomination	Percentage of Families with Incomes over $25,000
Baptist	59.0
Episcopalian	62.4
Methodist	69.0
Roman Catholic	70.4
Lutheran	71.5
Presbyterian	77.0
Jewish	81.1

Figure 5.6 Education and Denominations

There are sharp differences in the proportion of those with some college education by denomination.

SOURCE: Based on interviews with a representative sample of 35,000 adults and reproduced in the *Pew Forum on Religion and Public Life* 2008b:78–79, 84–85.

Denomination	Percentage with Some College Education
Baptist	21.7
Roman Catholic	32.7
Lutheran	33.0
Methodist	35.0
Presbyterian	44.2
Episcopalian	53.7
Jewish	65.7

representatives of the liberal and moderate faiths dominate the leadership of the military's chaplain corps. There are 16 Presbyterian soldiers for every Presbyterian chaplain, 121 Full Gospel worshippers for every Full Gospel chaplain, and 339 Muslim soldiers for every Muslim chaplain (Cooperman 2005).

As another example of denominational discrimination, in 1998, the Southern Baptist Convention amended its basic theological statements of beliefs to include a strong statement on family life. The statement included a declaration that a woman should "submit herself graciously" to her husband's leadership. There was widespread criticism of this position outside the Baptist Church, which many Baptists felt was inappropriate and a form of respectable bigotry. Many Baptists wondered why it was acceptable to attack them for their views on social issues when criticism was much more muted against more liberal faiths that are more tolerant of abortion (Bowman 1998; Niebuhr 1998).

Religion and the Courts

5.7 Understand court rulings on religion.

Religious pluralism owes its existence in the United States to the First Amendment declaration that "Congress shall make no law respecting an establishment of religion, or prohibiting the free exercise thereof." The U.S. Supreme Court has consistently interpreted this wording to mean not that government should ignore religion but that it should follow a policy of neutrality to maximize religious freedom. For example, the government may not help religion by financing a new church building, but it also may not obstruct religion by denying a church adequate police and fire protection. We examine five issues that continue to require clarification: company exemptions, school prayer, secessionist minorities and their rituals, creationism (including intelligent design), and the public display of religious (or sacred) symbols.

Company Exemptions

Businesses cannot typically discriminate in their hiring based on a person's religious beliefs, nor can they deny services to people based on their faith. While these laws may seem easy enough to enforce, in recent years the situation has grown more complex.

The effort to offer health insurance to more people led to the passage of the Patient Protection and Affordable Care Act (often called Obamacare), which mandates that more employers provide insurance options. By law, this insurance must include coverage for oral contraceptives, some of which pro-life people regard as bordering on abortion. The Supreme Court in 2014 ruled in favor of businesses being granted exceptions if the law ran contrary to the owner's beliefs. The company that brought the suit, Hobby Lobby, does not require that its 23,000 workers be Christian, but it does seek to create "a positive environment that happens to be based on biblical principles." For example, all its retail outlets are closed on Sundays, but it sells Hanukkah-related merchandise alongside Christmas-themed goods (Liptak 2014).

Another controversy has erupted in which businesses refuse to offer goods and services to people who embrace practices that the owners find religiously offensive. For example, some bakeries, event planners, and photography studios have refused to serve same-sex weddings since they became legal nationwide in 2015. Business owners have generally been unsuccessful in getting judicial support for such actions, but the Supreme Court has yet to rule definitively on the practice (Richey 2016).

School Prayer

Among the most controversial and ongoing disputes has been whether prayer has a role in U.S. public schools. The 1962 Supreme Court decision in *Engel v. Vitale*, which disallowed a purportedly nondenominational prayer drafted for use in the New York public schools, disturbed many people. The prayer was "Almighty God, we acknowledge our dependence upon Thee, and we beg Thy blessings upon us, our parents, our teachers, and our country." Subsequent decisions overturned state laws requiring Bible reading in public schools, laws requiring recitation of the Lord's Prayer, and laws permitting a daily one-minute period of silent meditation or prayer. Despite such judicial pronouncements, children in many public schools in the United States are led in regular prayer recitation or Bible reading. Contrary to what many people believe, religion has not been hounded out of public schools (Yemma 2013).

What about prayers at public gatherings? In 1992, the Supreme Court ruled 5–4 in *Lee v. Weisman* that prayer at a junior high school graduation in Providence, Rhode Island, violated the U.S. Constitution's mandate of separation of church and state. A rabbi had given thanks to God in his invocation. The district court suggested that the invocation would have been acceptable without that reference. The Supreme Court did not agree with the school board that a prayer at a graduation was not coercive. The Court did say in its opinion that it was acceptable for a student speaker voluntarily to say a prayer at such a program (Marshall 2001).

Public schools and even states have mandated a "moment of silence" at the start of the school day in what critics contend is a transparent attempt to get around *Lee v. Weisman*. While legislators clearly intended prayer or religious thoughts when they created these "moments," the courts have to date ruled such policies as constitutional and argued that the policy is secular, rather than sacred. Arkansas in 2013 became the latest state to mandate a minute of silence at the beginning of the school day (ABC Television 2013).

Secessionist Minorities

Several religious groups have been in legal and social conflict with the rest of society. Some can be called **secessionist minorities** in that they reject both assimilation and coexistence in some form of cultural pluralism. The Amish are one such group that comes into conflict with mainstream society because of the Amish beliefs and way of life. The Old Order Amish shun most modern conveniences and maintain a lifestyle dramatically different from that of larger society.

Are there limits to the free exercise of religious rituals by secessionist minorities? Today, tens of thousands of members of Native American religions believe that ingesting the powerful drug peyote is a sacrament and that those who partake of peyote will enter into direct contact with God. In 1990, the Supreme Court ruled that prosecuting people who use illegal drugs as part of a religious ritual is not a violation of the First Amendment guarantee of religious freedom. The case arose because Native Americans were dismissed from their jobs for the religious use of peyote and were then refused unemployment benefits by the state of Oregon's employment division. In 1991, however, Oregon enacted a new law permitting the sacramental use of peyote by Native Americans (*New York Times* 1991).

In another ruling on religious rituals, in 1993 the Supreme Court unanimously overturned a local ordinance in Florida that banned ritual animal sacrifice. The Court held that this law violated the free-exercise rights of adherents of the Santeria religion, in which the sacrifice of animals (including goats, chickens, and other birds) plays a central role. The same year, Congress passed the Religious Freedom Restoration Act, which said the government may not enforce laws that "substantially burden" the exercise of religion. Presumably, this legislation gives religious groups more flexibility in practicing their faiths. However, many local and state officials are concerned that the law has led to unintended consequences, such as forcing states to accommodate prisoners' requests for questionable religious activities or to permit a church to expand into a historic district in defiance of local laws (Greenhouse 1996).

The legal acceptance of different faiths has been illustrated in numerous decisions. For example, the courts have allowed Wiccan organizations to enjoy nonprofit status. In addition, the U.S. Department of Veterans Affairs approved of the pentacle symbol for use on national cemetery markers of those fallen soldiers who self-identify as Witches.

After lobbying by Wiccans, the U.S. Department of Veterans Affairs eventually approved the pentacle symbol for use on the cemetery markers of fallen soldiers who self-identify as Witches.

Creationism and Intelligent Design

Another area of contention has been whether the biblical account of creation should be or must be presented in school curricula and whether this account should receive the same emphasis as scientific theories. In the famous "monkey trial" of 1925, Tennessee schoolteacher John Scopes was found guilty of teaching the scientific theory of evolution in public schools. Since then, however, Darwin's evolutionary theories have been presented in public schools with little reference to the biblical account in the book of Genesis. People who support the literal interpretation of the Bible, commonly known as **creationists**, have formed various organizations to crusade for the teaching of creationism in U.S. public schools and universities.

In a 1987 Louisiana case, *Edwards v. Aguillard*, the Supreme Court ruled that states may not require the teaching of creationism alongside evolution in public schools if the primary purpose of such legislation is to promote a religious viewpoint. Creationists often seek to influence the choice of textbooks by a local school district or, in states with statewide adoptions by a state board of education; publishers who do not include creationism in their textbooks thus lose the opportunity to sell tens of thousands of textbooks in a particular state or district. The teaching of evolution and creationism has remained a controversial issue in many communities across the United States (Applebome 1996; Rich 2013).

Beginning in the 1980s, those who believe in a divine hand in the creation of life have advanced **intelligent design (ID)**, the idea that life is so complex that it could only have been created by a higher intelligence. Although ID is not explicitly based on the biblical account, many creationists feel comfortable with ID and advocate that it is a more accurate account than Darwinism or, at the very least, that it be taught as an alternative alongside the theory of evolution. In 2005, a federal judge in *Kitzmiller v. Dove Area School District* ended a Pennsylvania school district's intention to require the teaching of ID. In essence, the judge found ID to be "a religious belief" that was only a subtler way of finding God's fingerprints in nature than traditional creationism. Because the issue continues to be hotly debated, future court cases are certain to come (Clemmitt 2005; Goodstein 2005).

Public Displays

Another area of contention has been a battle over public displays that depict symbols of religion or appear to be sacred representations. Can manger scenes be erected on public property? Do people have a right to be protected from large displays such as a cross or a star atop a water tower overlooking an entire town? In a series of decisions in the 1980s and early 1990s, the Supreme Court ruled that tax-supported religious displays on public government property may be successfully challenged but may be permissible if made more secular. Displays that combine a crèche—the Christmas manger scene depicting the birth of Jesus—or the Hanukkah menorah and also include Frosty the Snowman or even Christmas trees have been ruled secular. These decisions have been dubbed "the plastic reindeer rules." In 1995, the Court clarified the issue by stating that privately sponsored religious displays may be allowed on public property if other forms of expression are permitted in the same location.

The issue is far from resolved, because these cases have been decided by close votes. Changes in the Supreme Court's composition in the next few years may lead to different decisions on future cases (Bork 1995; Hirsley 1991; Mauro 1995).

Conclusion

From his cramped basement apartment, Grigore Culian has been producing a biweekly Romanian-language paper called *New York Magazine* since 1997 that provides local news of interest to Romanians in the New York metro area and beyond. There are over 146,000 adults in the United States whose primary language is Romanian. While being a one-person operation is unusual, producing news for a small ethnic community is not. Foreign-language newspapers, radio stations, cable outlets, and video streaming keep ethnic ties alive and go beyond symbolic ethnicity. Media outlets foster a sense of community for hundreds of religious denominations, Christian and non-Christian alike (Lazar 2013).

Considering ethnicity and religion reinforces our understanding of the spectrum of intergroup relations first presented in Chapter 1. The Spectrum of Intergroup Relations (Figure 5.7) shows the rich variety of relationships as defined by people's ethnic and religious identities. The profiles of German, Irish, Italian, and Polish Americans reflect the variety of White ethnic experiences.

Any study of life in the United States, especially one that focuses on dominant and subordinate groups, cannot ignore religion and ethnicity. The two are closely related, as certain religious faiths predominate in certain nationalities. Both religious activity and interest by White ethnics in their heritage continue to be prominent features of contemporary society. People have been and continue to be ridiculed or deprived of opportunities solely because of their ethnic or religious affiliation.

Figure 5.7 Spectrum of Intergroup Relations: Ethnicity, Whiteness, and Religion

EXPULSION — SEGREGATION — ASSIMILATION

INCREASINGLY UNACCEPTABLE → MORE TOLERABLE

EXTERMINATION or genocide
- Holocaust (Jews in Poland)

SECESSION or partitioning

FUSION or amalgamation or melting pot
- German and Italian internment during World War II
- Ethnic neighborhoods (e.g., "Little Italy")
- All-White and All-Black churches
- Constructing social identity among Italian immigrants
- English language acquisition
- Ethnic paradox
- Immigrant groups becoming White

PLURALISM or multiculturalism
- First Amendment
- Secessionist minorities
- Symbolic ethnicity
- Religious pluralism
- Third-generation principle
- Civil religion
- Marco Polo Festival
- Blended identity

Religion is changing in the United States. As one commercial recognition of this fact, Hallmark created its first greeting card in 2003 for the Muslim holiday Eid-al-fitr, which marks the end of the month-long fast of Ramadan. The issue of the persistence of ethnicity is an intriguing one. Some people may only casually exhibit their ethnicity and practice what has been called symbolic ethnicity. However, can people immerse themselves in their ethnic culture without society punishing them for their desire to be different or to embrace their heritage? The tendency to put down White ethnics through respectable bigotry continues. Despite this intolerance, ethnicity remains a common source of identity for many Americans today. There is also the ethnic paradox, which finds that practicing one's ethnic heritage often strengthens people and allows them to move successfully into the larger society.

The issue of religious expression in all its forms also raises a variety of intriguing questions. How can a country that is increasingly populated by diverse and often non-Christian faiths maintain religious tolerance? How might this level of tolerance change in the decades ahead? How will the courts and society resolve the issues of religious freedom? This is a particularly important issue in areas such as company exemptions, school prayer, secessionist minorities, creationism, intelligent design, and public religious displays. Some examination of religious ties is fundamental to completing an accurate picture of a person's social identity.

Summary of Learning Objectives

5.1 Understand what is meant by ethnicity, including Whiteness.

1. While considering race and ethnicity in the United States, we often ignore how White people come to see themselves as a group and in relationship to others. Racial and ethnic groups may achieve "Whiteness" over a period of time.

2. Feelings of ethnicity may be fading among the descendants of Europeans, but they may reemerge as reflected in either the third-generation principle or, in a more limited fashion, through symbolic ethnicity.

5.2 Describe the German American experience.

3. German Americans are the largest White ethnic group but have been largely incorporated into the core population with little visible distinctive cultural presence apart from food.

5.3 Identify the major periods of Irish American immigration.

4. First regarded very much as "outsiders" and even as not White, people of Irish descent are the second-largest White ethnic group today. The Irish in the United States date back to the colonial period, but a major Irish immigration to the United States took place in the mid-nineteenth century as a result of a potato famine. The twenty-first century saw renewed Irish immigration as a result of economic difficulties in Ireland.

5.4 Explain the Italian American experience.

5. Like the Irish, immigrants from Italy first encountered resistance in the United States but moved up from their lower- and working-class status in the American social hierarchy.

5.5 Describe the Polish American immigration story.

6. Immigration from Poland has created a visible presence of Polonia in several American cities.

5.6 Define and explain religious pluralism.

7. The ethnic diversity of the United States is matched by the many denominations among Christians, as well as the sizable Jewish and Muslim presence.

5.7 Understand court rulings on religion.

8. In its interpretation of the First Amendment, the Supreme Court has tried to preserve religious freedom, but critics have argued that the Court has served to stifle religious expression.

Key Terms

blended identity, *page 132*
civil religion, *page 153*
creationists, *page 160*
denomination, *page 150*
ethnic paradox, *page 133*
intelligent design (ID), *page 160*
principle of third-generation interest, *page 133*
religion, *page 149*
respectable bigotry, *page 144*
secessionist minority, *page 159*
symbolic ethnicity, *page 135*
White privilege, *page 130*

Review Questions

1. How is Whiteness socially constructed?
2. In what ways can White ethnicity be rediscovered?
3. Explain the impact that World War II had on German Americans both before and after the war.
4. Explain how Irish Americans became "White."
5. How does stereotyping relate to contemporary Italian Americans?
6. What role does Polonia play in the lives of contemporary Polish Americans?
7. How has the non-Christian population been expanding in the United States?
8. How have court rulings affected religious expression?

Critical Thinking

1. In which situations do you see ethnicity becoming more apparent? When does it appear to occur only in response to other people advancing or celebrating their own ethnicity? In these situations, how can ethnic identity be both positive and perhaps counterproductive or even destructive?
2. How do White people you know seem to be aware or unaware of their ethnic roots? Of their Whiteness?
3. Why do you think we are so often reluctant to show our religion to others? Why might people of certain faiths be more hesitant than others?
4. How do religious denominations reflect conservative and liberal positions on social issues? Consider services for the homeless, the need for childcare, the acceptance or rejection of gay men and lesbians, and a woman's right to terminate a pregnancy versus the fetus's right to survive.

Chapter 6
The Nation as a Kaleidoscope

David Grossman/Alamy Stock Photo

⌄ Learning Objectives

6.1 Characterize the progress or lack of progress made by racial and ethnic minorities in the United States.

6.2 Explain the model minority image.

6.3 Describe the major educational issues facing African Americans.

6.4 Discuss how inequality has persisted.

6.5 Consider how intergroup communication occurs without true communication.

What metaphor do we use to describe a nation whose racial, ethnic, and religious minorities are now becoming numerical majorities in cities coast to coast; in the states of California, Hawai'i, New Mexico, and Texas; and in a growing proportion of all counties within the United States? A vast amount of statistical data and personal experience documents the nation's racial and ethnic diversity. The mosaic differs by region and by community, but the tapestry of racial and ethnic groups is always close at hand everywhere in the United States.

The U.S. motto *E Pluribus Unum* ("Out of many, one") is apparent in the increasing numbers of immigrants in the rural town of Garden City, Kansas, and in the emerging Bhutanese immigrant population in Manchester, New Hampshire. For several generations, the idea of the "melting pot" has been used as a convenient description of our culturally diverse nation. The phrase *melting pot* originated as the title of a 1908 play by Israel Zangwill. In this play, a young Russian Jewish immigrant to the United States composes a symphony that portrays a nation that serves as a crucible (or pot) where all ethnic and racial groups dissolve into a new, superior stock.

The perception of the United States as a melting pot became widespread in the first part of the twentieth century, particularly because it suggested that the United States had an almost divinely inspired mission to destroy artificial divisions and create a single national identity. However, the dominant group had indicated its unwillingness to welcome Native Americans, African Americans, Latinos, Jews, and Asians, among many others, into the melting pot.

Although the metaphor of the melting pot is still used today, astute observers recognized that the term hides as much about a multiethnic United States as it discloses. Therefore, in the 1970s the metaphor of the *salad bowl* emerged to describe our ethnically diverse country. Just as we can distinguish the lettuce, the tomatoes, and the peppers in a tossed salad, we also can see the wide variety of ethnic restaurants and the popularity of foreign-language newspapers. The dressing over the salad's ingredients is akin to the shared value system and culture covering, but not hiding, the different ingredients.

Yet even the notion of a salad bowl is wilting. Like its melting-pot predecessor, the image of a salad is static—and the United States is certainly not static. Nor does the idea of a salad call to mind the myriad cultural pieces that make up the fabric or mosaic of our diverse nation.

The kaleidoscope offers another familiar, more useful, analogy. Patented in 1817 by Scottish scientist Sir David Brewster, the kaleidoscope is both a toy and a conversation piece in upscale living rooms. When people turn the set of mirrors in the kaleidoscope, they see an almost endless variety of colors and patterns reflected off pieces of glass, tinsel, or beads. The growing popularity of the phrase "people of color" seems appropriate for the kaleidoscope that is the United States. The changing images correspond to the sometimes bewildering array of groups found in our country.

For more than 40 years, a million people have flocked to Little Havana in Miami for food, fun, and dancing at the annual Calle Ocho festival, which features a wide variety of live entertainment. Participants often attempt to break records set at previous years' festivals, such as the biggest piñata, longest cigar, most domino players, and longest conga line.

Figure 6.1 Changes in Minority School Population, 1995–2022

As recently as 1995, all racial and ethnic minorities combined accounted for just a little more than one out of three of the nation's schoolchildren. By 2022, the "minorities" will be the numerical majority.

NOTE: Data for public elementary and secondary schools. Race categories exclude Hispanics.

SOURCE: Hussar and Bailey 2014:33; National Center for Education Statistics 2013: Table 44.

1995
- Asian and Other 4.9%
- Hispanic 13.6%
- Black 16.8%
- White 64.7%

2022
- Asian and Other 9.5%
- Hispanic 29.6%
- Black 15.0%
- White 45.9%

As Figure 6.1 shows, estimates for the period 1995–2022 predict an increase in the proportion of racial and ethnic minorities in schools and a decline in the proportion of White non-Hispanics.

How easy is it to describe the images we see in a kaleidoscope to someone else? Unfortunately, it is easy to misspeak even in the midst of good intentions. For example, we can forgive the faux pas by the *Washington Post* writer who described the lack of Hispanic-speaking (rather than Spanish-speaking) police as a factor contributing to hostilities in the nation's capital. We can understand why Chicago politicians, who sought to maintain the boundaries of a Hispanic congressional district after the results of the 2010 Census, found themselves criticized by Blacks fearful of losing their districts and by Latinos who had hoped to achieve a second or third seat in Congress. We can forgive Marlon Brando for sending a Native American woman to refuse his Oscar, with the goal of protesting Hollywood's portrayal of Native Americans. Was he unaware of Italian Americans' discomfort regarding his award-winning performance in *The Godfather*, which played on Italian American stereotypes?

We also can understand why the African Americans traumatized by Hurricane Katrina would turn their antagonism from the White power structure (which they perceived as ignoring their needs) to the Latinos who took advantage of the employment opportunities provided by the reconstruction projects in New Orleans. The proportion of the city's population that was Hispanic increased by 77 percent between 2000 and 2015 (American Community Survey 2016b).

In short, it is difficult to describe the image created by a kaleidoscope because it changes dramatically with little effort. Similarly, we find it a challenge to describe the multiracial nature of our republic. Perhaps in viewing the multiethnic, multiracial United States as a kaleidoscope, we may take comfort that the Greek word *kalos* means "beautiful" (Schaefer 1992). To develop a better understanding of the changing image through the kaleidoscope, we will examine the progress that has taken place and explore why miscommunication among our diverse peoples seems to be the rule rather than the exception.

The Glass Half Empty

6.1 Characterize the progress or lack of progress made by racial and ethnic minorities in the United States.

A common expression makes reference to a glass of water being "half full" or "half empty." If one is thirsty, it is half empty and needs to be replenished. If one is attempting to clear dirty dishes, it is half full. Many people, especially Whites, see the progress of subordinate groups or minorities and find it difficult to understand calls for more programs and new reforms. They also find it difficult to understand why minority neighborhoods sometimes erupt in violence.

In absolute terms, the glass of water has been filling up. In other words, many racial and ethnic groups have made progress, but they believe that there is still a long way to go. For example, Latinos and African Americans often compare themselves to Whites today and therefore see the glass as half empty (at best).

Figure 6.2 shows the current picture and recent changes by comparing African Americans, Hispanics, and Whites. We see that the nation's largest minority groups—African Americans and Hispanics—have completed more schooling and enjoy longer life expectancy today than they did in 2002. However, household incomes are virtually unchanged. In contrast, White Americans have made strides in all three areas.

The greatest strides have been made in educational attainment. However, in other areas, the gap remains and has increased in some instances. Black household median incomes in 2015 have yet to match Whites income levels in 1975, more than four decades ago! Hispanics are not doing much better with regard to income. Latinos and African Americans still have more than double the poverty rates of Whites. Also, Black Americans today have barely the life expectancy that Whites had a generation ago.

Is There a Model Minority?

6.2 Explain the model minority image.

"Asian Americans are a success! They achieve! They succeed! They have no protests, no demands. They just do it!" This is the general image that people in the United States often hold of Asian Pacific Americans (APAs) as a group. APAs constitute a **model minority** because, although they have experienced prejudice and discrimination, they seem to have succeeded economically, socially, and educationally without resorting to political or violent confrontations with Whites.

Some observers point to the existence of a model minority as a reaffirmation that anyone can get ahead in the United States. Proponents of the model-minority view declare that because Asian Americans have achieved success, they have ceased to be subordinate and are no longer disadvantaged. This labeling is a variation of **blaming the victim**: With Asian Americans, it is praising the victim. Examining aspects of the family, educational, and economic status of Asian Americans allows a more thorough exploration of this view (Ryan 1976).

Figure 6.2 Changes in Schooling, Income, and Life Expectancy for African Americans, Hispanics, and Whites, 2002 to 2015–2016

NOTE: College, income, and poverty data for Whites are for White non-Hispanics.

SOURCES: Bureau of the Census 2017c; National Center for Health Statistics 2017a; Proctor, Semega, and Kollar 2016.

Adults Having Completed College

	Whites	Blacks	Hispanics
2002	27.3%	17.5%	11.2%
2016	37.3%	24.6%	17.4%

Median Household Income

	Whites	Blacks	Hispanics
2002	$81,833	$38,240	$45,611
2015	$85,585	$36,898	$45,148

Percentage of People Below Poverty Level

	Whites	Blacks	Hispanics
2002	8.0%	24.1%	21.8%
2015	9.1%	24.1%	21.4%

Life Expectancy in Years at Birth

	Whites	Blacks
2002	77.5	72.2
2015	79.0	75.5

The Family

Many point to the Asian American family as the social institution in which the excellence begins. Nonetheless, many older Asian Americans and new arrivals are dismayed by the more American behavior patterns of APA youth. Change in family life is one of the most difficult cultural changes to accept. Children questioning parental authority, which Americans grudgingly accept, is a painful experience for the tradition-oriented Chinese. The 2011 bestseller *Battle Hymn of the Tiger Mother* by legal scholar Amy Chua touched off heated discussions with its indictment of parents indulging their children and its insistence on parental guidance (and control) of children's activities and interests. We look at this controversy more closely in the Research Focus.

The tiger mother has resonated on two levels. First, Amy Chua has gone public with the fact that she entered into a legal contract with her daughters when she and her husband bought a Manhattan apartment and allowed their two 20-something daughters to live there. Today, the two young women claim their mom is now a "hands-off mother" (Chua 2016; *The Week* 2016).

Second, and more importantly, *Battle Hymn of the Tiger Mother* ignited scholarly research into the parenting techniques used by Chinese American parents. The studies have generally noted that there is great variety in parenting styles; the tiger approach is one parenting style, but it is not necessarily particularly successful. Generally, Chinese American parents are much more flexible than they are depicted in the best-selling memoir (Cheah, Leung, and Zhou 2013; Jung, Qin, and Park 2013; Kim, Wang, Orozco-Lapray, Shen, and Murtuza 2013).

Close families as depicted in *Battle Hymn of the Tiger Mother* and confirmed in other studies resonate in many immigrant communities. **Familism** means pride and closeness in the family, which results in family obligations and loyalty coming before individual needs. The Bureau of the Census (Bureau of the Census 2009a: D7) found, for example, that children under 12 in Asian and Hispanic households in the United States were more likely to eat dinner with a parent every day than children in White or Black households.

Educational Levels

As a group, Asian Americans have impressive school-enrollment rates in comparison to the total population. In 2010, half of Asian Americans 25 years of age or older held bachelor's degrees, compared with 28 percent of the White population. These rates vary among Asian American groups: Asian Indians, Filipino Americans, Korean Americans, Chinese Americans, and Japanese Americans have higher levels of educational achievement than other Asian American groups. In fact, Indian Americans as a group are more likely to have a college degree than Whites. Yet other groups, such as Vietnamese Americans, the Hmong, and Pacific Islanders (including Native Hawaiians), have much lower levels of education than White Americans (Bureau of the Census 2007b, 2011a; Guillermo 2015; Taylor 2013).

Many Asian Americans do have some qualifications that challenge the optimistic model minority view. According to a study of California's state university system, Asian Americans often are viewed as successful overachievers, but they have unrecognized and overlooked needs, and they have experienced discomfort and harassment on campus. As a group, they also lack Asian faculty and staff members to whom they can turn for support. They confront many identity issues and must also perform a "cultural balancing act" while facing all the usual pressures faced by college students. The report noted that an "alarming number" of Asian American students appeared to be experiencing intense stress and alienation, problems that have often been "exacerbated by racial harassment" (Ohnuma 1991; Teranishi 2010).

Research Focus

Tiger Mothers

It is not often that a memoir sparks a national debate about parenting that extends around the world, but such was the case with a memoir published by a Yale law professor. In 2011, Amy Chua published *Battle Hymn of the Tiger Mother*, in which she recounts how she raised her two American girls, who were teenagers at the time. Her parenting practices followed the approach to child-rearing common in China and other parts of Asia. Chua's Chinese parents, who had emigrated from the Philippines to Illinois, followed these practices.

The quick takeaway for readers, or even those who never opened the book, was the concept of "tiger moms"—Chinese American (or maybe all Asian Pacific American) mothers who raise their children in a stern but loving fashion that emphasizes competition for success. The term **tiger mother** has come to refer to a demanding mother who pushes her children to high levels of achievement.

Days are filled with music lessons, music practice, and handmade greeting cards but no sleepovers, no television or video games, and no tolerance for any grade but A. Married to a fellow law professor, Chua agreed to raise their children in his Jewish faith (Chua is Roman Catholic) but only if she could be a "Chinese mother." Her book came to be seen as an indictment of the more permissive U.S. child-rearing practices. The *Wall Street Journal* (*Wall Street Journal* 2011) titled its excerpt from the book "Why Chinese Mothers Are Superior."

Chua does not claim to be a child development specialist and contends that her book is the story of one mother who became frustrated when her second daughter became rebellious at age 13 and chose tennis over piano and violin. Since the ensuing firestorm about the book, Chua has admitted that she has some regrets about the way she raised her daughters, but she continues to defend her strictness and her overall approach as taking the best from "Asian cultures."

So is there really a single method of "Chinese parenting"? Studies of Chinese parenting indicate that there is no one way that most parents rear their children. In addition, Chua's relatively affluent lifestyle allowed her to hire many helpers and experts while still allowing her to work as a full-time professional. Such assistance is well beyond most parents' financial means. Chua's book also serves to reinforce the model minority stereotype. There is more emphasis in Asia and among Asian immigrant households on stressing respect for authority and self-discipline. These cultural expectations have their roots in the ethical and philosophical system developed from the teachings of the Chinese philosopher Confucius in the fifth century BCE. Confucian goals stress the importance of perseverance, working hard in school, being obedient, and being sensitive to parents' wishes.

Yet even if it is more common in Asia, this approach is not uniquely Chinese, as Chua has admitted. For example, NBC journalist Tom Brokaw told Chua that his working-class South Dakotan father was a "Chinese mom." There is also evidence that in China today, especially urban China, parents are becoming more relaxed with their children and growing critical of schools' emphasis on rote memorization.

Perhaps most revealing about the notion of the tiger mother and the ensuing debate is the way it speaks to views of Asia and particularly China as "threats" to America's superpower status. Chua makes explicit reference to the fact that children in other countries, especially China, are outperforming U.S. children on standardized tests. So, while the concept of the tiger mother offers some insight into the caregiving culture in Asia, it also highlights how Americans see Asian Americans and Asian Pacific Americans.

Sources: Chua 2011, 2016; Paul 2011; Pitt 2013; Russell, Crockett, and Chao 2010; Shah 2012; *Wall Street Journal* 2011.

Even the positive stereotype of Asian American students as academic stars or whiz kids can be burdensome to the people so labeled. Asian Americans who do only modestly well in school may face criticism from their parents or teachers for their failure to conform to the whiz-kid image. Some Asian American youths disengage from school when faced with these expectations or receive little support for their interest in vocational pursuits or athletics (Lee and Zhou 2014a).

While the widely held public perception is that Asian Americans have a fast track to college, many Asian Americans perceive that admissions policies work against them. The culprits, in their view, are:

- limits or quotas on the number of Asian Americans at highly selective universities and
- affirmative action that works against them by failing to consider them as eligible.

Recall that **affirmative action** refers to positive efforts to recruit subordinate group members for jobs, promotions, and educational opportunities. Asian Americans have been vocal in saying that they are not generally considered in such programs and that in fact they lose places to less-qualified Whites.

Indeed, some activist Asian American groups were conspicuously vocal in their disappointment in the *Fisher* Supreme Court case that ruled against the White plaintiff who felt she was unfairly passed over for admission to a Texas university. Efforts are under way to force elite institutions like Harvard, Yale, Dartmouth, and Brown to make public their admissions records. While Asian Americans account for 15 percent to 25 percent of Ivy League college enrollment, some argue that the percentage would be even greater if they were treated like White applicants or even like African American and Latino high school graduates. Many argue that this barrier to advancement continues in the labor market (Asian-American Coalition for Education 2017; Bachelder 2015; *The Economist* 2014).

Economic Status

APAs account for almost 6 percent of the U.S. population, but they represent fewer than 2 percent of *Fortune* 500 CEOs and corporate officers. Most of these standouts are immigrants who started up successful technological and information companies. A national survey showed that APAs who are successful in the corporate world must manage themselves so they don't seem "too ambitious" or have "too many ideas." Only 28 percent of Asian Americans feel very comfortable "being themselves" at the workplace, compared to 45 percent of African Americans, 41 percent of Latinos, and 42 percent of White workers (Center for Work-Life Policy 2011; Chin 2016).

Despite the widespread belief that they constitute a model minority, APAs are victims of both prejudice and violence. At issue is what has been termed the "perpetual foreigner" view of APAs. After the terrorist attacks of September 11, 2001, anti-Asian violence increased dramatically for several months in the United States. The first fatality was an Asian Indian American who was shot and killed by a gunman in Mesa, Arizona. The gunman shouted, "I stand for America all the way" (National Asian Pacific American Legal Consortium 2002; Xu and Lee 2013).

This anti–Asian American feeling is built on a long cultural tradition. The term *yellow peril* dates back to the view of Asian immigration, particularly from China, as unwelcome. **Yellow peril** came to refer to the generalized prejudice toward Asian people and their customs. The immigrants were characterized as heathen, morally inferior, drug addicted, savage, or lustful. Although the term was first used around the turn of the twentieth century, this anti-Asian sentiment is very much alive today. Many contemporary Asian Americans find this intolerance very unsettling given their conscientious efforts to extend their education, seek employment, and conform to the norms of society. Hate crimes against APAs persist and have even risen in recent years (Hurh 1994; Lee et al. 2007).

The resentment against APAs is not limited to overt expressions of violence. Like other subordinate groups, APAs are subject to institutional discrimination. As noted in Chapter 3, **institutional discrimination** is the denial of opportunities and equal rights to individuals and groups that results from the normal operations of a society.

For example, some APA groups have large families and find themselves subject to zoning laws stipulating the number of people per room, which makes it difficult for family members to live together. Kinfolk are unable to legally take in family members. Whereas laws may regard these family members as distant relatives, many Asian cultures view cousins, uncles, and aunts as relatives to whom the traditional nuclear family has a great deal of responsibility.

The marginal status of APAs leaves them vulnerable to both selective and collective oppression. In 1999, news stories implicated Wen Ho Lee, a nuclear physicist at Los Alamos National Laboratory in New Mexico, as a spy for China. Subsequent investigation, during which Lee was imprisoned under very harsh conditions, concluded that the naturalized citizen scientist had indeed downloaded secret files to an unsecured computer, but there was no evidence that the information ever went further.

In the aftermath of the Wen Ho Lee incident, a new form of racial profiling emerged. Recall that **racial profiling** is any police-initiated action that relies on race, ethnicity, or national origin rather than a person's behavior. Despite Lee being found not guilty, Asian Americans were viewed as security risks. A survey found that 32 percent of U.S. residents felt that Chinese Americans are more loyal to China than to the United States. In fact, the same survey showed that 46 percent were concerned about Chinese Americans passing secrets to China. Subsequent studies found that Asian Americans were avoiding top-secret science labs for employment because they became subject to racial profiling at higher security levels (Committee of 100 2001; Department of Energy 2000; Lee with Zia 2006; Wu 2002).

Another misleading sign of the apparent success of APAs is their high incomes as a group. APA family income approaches parity with that of Whites because of their greater achievement than Whites in formal schooling. If we look at specific educational levels, however, Whites earn more than their Asian counterparts of the same age. APAs' average earnings increased by at least $2,300 for each additional year of schooling, whereas Whites gained almost $3,000. APAs as a group have significantly more formal schooling but lower household family income. We should note that, to some degree, some APAs' education is from overseas and, therefore, may be devalued by U.S. employers. Yet, in the end, educational attainment does not pay off as much for those of Asian descent as it does for White non-Hispanics (Kim and Sakamoto 2010; Zeng and Xie 2004).

So even with all the "tools" to succeed—supportive family, high achievement, and a degree from a prestigious school—APAs often hit what has been termed a *bamboo ceiling*. The **bamboo ceiling** refers to the barrier that talented APAs face because of resentment and intolerance directed toward them. The bamboo ceiling is a nod to the term *glass ceiling*, which has historically been used to address barriers that women and minority-group men have faced in the workplace. For example, 11 percent of law-firm associates were APAs as of 2014, but only 3 percent of partners were APAs. The presence of the bamboo ceiling reflects the cultural values and social norms that affect Asian professionals' interactions with others and cause others to make negative judgments about them (*The Economist* 2015b; Hyun 2006, 2009).

Striking contrasts are evident among APAs. For every APA household in 2015 with an annual combined income of $200,000 or more, another APA household earns less than $20,000 a year. Collectively, 11.4 percent of APAs were below the poverty level in 2015, compared to 9.1 percent of White non-Hispanics. Almost every APA group has a higher poverty rate than White non-Hispanics. The lone exception is Filipinos, who tend to live in the relatively high-income states of Hawai'i and California (Proctor, Semega, and Kollar 2016: Table A-1; National CAPACD 2012).

At first, one might be puzzled to see criticism of a positive generalization such as "model minority." Why should the stereotype of adjusting without problems be a disservice to APAs? The answer is that this incorrect view excludes APAs from social programs and conceals unemployment and other social ills. When representatives of Asian groups seek assistance for those in need, people who have accepted the model-minority stereotype resent them. This problem is especially troubling given that issues of substance abuse and juvenile delinquency need to be addressed within the APA community.

According to research, the model minority myth seems to embraced by people who subscribe to **color-blind racism**—the use of race-neutral principles to defend the racially unequal status quo. Individuals who view APAs as uniformly successful are also likely to see discrimination as absent in both school and work; for them, inequality is essentially a thing of the past. They also endorse anti-APA sentiments such as seeing them as perpetual foreigners (Parks and Yoo 2016).

The positive stereotype of the model minority reaffirms the U.S. system of mobility, which holds that new immigrants, as well as established subordinate groups, ought to achieve more merely by working within the system. At the same time, viewed from the conflict perspective outlined in Chapter 1, the model-minority myth is yet another instance of blaming the victim: If Asian Pacific Americans have succeeded, then Blacks and Latinos must be responsible for their own low status, thus absolving society of any responsibility (Chen 2012; Chou and Feagin 2008; Xu and Lee 2013).

Acting White, Acting Black, or Neither

6.3 Describe the major educational issues facing African Americans.

A common view advanced by some educators is that African Americans, especially young men, do not succeed in school because they do not want to be caught "acting White." That is, they avoid at all costs taking school seriously and do not accept the authority of teachers and administrators. Whatever the accuracy of such a generalization, acting White clearly shifts the responsibility of low school attainment from the school to the individual and, therefore, can be seen as yet another example of blaming the victim. **Acting White** is also associated with speaking proper English or with cultural preferences like listening to rock music rather than hip-hop.

In the context of high achievers, to what extent do Blacks *not* want to act White? Many scholars have noted that individuals' efforts to avoid looking like they want an education has a long history and is not exclusive to any one race. Students of all colors fear accusations of being "too hardworking."

Back in the 1950s, one heard disparaging references to "teacher's pet" and "brownnosing." Does popularity come to members of the high-school debate team and National Honor Society or to cheerleaders and athletes? Academically oriented students are sometimes viewed as social misfits, nerds, and geeks and may be seen as socially inept, even if their skill-building will later make them more economically independent and more socially desirable. For minority youth, including African Americans, taking school seriously means overcoming the desire, shared with their White classmates, to be cool and not to be seen as geeks. In addition, to succeed in school, Black youth must embrace a curriculum and respect teachers who are much less likely to look or sound like them.

The acting-White thesis emphasizes personal responsibility rather than the structural features of the education system, such as quality of schools, curricula, and teachers. Therefore, it locates the source of Black miseducation—and, by implication, the remedy—in the African American household.

Of course, not all Whites "act White." To equate acting White with high academic achievement has little empirical or cultural support. Studies comparing attitudes and performance show that Black students have the same attitudes—good and bad—about achievement as their White counterparts. Too often, we tend to view White slackers who give a hard time to the advanced placement kids as "normal," but when low-performing African Americans do the same thing, it becomes a systemic pathology undermining everything good about schools. The research consensus is that the primary stumbling block is not acting White or acting Black but being presented with similar educational opportunities (Buck 2011; Covay 2013; Downey 2008; Fordham and Ogbu 1986; Lewis 2013; Ogbu 2004; Tyson 2011).

So if the notion that the difficulty that some Black students face in school is not due to their opposition to "acting White," why are so many people still advancing this incorrect explanation as a fact? Doing so allows us to blame the student and "Black culture" and not confront how our educational institutions are underperforming. This is another example of **color-blind racism**, in which we use race-neutral principles to defend the racially unequal status quo. Majority-minority schools today persist with far fewer educational resources. In addition, where African Americas attend more integrated schools, they are often relegated to less demanding curricular programs and face increased disciplinary actions compared to their fellow students.

The Persistence of Inequality

6.4 Discuss how inequality has persisted.

Progress has occurred. Some indignities and injustices have been eliminated, allowing us to focus on the remaining barriers to equity. But why do the gaps in income, wages, education, and life expectancy persist? Especially perplexing is the question of whether the glass is half full or half empty in light of the numerous civil-rights laws, study commissions, favorable court decisions, and efforts by nonprofits, faith-based organizations, and private sectors.

In trying to comprehend the persistence of inequality among racial and ethnic groups, sociologists and other social scientists have found it useful to think in terms of the role played by social and cultural capital. Popularized by French sociologist Pierre Bourdieu, these concepts refer to assets that are not necessarily economic but do affect economic capital for one's family and future. Lower levels of cultural and social capital may be passed on from one generation to the next, especially when prejudice and discrimination make it difficult to overcome deficits. Racial and ethnic minorities reproduce disadvantage while Whites are more likely to reproduce privilege (Bourdieu 1983; Bourdieu and Passeron 1990).

Cultural capital refers to noneconomic forces, such as family background and past investments in education, that are then reflected in knowledge about the arts and language. Cultural capital is not necessarily book knowledge but rather the kind of education valued by the elites. African Americans and Native Americans have in the past faced significant restrictions in receiving a quality education. Immigrants have faced challenges due to English not being spoken at home. Muslim immigrants face an immediate challenge in functioning in a culture that advantages a different form of spirituality and lifestyle. The general historical pattern has been for immigrants, especially those who came in large numbers and settled in ethnic enclaves, to take two or three generations to reach educational parity with the dominant culture. Knowledge of hip-hop and familiarity with Polish cuisine are forms cultural knowledge, but these are not valued and prestigious components of culture. Society privileges or values some lifestyles over others; being able to differentiate among the types of *pierogi* will not get you to the top of corporate America as fast as the ability to differentiate among wines. Of course, elitist ideas regarding cultural capital are not unique to the United States. Someone settling in Japan would have to deal with cultural capital that includes knowledge of Noh Theatre and tea ceremonies. In most countries, you are much better off following the run-up to the World Cup rather than the contenders for the next Super Bowl (DiMaggio 2005).

Social capital refers to the collective benefit of durable social networks and their patterns of reciprocal trust. Much has been written about the strength of family and friendship networks among racial and ethnic minorities. Family reunions are major events. Family history and storytelling are rich and full. Kinfolk are not merely acquaintances but truly living assets upon which one depends or, at the very least, feels comfortable to call upon repeatedly. Networks outside the family are critical to coping in a society that often seems to be determined to keep anyone who looks like you down. However, given past as well as current discrimination and prejudice, these social networks may help you become a construction worker, but they are less likely to get you onto a board of directors. Residential and school segregation make developing social capital more difficult. Immigrant professionals find that their skills or advanced degrees are devalued, and they are shut out of the networks of the educated and influential. However, working-class Latino and Black workers have begun to develop informal social ties with their White coworkers and neighbors. Professional immigrants, in time, become accepted as equals, but racial and ethnic minority communities continue to face (and resist) institutional marginalization (Coleman 1988; Cranford 2005).

Being even modestly successful can be difficult for members of racial and ethnic groups to sustain. The Speaking Out feature reproduces an excerpt from *Black Picket Fences: Privilege and Peril Among the Black Middle Class*. The author, sociologist Mary Pattillo, wrote about the Groveland neighborhood of Chicago, where she was doing ethnographic research on the precarious nature of maintaining a Black middle-class community.

Speaking Out

Black Picket Fences

Mary Pattillo

On a tour of Chicago's neighborhoods, our jumbo coach bus drove through a predominantly African American neighborhood not too far from Groveland. And just as middle class. It was a cold autumn morning, and the tree-lined streets were completely empty. Yet there were conspicuous clues that somebody cared deeply about this neighborhood. Matching lampposts stood like sentries at the edge of each home's neat lot. Welcoming block-club placards on the corners—"Please Drive Slowly"—conveyed a concern for children who might be too engrossed in play to mind the traffic. The occasional candy wrapper or grocery bag on a few lawns did not ruin the overall tidiness. The homes with fresh paint, edged grasses, and decorative screen doors outnumbered the properties of loafers who had ceded victory to the weeds, or refused to sweep the sidewalk.

As we took in the pleasant sights, our learned Chicago tour guide, who was white, reported to our

Mary Pattillo

group of sightseers, most of who were also white. "From looking at it, some you might think this is a predominantly white neighborhood, but actually this neighborhood is all black." He spoke as if he let us in on a little secret.

The guide's comment, dressed in its disclosing tone, initially struck me as narrow-minded, since I had, after all, grown up in a like neighborhood, and was not at all surprised by this find in Chicago. Yet with the near completeness of racial segregation in many large American cities, it would indeed be difficult for many whites to just happen upon a place like Groveland. For the most part—and especially in cities like Chicago, Milwaukee, St. Louis, Newark, Buffalo, Philadelphia, and so on—African Americans live on the "black side of town," and whites on the "white side of town." To a somewhat lesser extent and depending on the city, Hispanic and Asian American groups each year have their "side of town," too.

People's routine patterns ensure that they have little reason or opportunity to see Groveland and neighborhoods like it. The average nonblack citizen's ignorance of these enclaves is bolstered by the common belief in academia that the black middle class actually moved away from black neighborhoods after the 1960s, leaving behind their poorer former neighbors. Recognizing all this, perhaps black middle-class neighborhoods *are* a secret. And the black middle class, while far from a secret, is shrouded in misperception.

Groveland's first generation of residents who entered adulthood in the immediate post–World War II era remember a time of largesse. With their stable jobs and in search of better housing, African American college-educated professionals moved to Groveland. Along with them came customer service representatives, hairdressers, transit employees, and railroad workers. All earned enough to buy a home and perhaps send the children to Catholic school, or take a yearly trip back Down South. They replaced the white residents who were also benefiting from postwar prosperity, and were looking to move to the growing suburbs. Far from integration, the change in Groveland was complete racial turnover. As Groveland's African American residents established their stake in the neighborhood, the statues of Jesus in the old neighborhood churches were painted darker, the restaurants started serving soul food, and the drugstores stocked black hair-care products. In their new, attractive neighborhood, Groveland's first generation began to reap the benefits of the civil rights movement.

The expansion of the black middle class in the 1950s, 1960s, and very early 1970s came to a halt in the last two-and-a-half decades of the twentieth century. The generations that followed Groveland's African American pioneer settlers have found it progressively more difficult to match what their parents amassed in those days of plenty. Executive profit-hoarding, corporate and government downsizing, and global labor markets have pillaged the wallets of the American middle class, both white and black. But with lower incomes and a flimsier financial cushion, African Americans are more susceptible than whites to slipping back down the class ladder.

A contemporary profile of the black middle class reveals that higher-paid professionals and executives do not predominate as they do among the white middle class. Instead, office workers, salespeople, and technical consultants—all lower-middle-class jobs— make up the majority of black middle-class workers. Working-class African Americans, who have been even harder hit by production shifts, are also an integral part of neighborhoods like Groveland.

Linda Brewer, a Groveland resident in her mid-thirties, listed the jobs that anchored her parents' generation. "A lot of these people around here, you know, post office workers, steel mills. They father had two jobs," she reflected. "But them jobs are no longer here. So now they kids are poor." The second generation, of which Linda is a member, struggles to buy homes, or maintain the homes their parents purchased. Along with the third generation of teenagers and young adults, they are somewhat bewildered by the fact that without a college degree, they often have to live with their parents in order to get full consumption and leisure mileage out of their lower-middle-class paychecks. The black middle class is particularly fragile. As Anna Morris [born in Groveland and now raising her own family there] summarized, "I get enough to get by. I don't get any more. I take care of my children. I think we're sort of well-to-do, but who could say. You could go any way any day."

Source: Pattillo 2013: 201–203.

Members of the Black middle class are better off than poor African Americans, but studies show that in urban areas their surrounding social environment more closely mirrors that of poor Whites than middle-class Whites. This social environment has consequences for housing quality, access to retail and medical providers, and public safety (Reardon, Fox, and Townsend 2015; Sharkey 2014).

As the ranks of the powerful and important have been reached by all racial and ethnic groups, social capital is more widely shared, but this process has proven to be slower than advocates of social equality would wish. Perhaps accelerating it will be the tendency for successful minority members to be more likely to network with up-and-coming members of their own community, while Whites are more likely to be more comfortable, even complacent, with the next generation making it on their own. We are increasingly appreciative of the importance of aspirations and motivations that are often much more present among people with poor or immigrant backgrounds than those born of affluence. We know that bilingualism is an asset, not a detriment. Children who have translated for their parents develop "real-world" skills at a much earlier age than their monolingual English counterparts (Bauder 2003; Monkman, Ronald, and Théraméne 2005; Portes 1998; Yosso 2005).

Considering cultural and social capital does leave room for measured optimism. Racial and ethnic groups have shared their cultural capital, whether it is the music we listen to or the food we eat. As the barriers to privilege weaken and eventually fall, people of all colors will be able to advance. The particular strength that African Americans, tribal people, Latinos, Asian Americans, and arriving immigrants bring to the table is that they also have the ability to resist and to refuse to accept second-class status. The role that cultural capital and social capital play also points to the need to embrace strategies of intervention that will increasingly acknowledge the skills and talents found in a pluralistic society.

Talking Past One Another

6.5 Consider how intergroup communication occurs without true communication.

African Americans, Italian Americans, Korean Americans, Puerto Ricans, Native Americans, Mexican Americans, and many others live in the United States and interact daily, sometimes face-to-face and constantly through the media. As the state rankings in Table 6.1 show, the opportunities to interact with people of different backgrounds vary from state to state, but it is not difficult to encounter people of a different race, ethnicity, or religion than oneself.

Talking Face-to-Face

Communication does not mean we listen to, much less understand, one another. Sometimes we assume that, as we become an educated nation, we will set aside our prejudices. Yet even our college campuses have been the scenes of tension, insults, and even violence. Fletcher Blanchard, Teri Lilly, and Leigh Ann Vaughn (1991) conducted an experiment at Smith College and found that even overheard statements can influence expressions of opinion on the issue of racism.

Table 6.1 Top Ten Lists: Largest Concentrations of Different Groups, by Percentage and State, 2015

	White Americans (Non-Hispanic) (USA = 61.5%)		Foreign-Born (USA = 13.5%)		Speak Language Other Than English at Home (People 5 Years and Older) (USA = 21.5%)		Multiracial (Self-Identify as Two or More Races) (USA = 3.1%)		Hispanic or Latino (USA = 14.7%)		African Americans (USA = 12.7%)		Native Americans (American Indians and Alaska Natives) (USA = 0.8%)		Asian Pacific Americans (including Native Hawaiians) (USA = 5.4%)	
1. Maine	93.6%	1. California	27.3	1. California	44.6%	1. Hawai'i	24.5%	1. New Mexico	47.4%	1. Mississippi	37.7%	1. Alaska	13.7%	1. Hawai'i	46.5%
2. Vermont	93.4	2. New York	22.9	2. Texas	35.4	2. Alaska	8.6	2. California	38.4	2. Louisiana	32.2	2. New Mexico	9.3	2. California	14.6
3. West Virginia	92.3	3. New Jersey	22.1	3. New Mexico	34.3	3. Oklahoma	7.9	2. Texas	38.4	3. Georgia	31.3	3. South Dakota	8.3	3. New Jersey	9.5
4. New Hampshire	90.9	4. Florida	20.2	4. New York	30.9	4. Washington	5.5	4. Arizona	30.3	4. Maryland	29.5	4. Oklahoma	7.3	4. Nevada	8.6
5. Iowa	88.8	5. Nevada	19.3	5. New Jersey	30.8	5. Nevada	5.0	5. Nevada	27.5	5. South Carolina	27.5	5. Montana	6.3	5. Washington	8.5
6. Montana	86.6	6. Hawai'i	17.7	6. Nevada	30.2	6. California	4.5	6. Florida	23.7	6. Alabama	26.8	6. North Dakota	5.0	6. New York	8.4
7. North Dakota	85.9	7. Texas	17.0	7. Florida	29.0	7. Oregon	4.5	7. Colorado	21.1	7. North Carolina	21.6	7. Arizona	4.5	7. Alaska	7.3
8. Kentucky	85.2	8. Massachusetts	16.1	8. Arizona	27.1	8. Virginia	3.5	8. New Jersey	19.0	7. Delaware	21.6	8. Wyoming	2.2	8. Maryland	6.4
9. Wyoming	84.1	9. Maryland	15.2	9. Hawai'i	26.1	8. Colorado	3.5	9. New York	18.4	9. Virginia	19.2	9. Idaho	1.4	8. Virginia	6.4
10. South Dakota	82.8	10. Connecticut	14.5	10. Illinois/Massachusetts	23.0	10. New Mexico/Rhode Island	3.4	10. Illinois	16.5	10. Tennessee	16.8	10. Washington	1.3	10. Massachusetts	6.3

SOURCE: American Community Survey 2016a: Tables C03001, R0202, R0203, R0204, R0205, R0207, R0209, R0501, and R1601.

People of different races, religions, and ethnic backgrounds talk to one another, but do they also talk past one another?

The researchers asked a student to conduct an opinion poll for a class. The student was to approach seventy-two White students as each was walking across the campus. Each time the student researcher did so, she also stopped a second White student—actually a confederate working with the researchers—and asked her to participate in the survey as well. Both students were asked how Smith College should respond to anonymous racist notes actually sent to four African American students in 1989. However, the confederate was instructed to answer first. In some cases, she condemned the notes; in others, she justified them. Blanchard and his colleagues (1991) concluded that "hearing at least one other person express strongly antiracist opinions produced dramatically more strongly antiracist public reactions to racism than hearing others express equivocal opinions or opinions more accepting of racism" (pp. 102–103). In addition, when the confederate expressed sentiments justifying racism, the subjects were much less likely to express antiracist opinions than those who heard no other opinions. In this experiment, social control (through the process of conformity) influenced people's attitudes and the expression of those attitudes.

There is a growing realization that people do not always mean the same thing when they are addressing questions of race, ethnicity, gender, or religion. For example, a husband regularly does the dishes and feels he is an equal partner in doing the housework, not recognizing that he leaves the care of his infant daughter totally to his wife. Or a manager is delighted to hire a Puerto Rican salesperson but makes no effort to see that the new employee will fit into a workplace with an otherwise all-White, non-Hispanic staff.

We talk, but do we talk past one another? Surveys regularly show that different ethnic and racial groups have different perceptions, whether on immigration policies, on racial profiling, or on whether discrimination occurs in the labor force. Sociologist Robert Blauner (1969, 1972) drew our attention to how Blacks and Whites see racism differently. Minorities see racism as central to society, as ever present, whereas Whites regard it as a peripheral concern and a national concern only when accompanied by violence or involving a celebrity. African Americans and other minorities consider racist acts in a broader context. For example, some African Americans might say, "It is racist if my college fails to have Blacks significantly present as advisers, teachers, and administrators." Whites generally believe a racist act has occurred if a job was denied to an appropriately qualified minority member.

Furthermore, Whites apply the label "racist" only to the person or the few people who were responsible for the act. Members of minority groups are more willing to label most of the college's administrators or faculty racist for allowing racist practices to persist. For many Whites, the word *racism* is a red flag, and they are reluctant to use it as often as minorities do—that is, those who have been oppressed by racism. For example, a 2016 national survey showed that 65 percent of Blacks felt that is "a lot more difficult to be Black than White" compared to only 37 percent of Whites. In contrast, when asked if "White people benefit from advantages in society that Black people do not have," 62 percent of African Americans agreed, compared to only 13 percent of Whites (Lichtenberg 1992; Maniam 2016).

Community studies and fieldwork reveal the slights that African Americans feel in everyday interactions with Whites in places of public accommodation, such as restaurants and retail outlets. Not all these perceived slights are real, nor do they always reflect racial prejudice or discrimination. Nonetheless, African Americans and other racial minorities are much more likely to assess the perceived slights as the result of intolerance and typically dismiss them as "Here we go again" rather than drawing attention to bigotry. However, Whites are more likely to be annoyed that such slights could be interpreted as racial, and they generally perceive the same interactions quite differently or attribute them primarily to the obnoxious nature of the offending White person (Anderson 2011; Duneier 2013).

Communicating Online

A major change in society is our growing use and reliance on the Internet in general and on social media in particular. Online access affords us the opportunity to explore and understand cultures and lifestyles different from our own. In addition, online communication (including social media) can promote tolerance by reaching a broad audience.

However, online networking gives hate groups and extremist organizations the ability to gain followers and create an illusion of importance that otherwise would not exist. Even individual intolerance can find a new audience. The anonymity of the Internet allows those so inclined to express their offensive views.

Indeed, the majority of social media users feel that online discussions encourage people to say things that they never would say in person. In recent years, online political and social discussions appear to have become increasingly disrespectful. Offensive content is the main reason online users block or remove others from their feeds. Yet, as we noted in Chapter 3, browser searching typically builds on past searches, increasing the likelihood that one will encounter like-minded thinkers online (Duggan and Smith 2016; Glaser and Kahn 2004; Zittrain 2008).

A chilling development is the growing use of the Internet as a vehicle for anti-Semitism specifically and racism in general, either by delivering such messages or serving as a means of reaching Web sites that spread intolerance. The rise of social media has allowed the instantaneous transmission of messages of intolerance. According to studies in 2016 and 2017, a staggering 2.6 million anti-Semitic statements were found on Twitter in just one year. One-fourth of African Americans and 10 percent of Latinos feel racially harassed online compared to 3 percent of Whites (Anti-Defamation League 2016; Duggan 2017; Gladstone 2016; Mahler 2016).

Despite the proliferation of bias online, some people still espouse a doctrine of color-blind racism and see little evidence of intolerance except when confronted by a horrendous hate crime. Others contend that racism is often couched in a "backstage" manner through discussions of immigration, affirmative action, anti-poverty programs, and profiling for national security.

Is one view entirely correct—the broader minority perspective of widespread racism or the more limited White outlook of infrequent, isolated racist actions? No, but both are a part of the social reality in which we all live. We need to recognize both interpretations.

As we saw when we considered Whiteness in Chapter 5, the goal of acknowledging and confronting racism is not to make Whites feel guilty or absolve Blacks, Asians, Hispanics, and Native Americans of any responsibility for their present plight. Rather, to understand racism, past and present, is to understand how its impact has shaped both individual behavior and that of the entire society (Bonilla-Silva and Baiocchi 2001; Duke 1992).

In the book's final Spectrum of Intergroup Relations (Figure 6.3), we summarize how the country has either perpetuated racism or tried to confront it by creating a more tolerant society.

Figure 6.3 Spectrum of Intergroup Relations

EXPULSION — SEGREGATION — ASSIMILATION

INCREASINGLY UNACCEPTABLE → MORE TOLERABLE

EXTERMINATION or genocide
- American Indian–cavalry wars
- Ethnic cleansing
- Eugenics
- Hate crimes
- Holocaust

SECESSION or partitioning
- Alien Act of 1798
- Asylees (from native country)
- Chinese Exclusion Act
- Environmental refugees
- Refugees (from native country)
- Roma from France (2009)
- Creation of Kosovo
- Pakistan—India
- Palestinians

(Segregation)
- All-white and all-Black churches
- Apartheid
- Environmental justice
- Ethnic neighborhoods
- Glass ceiling
- Internment during World War II
- Nativism
- Occupational segregation
- Redlining
- Resegregation
- Roma schoolchildren in Czech Republic
- Xenophobia

FUSION or amalgamation or melting pot
- Colorism
- Intermarriage
- Acting White
- Birthright citizenship
- Civil Rights Act of 1964
- Constructing social identity among Italian Americans
- English language acquisition
- Ethnic paradox
- Immigrant groups becoming White
- Impact on health
- Marginality
- Naturalization

PLURALISM or multiculturalism
- Afrocentric perspective
- Bilingualism
- Blended identity
- Chain immigration
- Civil religion
- Marco Polo festival
- Religious pluralism
- Remittances
- Sanctuary city
- Symbolic ethnicity
- Third-generation principle
- Transnationals

Conclusion

As the United States promotes racial, ethnic, and religious diversity, it also strives to impose universal criteria on employers, educators, and real-estate agents so that subordinate racial and ethnic groups can participate fully in the larger society. In some instances, to bring about equality of results—not just equality of opportunity—programs have been developed to give competitive advantages to women and minority men. Only more recently have similar strides been made on behalf of people with disabilities. These latest attempts to move society closer to a general equality for all people have provoked much controversy over how to achieve the admirable goal of a multiracial, multiethnic society, undifferentiated in opportunity and rewards.

Relations among racial, ethnic, and/or religious groups take two broad forms, as situations characterized by either consensus or conflict. Consensus prevails where assimilation or fusion of groups has been completed. Consensus also prevails in a pluralistic society in the sense that members have agreed to respect differences among groups. By eliminating the contending group(s), extermination and expulsion also lead to a consensus society. In the study of intergroup relations, it is often easy to ignore conflict where there is a high degree of consensus because it is assumed that an orderly society has no problems. In some instances, however, this assumption is misleading. Through long periods of history, misery inflicted on a racial, ethnic, or religious group was judged to appropriate or even divinely inspired.

In recent history, harmonious relations among all racial, ethnic, and religious groups have been widely accepted as a worthy goal. The struggle against oppression and inequality is not new. It dates back at least to the revolutions in England, France, and the American colonies in the seventeenth and eighteenth centuries. The twentieth century was unique in the extension of equality to the less-privileged classes, many of whose members are racial and ethnic minorities. Conflict along racial and ethnic lines is especially bitter now because it evokes memories of slavery, colonial oppression, and overt discrimination. Today's African Americans are much more aware of slavery than contemporary poor people are of seventeenth-century debtors' prison.

Unquestionably, the struggle for justice among racial and ethnic groups has not completely met its goals. Many people are still committed to repression, although they may see it only as the benign neglect of those less privileged. Such repression leads to the dehumanization of both the subordinated individual and the oppressor. Growth in equal-rights movements and demands for self-determination in countries largely populated by non-White people continue the struggle against oppression. Meanwhile, the old ethnic battle lines now renewed in Iran, Kenya, Sudan, Syria, Turkey, and Ukraine have only added to the tensions.

Self-determination, whether for groups or individuals, often is impossible in societies as they are currently structured. Bringing about social equality, therefore, will entail significant changes in existing institutions. Because such changes are not likely to come about with everyone's cooperation, the social costs will be high. However, many believe that the social costs, however high, must be paid to achieve the goal of self-determination.

It would be naive to foresee a world of societies in which one person equals one vote and all are fully accepted without regard to race, ethnicity, religion, gender, age, disability status, or sexual identity. It is equally unlikely to expect to see a society, let alone a world, without a privileged class or prestigious jobholders. Contact between different peoples, as we have seen numerous times, precedes conflict. However, contact also may initiate mutual understanding and appreciation.

Assimilation does not necessarily bring with it acceptance, nor does it guarantee tolerance. Segregation persists. Efforts toward pluralism can be identified, but we also easily see counterefforts, whether they are the legal efforts to make English the official language of the United States or acts of intimidation by activists patrolling the nation's borders. However, the ever-changing population of the United States guarantees that we will continue to learn, work, and play in a more diverse society.

The task of making this kaleidoscopic image of diverse cultures, languages, colors, and religions into a picture of harmony may seem overwhelming. The images of failure in this noble goal, some of which we witness on the nightly news, are frightening. We can applaud success and even take time to congratulate ourselves, but we must also review the unfinished agenda and commit to continued progress.

Summary of Learning Objectives

6.1 Characterize the progress or lack of progress made by racial and ethnic minorities in the United States.

1. Racial and ethnic minority groups have made great strides during the past two generations in the United States, but typically the gap between them and Whites has remained the same.

6.2 Explain the model minority image.

2. Often Asian Americans are labeled as a model minority. This stereotype overlooks the many problems they face and serves to minimize the challenges of succeeding despite prejudice and discrimination.

6.3 Describe the major educational issues facing African Americans.

3. African Americans have made gains in all levels of formal schooling but still fall behind the gains made by others. Debate continues over the accuracy of the notion that Black youths avoid appearances of acting White.

6.4 Discuss how inequality has persisted.

4. Inequality persists despite visible improvement because most racial and ethnic groups are unable to accumulate social and cultural capital.

6.5 Consider how intergroup communication occurs without true communication.

5. While interaction across racial and ethnic lines occurs continues to increase, it is less clear whether we are all listening to one another. White people generally apply the charge of racism when it is operating explicitly, whereas members of racial and ethnic groups are more likely to see racism more generally where disadvantages persist. Online communication offers a new medium for furthering both tolerance and prejudice.

Key Terms

acting White, *page 174*
affirmative action, *page 171*
bamboo ceiling, *page 173*
blaming the victim, *page 167*
color-blind racism, *page 173*

cultural capital, *page 175*
familism, *page 169*
institutional discrimination, *page 172*
model minority, *page 167*

racial profiling, *page 172*
social capital, *page 176*
tiger mother, *page 169*
yellow peril, *page 172*

Review Questions

1. Choose an issue facing contemporary society. Then explain the "half full" and the "half empty" approach to that issue.
2. Why is it harmful to be viewed as a model minority?
3. What are the accurate and inaccurate aspects of identifying people as "acting White" or "acting Black"?
4. Select three measures that show how inequality among racial or ethnic groups has declined or persisted over the past generation.
5. Increased intergroup contact is usually encouraged, but how might the communication that naturally follows be misunderstood?

Critical Thinking Questions

1. What contributes to the changing image of diversity in the United States?
2. How do stereotypes affect both the people who are stereotyped as well as those who express those stereotypes?
3. Consider conversations you have with people very different than yourself. Why do you feel those people are different? To what degree do you talk to them or past them? To what degree do they talk to you or past you?
4. How have places where you have worked, even part time, been different from those of your parents or grandparents in terms of diversity of the workforce? What explains these changes?

Glossary

Parenthetical numbers refer to the pages on which the term is introduced.

absolute deprivation The minimum level of subsistence below which families or individuals should not be expected to exist. (70)

acting White Taking school seriously and accepting the authority of teachers and administrators. (174)

affirmative action Positive efforts to recruit subordinate group members, including women, for jobs, promotions, and educational opportunities. (85)

Afrocentric perspective An emphasis on the customs of African cultures and how they have pervaded the history, culture, and behavior of Blacks in the United States and around the world. (32)

amalgamation The process by which a dominant group and a subordinate group combine through intermarriage to form a new group. (28)

annexation The incorporation or attachment of land by a nation. (22)

anti-Semitism Anti-Jewish prejudice or discrimination. (45)

apartheid The policy of the South African government intended to maintain separation of Blacks, Coloureds, and Asians from the dominant Whites. (25)

assimilation The process by which a subordinate individual or group takes on the characteristics of the dominant group. (29)

asylees Foreigners who have already entered the United States and now seek protection because of persecution or a well-founded fear of persecution. (121)

authoritarian personality A psychological construct of a personality type likely to be prejudiced and to use others as scapegoats. (46)

bamboo ceiling The barrier that talented Asian Americans face because of resentment and intolerance directed toward them. (173)

bilingual education A program designed to allow students to learn academic concepts in their native language while they learn a second language. (112)

bilingualism The use of two or more languages in places of work or education and the treatment of each language as legitimate. (112)

biological race The mistaken notion of a genetically isolated human group. (10)

blaming the victim Portraying the problems of racial and ethnic minorities as their fault rather than recognizing society's responsibilities. (19)

blended identity Self-image and worldview that is a combination of religious faith, cultural background based on nationality, and current residency. (132)

Bogardus scale Technique to measure social distance toward different racial and ethnic groups. (59)

brain drain Immigration to the United States of skilled workers, professionals, and technicians who are desperately needed in their home countries. (107)

chain immigration Immigrants sponsor several other immigrants who, on their arrival, may sponsor still more. (98)

civil religion The religious dimension in American life that merges the state with sacred beliefs. (153)

class As defined by Max Weber, people who share similar levels of wealth. (16)

colonialism A foreign power's maintenance of political, social, economic, and cultural dominance over people for an extended period. (22)

color-blind racism Use of race-neutral principles to defend the racially unequal status quo. (50)

colorism The ranking or judging of individuals based on skin tone. (7)

conflict perspective A sociological approach that assumes that the social structure is best understood in terms of conflict or tension between competing groups. (18)

contact hypothesis An interactionist perspective stating that intergroup contact between people of equal status in noncompetitive circumstances will reduce prejudice. (59)

creationists People who support a literal interpretation of the biblical book of Genesis on the origins of the universe and argue that evolution should not be presented as established scientific thought. (160)

cultural capital Noneconomic forces such as family background and past investments in education that are then reflected in knowledge about the arts and language. (175)

denomination A large, organized religion not officially linked with the state or government. (150)

discrimination The denial of opportunities and equal rights to individuals and groups because of prejudice or for other arbitrary reasons. (41, 69)

dysfunction An element of society that may disrupt a social system or decrease its stability. (18)

emigration Leaving a country to settle in another. (21)

environmental justice Efforts to ensure that hazardous substances are controlled so that all communities receive protection regardless of race or socioeconomic circumstances. (84)

environmental refugees People forced to leave their communities because of natural disasters or the effects of climate change and global warming. (123)

ethnic cleansing Forced deportation of people accompanied by systematic violence. (24)

ethnic group A group set apart from others because of its members' national origin or distinctive cultural patterns. (7)

ethnic paradox The maintenance of one's ethnic ties in a way that can assist with assimilation in larger society. (133)

ethnocentrism The tendency to assume that one's culture and way of life are superior to all others. (40)

ethnophaulisms Ethnic or racial slurs, including derisive nicknames. (41)

eugenics The belief that human genetic quality can be improved through selective breeding. (10)

Eurocentrism Emphasizing the customs and traditions of European culture. (33)

exploitation theory A Marxist theory that views racial subordination in the United States as a manifestation of the class system inherent in capitalism. (46)

familism Pride and closeness in the family that result in placing family obligation and loyalty before individual needs. (169)

functionalist perspective A sociological approach emphasizing how parts of a society are structured to maintain its stability. (17)

fusion A minority and a majority group combining to form a new group. (28)

genocide The deliberate, systematic killing of an entire people or nation. (23)

glass ceiling The barrier that blocks the promotion of a qualified worker because of gender or minority membership. (90)

glass escalator The male advantage experienced in occupations dominated by women. (92)

glass wall A barrier to moving laterally in a business to positions that are more likely to lead to upward mobility. (92)

globalization Worldwide integration of government policies, cultures, social movements, and financial markets through trade, movements of people, and the exchange of ideas. (22, 120)

hate crime Criminal offense committed because of the offender's bias against a race, religion, ethnic or national origin group, or sexual orientation group. (71)

Holocaust The state-sponsored systematic persecution and annihilation of European Jewry by Nazi Germany and its collaborators. (23)

homophobia The fear of and prejudice toward homosexuals. (48)

immigration Coming into a new country as a permanent resident. (21)

income Salaries, wages, and other money received. (76)

institutional discrimination A denial of opportunities and equal rights to individuals or groups resulting from the normal operations of a society. (74)

intelligence quotient (IQ) The ratio of a person's mental age (as computed by an IQ test) to his or her chronological age, multiplied by 100. (11)

intelligent design View that life is so complex that it must have been created by a higher intelligence. (160)

intersectionality The overlapping and interdependent system of advantage and disadvantage that positions people in society on the basis of race, class, gender, and other characteristics. (33)

Islamophobia A range of negative feelings toward Muslims and their religion that ranges from generalized intolerance to hatred. (49)

labeling theory A sociological approach introduced by Howard Becker that attempts to explain why certain people are viewed as deviants but others engaging in the same behavior are not. (19)

marginality The status of being between two cultures at the same time, such as the status of Jewish immigrants in the United States. (15)

melting pot Diverse racial or ethnic groups or both, forming a new cultural entity. (28)

microaggressions Commonplace verbal indignities experienced daily by members of a minority group. (41)

migration A general term that describes any transfer of population. (21)

minority group A subordinate group whose members have significantly less control or power over their own lives than do the members of a dominant or majority group. (5)

mixed status Families in which one or more members are citizens and one or more members are noncitizens. (109)

model minority A group that, despite past prejudice and discrimination, succeeds economically, socially, and educationally without resorting to political or violent confrontations with Whites. (167)

nativism Beliefs and policies favoring native-born citizens over immigrants. (101)

naturalization Conferring of citizenship on a person after birth. (117)

normative approach The view that prejudice is influenced by societal norms and situations that encourage or discourage the tolerance of minorities. (47)

occupational segregation The tendency for racial, ethnic, or gender groups to be employed in different occupations from each other. (47)

panethnicity The development of solidarity between ethnic subgroups as reflected in the terms *Hispanic* and *Asian American*. (15)

pluralism Mutual respect for one another's culture, a respect that allows minorities to express their own culture without suffering prejudice or discrimination. (30)

prejudice A negative attitude toward an entire category of people, such as a racial or ethnic minority. (41)

principle of third-generation interest Marcus Hansen's contention that ethnic interest and awareness increase in the third generation, among the grandchildren of immigrants. (133)

racial formation A sociohistorical process by which racial categories are created, inhibited, transformed, and destroyed. (13, 162)

racial group A group that is socially set apart because of obvious physical differences. (7)

racial profiling Any arbitrary police-initiated action based on race, ethnicity, or national origin rather than a person's behavior. (48)

racism A doctrine that one race is superior. (12)

redlining The pattern of discrimination against people trying to buy homes in minority and racially changing neighborhoods. (80)

refugees People living outside their country of citizenship for fear of political or religious persecution. (121)

relative deprivation The conscious experience of a negative discrepancy between legitimate expectations and present actualities. (70)

religion A unified system of sacred beliefs and practices that encompass elements beyond everyday life that inspire awe, respect, and even fear. (149)

remittances The monies that immigrants return to their countries of origin. (114)

resegregation The physical separation of racial and ethnic groups reappearing after a period of relative integration. (27)

respectable bigotry Attitudes linking a minority group with crime and characterizing its members as criminals. (144)

reverse discrimination Actions that cause better-qualified White men to be passed over for women and minority men. (89)

sanctuary cities Areas in which local law-enforcement officers do not actively hand over illegal immigrants to federal enforcement agents. (116)

scapegoating theory A person or group blamed irrationally for another person's or group's problems or difficulties. (45)

secessionist minority Groups that reject assimilation and promote coexistence and pluralism. (159)

segmented assimilation The outcome of immigrants and their descendants moving into different classes of the host society. (30)

segregation The physical separation of two groups, often imposed on a subordinate group by the dominant group. (25)

self-fulfilling prophecy The tendency to respond to and act on the basis of stereotypes, a predisposition that can lead one to validate false definitions. (20)

sexism The ideology that one sex is superior to the other. (48)

sharing economy Online economic transactions that place buyers and sellers in direct peer-to-peer contact with no change in the ownership of goods and services; purchases can range from car rides to short-term accommodations. (81)

sinophobes People with a fear of anything associated with China. (102)

social capital Collective benefits of durable social networks and their patterns of reciprocal trust. (176)

social distance Tendency to approach or withdraw from a racial group. (59)

sociology The systematic study of social behavior and human groups. (16)

stereotypes Unreliable, exaggerated generalizations about all members of a group that do not take individual differences into account. (19, 48)

stratification A structured ranking of entire groups of people that perpetuates unequal rewards and power in a society. (16)

symbolic ethnicity Herbert Gans's term that describes emphasis on ethnic food and ethnically associated political issues rather than deeper ties to one's heritage. (135)

tiger mother A demanding mother who pushes her children to high levels of achievement following practices common in China and other parts of Asia. (170)

transnationals Immigrants who sustain multiple social relationships that link their societies of origin and settlement. (120)

wealth An inclusive term encompassing all of a person's material assets, including land and other types of property. (76)

White privilege Rights or immunities granted as a particular benefit or favor for being White. (43, 130)

world systems theory A view of the global economic system as divided between nations that control wealth and those that provide natural resources and labor. (23)

xenophobia The fear or hatred of strangers or foreigners. (101)

yellow peril A term denoting a generalized prejudice toward Asian people and their customs. (172)

References

Cyan color type denotes reference citations new to this ninth edition.

Abbott, Andrew, and Ranier Egloff. 2008. The Polish Peasant in Oberlin and Chicago. The Intellectual Trajectory of W. I. Thomas. *American Sociologist*, 39: 217–258.

ABC Television. 2013. Arkansas Schools to Start Moment of Silence When Classes Begin. August 2. Accessible at www.4029tv.com.

Adorno, T. W., Else Frenkel-Brunswik, Daniel J. Levinson, and R. Nevitt Sanford. 1950. *The Authoritarian Personality*. New York: Wiley.

Allport, Gordon W. 1979. *The Nature of Prejudice*, 25th anniversary ed. Reading, MA: Addison-Wesley.

American Community Survey. 2016a. 2015 ACS 1-Year Estimates. Accessible at www.census.gov.

———. 2016b. 2015 American Community Survey 5-Year Estimates. Accessible at www.census.gov.

American Social and Economic Supplement. 2016. Current Population Survey (CPS) 2015 Annual Social and Economic (ASEC) Supplement. Accessible at www.census.gov.

Anderson, Elijah. 2011. *The Cosmopolitan Canopy: Race and Civility in Everyday Life*. New York: W. W. Norton and Company.

Angwin, Julia, and Terry Parris, Jr. 2016. Facebook Lets Advertisers Exclude Users by Race. *ProPublica* (October 28). Accessible at www.propublica.org.

Anti-Defamation League. 2016. *Audit of Anti-Semitic Incidents, 2015*. Accessible at www.adl.org.

Applebome, Peter. 1996. 70 Years After Scopes Trial, Creation Debate Lives. *New York Times* (March 10): 1, 22.

Aptekar, Sofya. 2016. Celebrating New Citizens, Defining the Nation. *Contexts*, 15 (Spring): 47–51.

Apuzzo, Matt, and Joseph Goldstein. 2014. New York Drops Unit That Spied Among Muslims. *New York Times* (April 16): A1, A3.

Archibold, Randal C. 2007. A City's Violence Feeds on Black-Hispanic Rivalry. *New York Times* (January 17): A1, A15.

Asante, Molefi Kete. 2007. *An Afrocentric Manifesto: Toward an African Renaissance*. Cambridge, UK: Polity.

———. 2008. Afrocentricity. Pp. 41–42 in vol. 1, *Encyclopedia of Race, Ethnicity, and Society*, Richard T. Schaefer, ed. Thousand Oaks, CA: Sage.

———. 2015. Book Review of *The Afrocentric Praxis of Teaching for Freedom: Connecting Culture to Learning*. *Journal of Black Studies*, 47 (1): 88–89.

Asian-American Coalition for Education. 2017. Homepage. Accessible at www.asianamericanforeducation.org.

Aust, Scott. 2016. No. 1: Community Comes Together Following Foiled Attack Plot. *The Garden City Telegram* (December 30). Accessible at www.gctelegram.com.

Awad, Nihad. 2015. May America Be True to Her Dream. July 4. Accessible at www.cair.com.

Bachelder, Kate. 2015. Harvard's Chinese Exclusion Act. *Wall Street Journal* (June 6): A9.

Badgett, M. V. Lee, and Heidi I. Hartmann. 1995. The Effectiveness of Equal Employment Opportunity Policies. Pp. 55–83 in *Economic Perspectives in Affirmative Action*, Margaret C. Simms, ed. Washington, DC: Joint Center for Political and Economic Studies.

Baker, Bryan C. 2009. *Trends in Naturalization Rates: 2008 Update*. Washington, DC: Department of Homeland Security.

Baltzell, E. Digby. 1964. *The Protestant Establishment: Aristocracy and Caste in America*. New York: Vintage Books.

Bamshad, Michael J., and Steve E. Olson. 2003. Does Race Exist? *Scientific American* (December): 78–85.

Banton, Michael. 2008. The Sociology of Ethnic Relations. *Ethnic and Racial Studies* (May): 1–19.

———. 2012. The Colour Line and the Colour Scale in the Twentieth century. *Ethnic and Racial Studies*, 35 (July): 1109–1131.

Barrett, James. 2016. "Yes, Obama's Really a Muslim," Claim Muslims…? *Daily Wire* (January 21). Accessible at www.dailywire.com.

Bash, Harry M. 2001. *If I'm So White, Why Ain't I Right? Some Methodological Misgivings on Taking Identity Ascriptions at Face Value*. Paper presented at the annual meeting of the Midwest Sociological Society, St. Louis.

Bauder, Harald. 2003. Brain Abuse, or the Devaluation of Immigrant Labour in Canada. *Antipode* 35 (September): 699–717.

Bean, Frank D., and G. Stevens. 2003. *America's Newcomers and the Dynamics of Diversity*. New York: Russell Sage Foundation.

Bell, Derrick. 1994. The Freedom of Employment Act. *The Nation* (May 23), 258: 708, 710–714.

Bell, Wendell. 1991. Colonialism and Internal Colonialism. Pp. 52–53 in *The Encyclopedic Dictionary of Sociology*, 4th ed., Richard Lachmann, ed. Guilford, CT: Dushkin Publishing Group.

Bellafante, Ginia. 2005. Young South Asians in America Embrace "Assisted" Marriages. *New York Times* (August 23): A1, A15.

Bellah, Robert. 1967. Civil Religion in America. *Daedalus* 96 (Winter): 1–21.

Bernard, Tara Siegel. 2015. How to Help in a Global Refugee Crisis. *New York Times* (December 25). Accessible at www.nytimes.com.

———. 2017. How You Can Help Refugees Around the World. *New York Times* (February 17). Accessible at www.nytimes.com.

Bernstein, Mary, and Verta Taylor, eds. 2013. *The Marrying Kind?* Minneapolis: University of Minnesota Press.

Biagas, Jr., David E., and Alison J. Bianchi. 2015. The Latin Americanization Thesis: An Exception States Approach. *Social Forces,* 94 (March): 1335–1358.

Bialik, Kristen. 2017. Key Facts About Race and Marriage, 50 Years After *Loving v. Virginia.* June 12. Accessible at www.pewresearch.org.

Bjerk, David. 2008. Glass Ceilings or Sticky Floors? Statistical Discrimination in a Dynamic Model of Hiring and Promotion. *The Economic Journal,* 118 (530): 961–982.

Blanchard, Fletcher A., Lilly, Teri, and Vaughn, Leigh Ann. 1991. Reducing the Expression of Racial Prejudice. *Psychological Science* (March 2): 101–105.

Blas, Lorena. 2016. Niche Cable Networks Target Diverse Audiences. *USA Today* (November 2): 3D.

Blauner, Robert. 1969. Internal Colonialism and Ghetto Revolt. *Social Problems* 16 (Spring): 393–408.

Blauner, Robert. 1972. *Racial Oppression in America.* New York: Harper & Row.

Blazak, Randy. 2011. Isn't Every Crime a Hate Crime? The Case for Hate Crime Laws. *Sociology Compass,* 5 (4): 244–255.

Bloom, Leonard. 1971. *The Social Psychology of Race Relations.* Cambridge, MA: Schenkman Publishing.

Bobo, Lawrence. 2013. The Antinomes of Racial Change. *DuBois Review,* 10 (1): 1–5.

Bogardus, Emory. 1968. Comparing Racial Distance in Ethiopia, South Africa, and the United States. *Sociology and Social Research,* 52 (January): 149–156.

Bohmer, Susanne, and Kayleen V. Oka. 2007. Teaching Affirmative Action: An Opportunity to Apply, Segregate, and Reinforce Sociological Concepts. *Teaching Sociology* (October), 35: 334–349.

Bonilla-Silva, Eduardo. 1996. Rethinking Racism: Toward a Structural Interpretation. *American Sociological Review* (June), 62: 465–480.

———. 2002. The Linguistics of Color Blind Racism: How to Talk Nasty About Blacks Without Sounding Racist. *Critical Sociology,* 28 (1–2): 41–64.

———. 2006. *Racism Without Racists.* 2nd ed. Lanham, MD: Rowman & Littlefield.

———. 2012. The Invisible Weight of Whiteness: The Racial Grammar of Everyday Life in Contemporary America. *Ethnic and Racial Studies* (February), 35: 173–194.

Bonilla-Silva, Eduardo, and Gianpaolo Baiocchi. 2001. Anything but Racism: How Sociologists Limit the Significance of Racism. *Race and Society* 4: 117–131.

Bonilla-Silva, Eduardo, and David Dietrich. 2011. The Sweet Enchantment of Color-Blind Racism in Obamerica. *The ANNALS of the American Academy of Political and Social Science* (March), 634: 190–206.

Bonilla-Silva, Eduardo, and David G. Embrick. 2007. "Every Place Has a Ghetto..." The Significance of Whites' Social and Residential Segregation. *Symbolic Interaction,* 30 (3): 323–345.

Bonilla-Silva, Eduardo, and David G. Embrick, with Louise Seamster. 2011. The Sweet Enchantment of Color Blindness in Black Face: Explaining the "Miracle," Debating the Politics, and Suggesting a Way for Hope to Be "For Real" in America. *Political Power and Social Theory* (22): 139–175.

Bork, Robert H. 1995. What to Do About the First Amendment. *Commentary* (February), 99: 23–29.

Bourdieu, Pierre. 1983. The Forms of Capital. Pp. 241–258 in *Handbook of Theory and Research for the Sociology of Education,* J. G. Richardson, ed. Westport, CT: Greenwood.

Bourdieu, Pierre, and Jean-Claude Passeron. 1990. *Reproduction in Education, Society, and Culture,* 2nd ed. London: Sage. Orignally published as *La reproduction.*

Bowman, Tom. 1998. Evangelicals Allege Bias in U.S. Navy, Marine Chaplain Corps. *Baltimore Sun,* 23 (August): A12.

Bowser, Benjamin, and Raymond G. Hunt, eds. 1996. *Impacts of Racism on White Americans.* Beverly Hills, CA: Sage Publications.

Brennan Center. 2006. *Citizens Without Proof.* November. New York: Brennan Center for Justice at NYU School of Law.

Brennan, Christopher. 2017. Black 15-Year-Old Wins Essay Contest on White Privilege in Affluent Connecticut Town. *New York Daily News* (April 6). Accessible at www.nydailynews.com.

Brown, Hana, and Jennifer A. Jones. 2015. Rethinking Panethnicity and the Race-Immigration Divide: An Ethnoracialization Model of Group Formation. *Sociology of Race and Ethnicity,* 1 (1): 181–191.

Brown, Ryan Lenora. 2015. Nigeria's Export—Fervent Christianity. *Christian Science Monitor* (September 28): 21–23.

Brulliard, Karin. 2006. A Proper Goodbye: Funeral Homes Learn Immigrants' Traditions. *Washington Post National Weekly Edition* (May 7): 31.

Bruinius, Harry. 2017. What's the Same, What's Different. *Christian Science Monitor Weekly* (February 27): 10–11.

Buchanan, Angela B., Nora G. Albert, and Daniel Beaulieu. 2010. *The Population with Haitian Ancestry in the United States: 2009.* ACSR/09-18. Accessible at www.census.gov.

Buck, Stuart. 2011. *Acting White: The Ironic Legacy of Desegregation.* New Haven: Yale University Press.

Budig, Michelle J. 2002. Male Advantage and the Gender Composition of Jobs: Who Rides the Glass Escalator? *Social Problems,* 49 (2): 258–277.

Bukowczyk, John J. 2007. *A History of Polish Americans.* New Brunswick, NJ: Transaction Books.

Bureau of the Census. 2007b. *The American Community—Pacific Islanders: 2004.* ACS-06. Washington, DC: U.S. Government Printing Office.

———. 2009a. *Asian and Hispanic Children More Likely to Dine with Their Parents.* March 4. Accessible at www.census.gov/Press-Release/www/releases/archives/children/013383.html.

———. 2009b. *Irish-American Heritage Month (March) and St. Patrick's Day (March 17th): 2009.* Washington, DC: U.S. Census Bureau.

———. 2010a. *Statistical Abstract of the United States, 2011.* Washington, DC: U.S. Government Printing Office.

———. 2011a. *Statistical Abstract of the United States: 2012.* Accessible at www.census.gov.

———. 2011b. *Irish-American Heritage Month (March) and St. Patrick's Day (March 17): 2011.* Census Brief CB11-FF, 03, January 13.

———. 2012d. *Most Children Younger Than Age 1 Are Minorities, Census Bureau Reports.* May 17. Accessible at www.census.gov/newsroom/releases/archives/population/cb12-90.html.

———. 2015a. Detailed Languages Spoken at Home and Ability to Speak English for the Population 5 Years and Over: 2009–2013. October 2015. Accessible at www.census.gov.

———. 2016i. CPS Income Tables. Accessible at www.census.gov.

———. 2017c. Educational Attainment in the United States: 2016. March 2017. Accessible at www.census.gov.

———. 2017e. Educational Attainment in the United States: 2016. March 2017. Accessible at www.census.gov.

Burgess, Melinda, Karen E. Dill, S. Paul Stermer, Stephen R. Burgess, and Brian P. Brown. 2011. Playing with Prejudice: The Prevalence and Consequences of Racial Stereotypes in Video Games. *Media Psychology,* 14: 289–311.

Calavita, Kitty. 2007. Immigration Law, Race, and Identity. *Annual Reviews of Law and Social Sciences,* 3: 1–20.

Callahan, Rebecca M., and Patricia C. Gándara (eds.). *The Bilingual Advantage: Language, Literacy, and the U.S. Labor Market.* September 17. Los Angeles: UCLA Civil Rights Project. Accessible at www.civilrightsproject.ucla.edu.

Camarota, Steven A. 2007a. *Immigrants in the United States, 2007: A Profile of America's Foreign-Born Population.* Washington, DC: Center for Immigrant Statistics.

Cameron, Darla. 2017. How Sanctuary Cities Work, and How Trump's Executive Order Might Affect Them. *Washington Post* (January 25). Accessible at www.washingtonpost.com.

Campbell, Alexia Fernández. 2016. The Truth About Undocumented Immigrants and Taxes. *The Atlantic* (September 12). Accessible at www.theatlantic.com.

Capps, Randy, Ku Leighton, and Michael Fix. 2002. *How Are Immigrants Faring After Welfare Reform? Preliminary Evidence from Los Angeles and New York City.* Washington, DC: Urban Institute.

Carroll, Joseph. 2006. Public National Anthem Should Be Sung in English. *The Gallup Poll* (May): 3.

Casey, Nicholas. 2015. Buyers' Rule in L.I. Town Is Relic of Nazi Past. *New York Times* (October 20): A1, A23.

Catalyst. 2001. *Women Satisfied with Current Job in Financial Industry but Barriers Still Exist.* Press release July 25, 2001. Accessible at www.catalystwomen.org.

Center for Constitutional Rights. 2011. *Stop-and-Frisks of New Yorkers in 2010 Hit All-Time High at 600, 601; 87 Percent of Those Stopped Black and Latino.* Accessible at ccrjustice.org.

Center for Work-Life Policy. 2011. *Asian-Americans Still Feel Like Outsiders in Corporate America, New Study from the Center for Work-Life Policy Finds.* July 20. New York: Center for Work-Life Policy.

Chakravorty, Sanjoy, Deuesh Kapur, and Niruikar Singh. 2017. *The Other One Percent: Indians in America.* New York: Oxford University Press.

Chazan, Guy, and Ainsley Thomson. 2011. Tough Irish Economy Turns Migration Influx to Exodus. *Wall Street Journal* (January 21): A8.

Cheah, Charissa S. L., Christy Y. L. Leung, and Nan Zhou. 2013. Understanding "Tiger Parenting" Through the Perceptions of Chinese Immigrant Mothers: Can Chinese and U.S. Parenting Coexist? *Asian American Journal of Psychology,* 4 (1): 30–40.

Chen, Carolyn. 2012. Asians: Too Smart for Their Own Good? *New York Times* (December 20): A35.

Chin, Margaret M. 2016. Asian Americans, Bamboo Ceilings, and Affirmative Action. *Contexts* (Winter): 70–73.

Chirot, Daniel, and Jennifer Edwards. 2003. Making Sense of the Senseless: Understanding Genocide. *Contexts,* 2 (Spring): 12–19.

Chou, Roslaind S., and Joe R. Feagin. 2008. *The Myth of the Model Minority: Asian Americans Facing Racism.* Boulder: Paradigm Publishers.

Chua, Amy. 2011. *Battle Hymn of the Tiger Mother.* New York: Penguin Press.

———. 2016. The "Tiger Mother" Has a Contract for Her Cubs. *Wall Street Journal* (June 11): C3.

Citrin, Jack, Amy Lerman, Michael Murakami, and Kathryn Pearson. 2007. Testing Huntington: Is Hispanic Immigration a Threat to American Identity? *Perspectives on Politics* (March), 5: 31–48.

Clemmitt, Marcia. 2005. Intelligent Design. *CQ Researcher* (July 29), 95: 637–660.

Cognard-Black, Andrew J. 2004. Will They Stay, or Will They Go? Sex—Atypical Among Token Men Who Teach. *Sociological Quarterly,* 45 (1): 113–139.

Cohen, Adam. 2016. *Imbeciles: The Supreme Court, American Eugenics, and the Sterilization of Carrie Buck.* New York: Penguin Press.

Coker, Tumaini, et al. 2009. Perceived Racial/Ethnic Discrimination Among Fifth-Grade Students and Its Association with Mental Health. *American Journal of Public Health,* 99 (5): 878–884.

Colby, Sandra L., and Jennifer M. Ortman. 2015. Projections of the Size and Composition of the U.S. Population: 2014 to 2060. March. *Current Population Reports P25-1143.* Washington, DC: U.S. Government Printing Office.

Coleman, James S. 1988. Social Capital in the Creation of Human Capital. *American Journal of Sociology* 94 (Suppl.): S95–S120.

Collier, Paul. 2013. How Migration Hurts Poor Countries. *New York Times* (December 1), sect. SR, p. 3.

Collins, Patricia Hill. 2000. *Black Feminist Thought: Knowledge, Consciousness, and the Politics of Empowerment*, 2nd ed. New York: Routledge.

Collins, Patricia Hill, and Sirma Bilge. 2016. *Intersectionality*. Cambridge, MA: Polity Press.

Commission on Civil Rights. 1976. *Fulfilling the Letter and Spirit of the Law: Desegregation of the Nation's Public Schools*. Washington, DC: U.S. Government Printing Office.

———. 1981. *Affirmative Action in the 1980s: Dismantling the Process of Discrimination*. Washington, DC: U.S. Government Printing Office.

Committee of 100. 2001. *American Attitudes Towards Chinese Americans and Asian Immigrants*. New York: Committee of 100.

Connor, Phillip. 2016. Migrant Remittances Worldwide Drop in 2015 for First Time Since Great Recession. August 31. Accessible at www.pewresearch.org.

Conyers, James L., Jr. 2004. The Evolution of Africology: An Afrocentric Appraisal. *Journal of Black Studies* (May), 34: 640–652.

Cooperman, Alan. 2005. One Way to Pray? *Washington Post National Weekly Edition* (September 5), 22: 10–11.

Cornacchia, Eugene J., and Dale C. Nelson. 1992. Historical Differences in the Political Experiences of American Blacks and White Ethnics: Revisiting an Unresolved Controversy. *Ethnic and Racial Studies* (January 15): 102–124.

Cose, Ellis. 1993. *The Rage of a Privileged Class*. New York: HarperCollins.

———. 2008. So What If He Were Muslim? *Newsweek* (September 1): 37.

Covay, Elizabeth. 2013. Book Review Essay. *Social Forces*, 92 (September): 407–411.

Cox, Oliver C. 1942. The Modern Caste School of Social Relations. *Social Forces* (December), 21: 218–226.

Cranford, Cynthia J. 2005. Networks of Exploitation: Immigrant Labor and the Restructuring of the Los Angeles Janitorial Industry. *Social Problems* 52 (3): 379–397.

Crenshaw, Kimberlé. 1989. *Demarginalizing the Intersection of Race and Sex: A Black Feminist Critique of Antidiscrimination Doctrine, Feminist Theory, and Antiracist Politics*. Chicago, IL: University of Chicago Legal Foundation.

———. 2015. Why Intersectionality Can't Wait. *The Washington Post* (December 24). Accessible at www.washingtonpost.com.

DaCosta, Kimberly McClain. 2007. *Making Multiracials: State, Family, and Market in the Redrawing of the Color Line*. Stanford, CA: Stanford University Press.

Dade, Corey. 2012b. *The Fight Over Voter ID Laws Goes to the United Nations*. March 9. Accessible at www.npr.org.

Dally, Chad. 2011. Hmong Heritage Month Refocuses on Health. *Wausau Daily Herald* (April 3): A3.

Davis, James A., Tom W. Smith, and Peter V. Marsden. 2007. *General Social Surveys, 1972–2006: Cumulative Codebook*. Chicago: NORC.

Davis, Michelle R. 2008. Checking Sources: Evaluating Web Sites Requires Careful Eye. (Released by *Education Week*, March 6). Accessible at www.edweek.org.

DellaPergola, Sergio. 2007. World Jewish Population, 2007. Pp. 551–600 in *American Jewish Yearbook 2007*, David Singer and Lawrence Grossman, eds. New York: American Jewish Committee.

Department of Energy. 2000. *Final Report: Task Force Against Racial Profiling*. Washington, DC: U.S. Government Printing Office.

Department of Homeland Security. 2017. Welcome to the Civics Practice Test! Accessible at www.dhs.gov.

Department of Justice. 2001. *Report to the Congress of the United States: A Review of Restrictions on Persons of Italian Ancestry During World War II*. Accessible at www.house.gov/judiciary/Italians.pdf.

Department of State. 2013. *US State Department Services Dual Nationality*. Accessible at travel.state.gov/travel/cis_pa_tw/cis/cis_1753.html.

———. 2017. Summary of Refugee Admissions as of 31 January 2017. Accessible at www.ds.gov.

DeSante, Christopher D. 2013. Working Twice as Hard to Get Half as Far: Race, Work Ethic, and America's Deserving Poor. *American Journal of Political Science*, 57 (April): 342–356.

Desmond, Scott A., and Charise E. Kubrin. 2009. The Power of Place: Immigrant Communities and Adolescent Violence. *Sociological Quarterly*, 50: 581–607.

Diamond, Jared. 2003. Globalization, Then. *Los Angeles Times* (September 14): M1, M3.

Dickson, Lisa M. 2006. Book Review: Italians Then, Mexicans Now. *Industrial and Labor Relations Review*, 60 (2): 293–295.

DiMaggio, Paul. 2005. Cultural Capital. Pp. 167–170 in *Encyclopedia of Social Theory*, George Ritzer, ed. Thousand Oaks, CA: Sage Publications.

DiTomaso, Nancy, Corinne Post, and Rochelle Parks-Yancy. 2007. Workforce Diversity and Inequality: Power, Status, and Numbers. *Annual Review of Sociology*, 33: 473–501.

Dobbin, Frank, Alexandra Kalev, and Erin Kelly. 2007. Diversity Management in Corporate America. *Contexts*, 6 (4): 21–27.

Dobbin, Frank, Soohan Kim, and Alexandra Kalev. 2011. You Can't Always Get What You Need: Organizational Determinants of Diversity Programs. *American Sociological Review*, 76 (3): 386.

Dolan, Sean, and Sandra Stotsky. 1997. *The Polish Americans*. New York: Chelsea House.

Dolan, Timothy. 2013. Immigration and the Welcome Church. *Wall Street Journal* (October 18): A11.

Downey, Douglas B. 2008. Black/White Differences in School Performance: The Oppositional Culture Explanation. *Annual Review of Sociology*, 34: 107–126.

Du Bois, W. E. B. 1903. *The Souls of Black Folks: Essays and Sketches* (reprint). New York: Facade Publications, 1961.

———. 1969a. *An ABC of Color* [1900]. New York: International Publications.

Duggan, Maeve. 2017. 1 in 4 Black Americans Have Faced Online Harassment Because of Their Race or Ethnicity. July 25. Accessible at www.pewresearch.org.

Duggan, Maeve, and Aaron Smith. 2016. The Political Environment on Social Media. October 25. Accessible at www.pewresearchcenter.org.

Duke, Lynne. 1992. You See Color-Blindness, I See Discrimination. *Washington Post National Weekly Edition*, 9 (June 15): 33.

Duneier, Mitchell. 2013. Elijah Anderson on Race Relations and Public Space: Beyond the Primacy of the Street. *Contemporary Sociology* 42 (6): 809–814.

Durkheim, Émile. 2001. *The Elementary Forms of Religious Life* [1912]. New translation by Carol Cosman. New York: Oxford University Press.

Duszak, Thomas. 1997. Lattimer Massacre Centennial Commemoration. *Polish American Journal* (August). Accessible at www.polamjournal.com/Library/APHistory/Lattimer/lattimer.html.

Eckstrom, Kevin. 2001. New, Diverse Take Spot on Catholic Altars. *Chicago Tribune* (August 31): 8.

The Economist. 2014. Not Black and White. (March 22): 33.

———. 2015b. The Model Minority Is Losing Patience. (October 3): 23–25.

Edelman, Benjamin, Michael Luca, and Dan Svirsky. 2017. Racial Discrimination in the Sharing Economy: Evidence from a Field Experiment. *American Economic Journal: Applied Economics*. Forthcoming.

El-Haj, Nadia Abu. 2007. The Genetic Reinscription of Race. *Annual Review of Anthropology*, 16: 283–300.

Eligon, John. 2013. Down-Home American, Korean Style. *New York Times* (January 6): 17, 21.

Erdmans, Mary Patrice. 1998. *Opposite Poles: Immigrants and Ethnics in Polish Chicago, 1976–1990*. University Park: Pennsylvania State University.

———. 2006. New Chicago Polonia: Urban and Suburban. Pp. 115–127 in *The New Chicago*, John Koval et al., eds. Philadelphia: Temple University Press.

Espiritu, Yen Le. 1992. *Asian American Panethnicity: Bridging Institutions and Identities*. Philadelphia: Temple University Press.

Fallows, Marjorie R. 1979. *Irish Americans: Identity and Assimilation*. Englewood Cliffs, NJ: Prentice Hall.

Farkas, Steve. 2003. *What Immigrants Say About Life in the United States*. Washington, DC: Migration Policy Institute.

Feagin, Joe R., and José A. Cobas. 2008. Latinos/as and White Racial Frame: The Procrustean Bed of Assimilation. *Sociological Inquiry* (February), 78: 39–53.

Feagin, Joe R., and Karyn D. McKinney. 2003. *The Many Costs of Racism*. Lanham, MD: Rowan and Littlefield.

Feagin, Joe R., and Eileen O'Brien. 2003. *White Men on Race, Power, Privilege, and the Shaping of Cultural Consciousness*. Boston: Beacon Press.

Feagin, Joe R., Hernán Vera, and Pinar Batur. 2000. *White Racism*, 2nd ed. New York: Routledge.

Federal Bureau of Investigation. 2016a. *2015 Hate Crime Statistics*. Accessible at www.ucr.fbi.gov.

Feldman, Marcus W. 2010. The Biology of Race. Pp. 136–159 in *Doing Race*, Hazel Rose Markus and Paula M. L. Moya, eds. New York: W. W. Norton.

Ferber, Abby L. 2008. Privilege. Pp. 1073–1074 in vol. 3, *Encyclopedia of Race, Ethnicity, and Society*, Richard T. Schaefer, ed. Thousand Oaks, CA: Sage.

Fihel, Agnieszka, and Izabela Grabowski-Lusinska. 2014. Labour Market Behaviours of Back-and-Forth Migrants from Poland. *International Migration*, 52 (1): 22–35.

Fordham, Signithia, and John U. Ogbu. 1986. Black Students' School Success: Coping with the Burden of "Acting White." *Urban Review*, 18 (3): 176–206.

Fox, Stephen. 1990. *The Unknown Internment*. Boston: Twayne.

Frey, William H. 2016. Analysis of 2000 Census and 2011–2015 American Community Survey (Released December 8, 2016). Table 2: Segregation Measured by Dissimilarity Index: Metropolitan Areas over One Million Population, 2000 and 2011–2015. Accessible at https://www.brookings.edu/wp-content/.../2016/12/freywhiteneighborhoods_table2.xls.

Fryer, Roland G., Lisa Kahn, Steven D. Levitt, and Jörg L. Spenkuch. 2012. The Plight of Mixed Race Adolescents. *Review of Economics and Statistics* (August), 94: 6231–6234.

Gans, Herbert J. 1979. Symbolic Ethnicity: The Future of Ethnic Groups and Cultures in America. *Ethnic and Racial Studies* 2 (January): 1–20.

———. 2014. The Coming Darkness of Late-Generation European American Ethnicity. *Ethnic and Racial Studies*, 37 (5): 757–765.

Gates, Gary J. 2017. U.S. Satisfaction with Immigration Levels Reaches New High. January 18. Accessible at www.gallup.com.

Gelles, David. 2016. For Standing Up, Scorn. *New York Times* (November 1): B1–B2.

Gerth, H. H., and C. Wright Mills. 1958. *From Max Weber: Essays in Sociology*. New York: Galaxy Books.

Girardelli, Davide. 2004. Commodified Identities: The Myth of Italian Food in the United States. *Journal of Communication Inquiry* (October), 28: 307–324.

Giroux, Henry A. 1997. Rewriting the Discourse of Racial Identity: Towards a Pedagogy and Politics of Whiteness. *Harvard Educational Review* (Summer) 67: 285–320.

GLAAD. 2016. *Where We Are on TV: 16–17*. Accessible at www.glaad.org.

Gladstone, Benjamin. 2016. Anti-Semitism at My University. *New York Times* (October 2): SR2.

Glaser, Jack, and Kimberly Kahn. 2004. Prejudice, Discrimination, and the Internet. Draft Paper, July 1. Accessible at www.gspp.berkeley.edu.

Gleason, Philip. 1980. American Identity and Americanization. Pp. 31–58 in *Harvard Encyclopedia of American Ethnic Groups*, Stephen Therstromm, ed. Cambridge, MA: Belknap Press of Harvard University Press.

Glusac, Elaine. 2016. My House Is Your House. Or Is It? *New York Times* (June 26): sect. TR, 8.

Goering, John M. 1971. The Emergence of Ethnic Interests: A Case of Serendipity. *Social Forces* (March), 48: 379–384.

Gomez, Alan. 2014. Obama Could Reshape a Rural Landscape. *USA Today* (December 9): 1A, 5A.

Gonzales, Roberto G. 2011. Learning to Be Illegal: Undocumented Youth and Shifting Legal Contexts in the Transition to Adulthood. *American Sociological Review*, 76 (45): 602–619.

Gonzalez, David. 2009. A Family Divided by 2 Worlds, Legal and Illegal. *New York Times* (April 26): 1, 20–21.

Goodstein, Laurie. 2005. Issuing Rebuke: Judge Rejects Teaching of Intelligent Design. *New York Times* (December 21): A1, A21.

Goodstein, Laurie, and Jennifer Steinhauer. 2010. Pope Picks Latino to Lead Los Angeles Archdiocese. *New York Times* (April 7): A17.

Gordon, Milton M. 1964. *Assimilation in American Life: The Role of Race, Religion, and National Origins*. New York: Oxford University Press.

Gorski, Phillip S. 2010. *Civil Religion Today* (ARDA Guiding Paper Series). State College, PA: Association of Religion Data Archives at the Pennsylvania State University. Accessible at www.thearda.com/rrh/papers/guidingpapers.asp.

Gose, Ben. 2013. Diversity Offices Aren't What They Used to Be. *Chronicle of Higher Education* (June 14): A14–A15, A17.

Gray-Little, Bernadette, and Hafdahl, Adam R. 2000. Factors Influencing Racial Comparisons of Self-Esteem: A Qualitative Review. *Psychological Bulletin*, 126 (1): 26–54.

Greeley, Andrew M. 1981. *The Irish Americans: The Rise to Money and Power*. New York: Harper & Row.

Greenhouse, Linda. 1996. Court Accepts Case Tied to Separation Powers. *New York Times* (October 16). Accessible at www.nytimes.com/1996/10/16/us/court-accepts-case-tied-to-separation-of-powers.html?pagewanted=all&src=pm.

Greenhouse, Steven. 2012. Equal Opportunity Panel Updates Hiring Policy. *New York Times* (April 26): B3.

Guerrero, Diane. 2014. "Orange Is the New Black" Actress: My Parents Were Deported. *Los Angeles Times*. November 15. Accessible at www.latimes.com.

Guest, Kenneth J. 2003. *God in Chinatown: Religion and Survival in New York's Evolving Immigrant Community*. New York: University Press.

Guglielmo, Jennifer, and Salvatore Salerno, eds. 2003. *Are Italians White?* New York: Routledge.

Guillermo, Emil. 2015. Model Minority? In St. Paul, Asian-American Test Scores Lag. (May 5). Accessible at www.nbcnews.com.

Guo, Jeff. 2016. The Sharing Economy Has a Serious Racism Problem—But There May Be a Way to Fix It. Wonkblog. November 2. Accessible at www.washingtonpost.com.

Guynn, Jessica. 2016. Airbnb Seeks Help from Civil Rights Leaders. *USA Today* (June 23): 3B.

———. 2017. Jackson to Uber: Release Diversity Data. *USA Today* (January 6): 1B–2B.

Hakimzadeh, Shirin, and D'Vera Cohn. 2007. *English Usage Among Hispanics in the United States*. Washington, DC: Pew Hispanic Center.

Haller, William, Alejandro Portes, and Scott M. Lynch. 2011. Dreams Fulfilled, Dreams Shattered: Determinants of Segmented Assimilation in the Second Generation. *Social Forces*, 89 (3): 733–762.

Halpern, Sue, and Bill McKibben. 2014. Manchester's Melting Pot. *Smithsonian* (April): 25–30.

Halstead, Mark L. 2008. Islamophobia. Pp. 762–764 in vol. 2, *Encyclopedia of Race, Ethnicity, and Society*, Richard T. Schaefer, ed. Thousand Oaks, CA: Sage.

Handlin, Oscar. 1951. *The Uprooted: The Epic Story of the Great Migrations That Made the American People*. New York: Grossett and Dunlap.

Hansen, Marcus Lee. 1952. The Third Generation in America. *Commentary* (November 14): 493–500.

Harlow, Caroline Wolf. 2005. *Hate Crime Reported by Victims and Police*. Bureau of Justice Statistics Special Report (November). Accessible at www.ojp.usdoj.gov/bjs/pub/pdf/hcrvp.pdf.

Harzig, Christine. 2008. German Americans. Pp. 540–544 in vol. 1, *Encyclopedia of Race, Ethnicity, and Society*, Richard T. Schaefer, ed. Thousand Oaks, CA: Sage.

Hassrick, Elizabeth McGhee. 2007. *The Transnational Production of White Ethnic Symbolic Identities*. Paper presented at the Annual Meeting of the American Sociological Association.

Herbert, Bob. 2010. Jim Crow Policy. *New York Times* (February 2): A27.

Herrnstein, Richard J., and Charles Murray. 1994. *The Bell Curve: Intelligence and Class Structure in American Life*. New York: Free Press.

Hirsley, Michael. 1991. Religious Display Needs Firm Count. *Chicago Tribune* (December 20), section 2: 10.

Hisnanick, John J., and Katherine G. Giefer. 2011. *Dynamics of Economic Well-Being: Fluctuations in the U.S. Income Distribution 2004–2007*. Washington, DC: U.S. Government Printing Office.

Hispanic Association on Corporate Responsibility. 2013. *2013 HACR Corporate Governance Study*. Accessible at www.hacr.org.

Hoover, Eric. 2013. Colleges Contemplate a "Race Neutral" Future. *Chronicle of Higher Education* (October 18): 30, 32–33.

Hout, Michael. 2016. Saint Peter's Leaky Boat: Falling Intergenerational Persistence Among U.S.-Born Catholics Since 1974. *Sociology of Religion*, 77 (1): 1–17.

Hughley, Matthew W., and Jessie Daniels. 2013. Racist Comments at Online News Sites: A Methodological Dilemma for Discourse Analysis. *Media, Culture & Society*, 35 (3): 332–347.

Humes, Karen R., Nicholas A. Jones, and Roberto R. Ramirez. 2011. Overview of Race and Hispanic Organization. *2010 Census Briefs.* C2010 BR-02.

Hunter, Lori M., Jessie K. Luna, and Rachel M. Norton. 2015. Environmental Dimensions of Migration. *Annual Review of Sociology* 41: 377–397.

Huntington, Samuel P. 1993. The Clash of Civilizations? *Foreign Affairs,* 73 (3), (Summer): 22–49.

———. 1996. *The Clash of Civilizations and the Remaking of World Order.* New York: Simon & Schuster.

Hurh, Won Moo. 1994. Majority Americans' Perception of Koreans in the United States: Implications of Ethnic Images and Stereotypes. Pp. 3–21 in *Korean Americans: Conflict and Harmony,* H. Kwon, ed. Chicago: Center for Korean Studies.

Hussar, William J., and Tabitha M. Bailey. 2014. *Projection of Education Statistics to 2022,* 41st ed. February. Accessible at www.nces.gov.

Hyun, Jane. 2006. *Breaking the Bamboo Ceiling: Career Strategies for Asians.* New York: Harper Business.

———. 2009. Better Luck Tomorrow: Breaking the Bamboo Ceiling. Interview with Peter Nguyen. (October 14). Accessible at diversitymbamagazine.com.

IAAMS. 2009. *Italian-Americans Against Media Stereotypes.* Accessible at iaams.blogspot.com.

Ignatiev, Noel. 1994. Treason to Whiteness Is Loyalty to Humanity. Interview with Noel Ignatiev. *Utne Reader* (November–December): 83–86.

———. 1995. *How the Irish Became White.* New York: Routledge.

Institute for Jewish and Community Research. 2008. *How Many Jews Are in World Today.* Accessible at bechollashon.org/population/today.php.

Isaac, Mike, 2017. Uber Chief, Facing Worker Ire, Quits Team of Trump Advisers. *New York Times* (February 3): 1, 13.

Jaroszyn'ska-Kirchmann, A. 2004. *The Exile Mission: The Polish Political Diaspora and Polish Americans, 1939–1956.* Athens: Ohio University Press.

Jefferies, Sierra M. 2007. Environmental Justice and the Skull Valley Goshute Indians' Proposal to Store Nuclear Waste. *Journal of Land, Resources, and Environmental Law,* 27 (2): 409–429.

Jefferys, Kelly. 2006. *Refugees and Asylees: 2005.* June. Washington, DC: Department of Homeland Security. Accessible at www.dhs.gov.

Jiménez, Tomás R. 2007. The Next Americans. *Los Angeles Times* (May 27): M1, M7.

Johnson, David R., and Lauren K. Bachan. 2013. What Can We Learn from Studies Based on Small Sample Sizes? Comment on Regan, Lakhanpal, and Anguiano. *Psychological Reports: Relationships & Communications,* 113 (1): 221–224.

Johnston, Tim. 2008. Australia to Apologize to Aborigines for Past Mistreatment. *New York Times* (January 31).

Jones-Puthoff, Alexa. 2013. *Is the U.S. Population Getting Older and More Diverse?* (June 14). Accessible at www.census.gov/newsroom/cspan/pop_diverse/.

Jonsson, Patrik 2016a. Ellis Island of the South. *Christian Science Monitor* (January 18): 26–32.

Jung, Linda P., Desiree Baolin Qin, and Irene J. K. Park. 2013. Deconstructing the Myth of the "Tiger Mother": An Introduction to the Special Issue on Tiger Parenting, Asian-Heritage Families, and Child/Adolescent Well-Being. *Asian American Journal of Psychology,* 4 (1): 1–6.

Kahlenberg, Richard D. 2010. 10 Myths About Legacy Preference in College Admissions. *Chronicle of Higher Education* (October 1): A23–A25.

Kalev, Alexandria, Frank Dobbin, and Erin Kelly. 2006. Best Practices or Best Guesses? Diversity Management and the Remediation of Inequality. *American Sociological Review,* 71: 589–617.

Katz, Jeffrey. 2012. Google's Monopoly and Internet Freedom. *Wall Street Journal* (June 8): A15.

Katz, Michael B., Mark J. Stern, and Jamie J. Fader. 2007. The Mexican Immigration Debate. *Social Science History,* 3 (Summer): 157–189.

Kelly, Cara. 2016. *The Bachelor's Chance to Break the Diversity Stalemate. USA Today* (March 7).

Kenji America. 2013. *Cheerios Parody "Just Checking" Response to Haters.* Accessible at www.youtube.com/user/kenjiamerica.

Keveney, Bill. 2016. Opportunity Still Lags Behind the Scenes. *USA Today* (November 2): 2D.

Kim, Chang Hwan, and Arthur Sakamoto. 2010. Have Asian American Men Achieved Labor Market Parity with White Men? *American Sociological Review,* 73 (6): 934–957.

Kim, Su Yeong, Yijie Wang, Diana Orozco-Lapray, Yishan Shen, and Mohammed Murtuza, 2013. Does "Tiger Parenting" Exist? Parenting Profiles of Chinese Americans and Adolescent Development Outcomes. *Asian American Journal of Psychology,* 4 (1): 7–18.

King, J. E., and E. E. Swartz. 2015. *The Afrocentric Praxis of Teaching for Freedom: Connecting Culture to Learning.* New York: Routledge.

Kinloch, Graham C. 1974. *The Dynamics of Race Relations: A Sociological Analysis.* New York: McGraw-Hill.

Koch, Wendy. 2006. Push for "Official" English Heats Up. *USA Today* (October 9): 1A.

Kochhar, Rakesh. 2006. *Growth in the Foreign-Born Workforce and Employment of the Native Born.* Washington, DC: Pew Hispanic Center.

Kochhar, Rakesh, and Richard Fry. 2014. Wealth Inequality Has Widened Along Racial, Ethnic Lines Since End of Great Recession. December 12. Accessible at www.pewresearch.org/fact-tank/2014/12/12/racial-wealthgaps-great-recession/.

Kolowich, Steve. 2015. Diversity Training Is in Demand. Does It Work? *Chronicle of Higher Education* (November 27): A6.

Kopacz, Maria A., and Bessie Lee Lawton. 2013. Talking About the YouTube Indians: Images of Native Americans and Viewer Comments on a Viral Video Site. *Howard Journal of Communications,* 24: 17–37.

Krase, Jerome. 2006. Seeing Ethnic Succession in Little Italy: Change Despite Resistance. *Modern Italy,* 11 (February): 79–95.

Kroeger, Brooke. 2004. When a Dissertation Makes a Difference. *New York Times* (March 20). Accessible at www.racematters.org/devahpager.htm.

Krogstad, Jens Manuel. 2016. 5 Facts About Illegal Immigration in the U.S. September 3. Accessible at www.pewresearch.org.

Krysan, Maria, Reynolds Farley, and Mick P. Couper. 2008. In the Eye of the Beholder. *DuBois Review,* 5 (1): 5–26.

LaFraniere, Sharon, and Andrew W. Lehren. 2015. The Disproportionate Risk of Driving While Black. *New York Times* (October 25): A1, A22–23.

Lai, K. K. Rebecca, and Jasmine C. Lee. 2016. 10 Percent of Florida Adults Are Ineligible to Vote. Why? *New York Times* (October 7): A13.

Lal, Barbara Ballis. 1995. Symbolic Interaction Theories. *American Behavioral Scientist* (January), 38: 421–441.

Lazar, Louie. 2013. Delivering News from the Homeland. *Wall Street Journal* (September 6): A16, A17.

Leavitt, Paul. 2002. Bush Calls Agent Kicked Off Flight "Honorable Fellow." *USA Today* (January 8).

Lee, J. J., and Marion R. Casey. 2006. *Making the Irish American.* New York: New York University Press.

Lee, Jennifer, and Frank D. Bean. 2007. Redrawing the Color Line. *City and Community* (March), 6: 49–62.

Lee, Jennifer, and Min Zhou. 2014a. The Success Frame and Achievement Paradox: The Costs and Consequences for Asian Americans. *Racial and Social Problems,* 6: 38–55.

Lee, Wen Ho, with Helen Zia. 2006. *My Country Versus Me: The First-Hand Account by the Los Alamos Scientist Who Was Falsely Accused of Being a Spy.* New York: Hyperion.

Lee, Yueh-Ting, Sandy Vue, Richard Seklecki, and Yue Ma. 2007. How Did Asian Americans Respond to Negative Stereotypes and Hate Crimes? *American Behavioral Scientist* (October), 51: 271–293.

Leehotz, Robert. 1995. Is Concept of Race a Relic? *Los Angeles Times* (April 15): A1, A14.

Levin, Jack, and Jim Nolan. 2011. *The Violence of Hate: Confronting Racism, Anti-Semitism, and Other Forms of Bigotry,* 3rd ed. Upper Saddle River, NJ: Pearson.

Levitt, Peggy, and B. Nadya Jaworsky. 2007. Transnational Migration Studies: Past Developments and Future Trends. *Annual Review of Sociology,* 33: 129–156.

Lewin, Tamar. 2006. Campaign to End Race Preferences Splits Michigan. *New York Times* (October 31): A1, A19.

Lewis, Amanda E. 2004. "What Group?" Studying Whites and Whiteness in the Era of "Color-Blindness." *Sociological Theory* (December), 22: 623–646.

———. 2013. The "Nine Lives" of Oppositional Culture? *DuBois Review,* 10 (1): 279–289.

Lichtenberg, Judith. 1992. Racism in the Head, Racism in the World. *Report from the Institute for Philosophy and Public Policy* 12 (Spring–Summer): 3–5.

Lieber, Ron. 2017. Refugees Need Help Here. But How? *New York Times* (February 8): B1, B2.

Lindner, Eileen. 2012. *Yearbook of American and Canadian Churches 2011.* Nashville, TN: Abingdon Press.

Lindsey, Brink. 2013. Why People Keep Misunderstanding the "Connection" Between Race and IQ. *The Atlantic* (May 15). Accessible at www.theatlantic.com.

Lipka, Michael. 2016. Muslims and Islam: Key Findings in the U.S. and Around the World. July 25. Accessible at www.pewresearch.org.

Liptak, Adam. 2014. Supreme Court Rejects Contraceptives Mandate for Some Corporations. *New York Times* (June 30). Accessible at www.nytimes.com.

Llosa, Alvaro Vargas. 2013. *Global Crossings: Immigration, Civilization, and America.* Oakland, CA: The Independent Institute.

Lofquist, Daphne, Terry Lugaila, Martin O'Connell, and Sarah Feliz. 2012. *Households and Families: 2010.* C2012BR-14. Accessible at www.census.gov/newsroom/releases/archives/2012_census/cb12-68.html.

Logan, John R., and Brian J. Stults. 2011. *The Persistence of Segregation in the Metropolis: New Findings from the 2010 Census.* Providence RI: US 2010 Project.

Lopata, Helena Znaniecki. 1994. *Polish Americans,* 2nd ed. New Brunswick, NJ: Transaction Books.

Lopez, Julie Amparano. 1992. Women Face Glass Walls as Well as Ceilings. *Wall Street Journal* (March 3).

Lopez, Mark Hugo, and Ana Gonzalez-Barrera. 2013. If They Could, How Many Unauthorized Immigrants Would Become U.S. Citizens? (June 27). Accessible at www.pewresearch.org.

Lopez, Mark Hugo, Jeffrey Passel, and Molly Rohal. 2015. Modern Immigration Wave Brings 59 Million to U.S., Driving Population Growth and Change Through 2065. September 28. Accessible at www.pewresearch.org.

Luconi, Stefano. 2001. *From Peasant to White Ethnics: The Italian Experience in Philadelphia.* Albany: State University Press of New York.

Lytle, Ashley, and Sharon R. Levy. 2015. Reducing Heterosexuals' Prejudice Toward Gay Men and Lesbian Women via an Induced Cross-Orientation Friendship. *Psychology of Sexual Orientation and Gender Diversity,* 2 (4): 447–455.

Mack, Raymond W. 1996. Whose Affirmative Action? *Society* 33 (March–April): 41–43.

Maheshwari, Sapna, and Mike Isaac. 2016. Facebook Limits Ads Targeted by Race. *New York Times* (November 12): B1.

Mahler, Jonathan. 2016. Report Cites Rise in Anti-Semitic Posts on Twitter, Many by Trump Backers. *New York Times* (October 16): A14.

Malhotra, Nei, and Yotam Margalit. 2009. State of the Nation: Anti-Semitism and the Economic Crisis. *Boston Review* (May/June). Accessible at bostonreview.net/BR34.3/malhotra_margalit.php.

Maniam, Shiva. 2016. Sharp Differences Over Who Is Hurt, Helped by Their Race. July 18. Accessible at www.pewresearch.org.

Manning, Robert D. 1995. Multiculturalism in the United States: Clashing Concepts, Changing Demographics, and Competing Cultures. *International Journal of Group Tensions* (Summer): 117–168.

Marist Poll. 2015. PBS NewsHour/Marist Poll. Summary of National Findings. September 2015. Accessible at www.pbs-newshour-marist-poll-sep2015.pdf.

Marshall, Patrick. 2001. Religion in Schools. *CQ Researcher* (July 12), 11: 1–24.

Martin, Daniel C., and James E. Yankay. 2013. *Refugees and Asylees: 2012*. Washington, DC: Office of Immigration Statistics.

Marx, Karl, and Frederick Engels. 1955. *Selected Works in Two Volumes*. Moscow: Foreign Languages Publishing House.

Massey, Douglas S. 2011. The Past and Future of American Civil Rights. *Daedalus*, 140 (Spring): 37–54.

———. 2012. Reflections on the Dimensions of Segregation. *Social Forces*, 91 (1): 39–43.

———. 2016. Residential Segregation Is the Linchpin of Racial Stratification. *City & Community*, 15 (March): 4–7.

Massey, Douglas S., and Nancy A. Denton. 1993. *American Apartheid: Segregation and the Making of the Underclass*. Cambridge, MA: Harvard University Press.

Massey, Douglas S., and Margarita Mooney. 2007. The Effects of America's Three Affirmative Action Programs on Academic Performance. *Social Problems*, 54 (1): 99–117.

Mastony, Colleen. 2013. Poland Calling Them Home. *Chicago Tribune* (January 13): 1, 12.

Matar, Shadi. 2015. Arab Portrayal in Film: A History of Stereotypes. March 20. Blog at Arab-American Anti-Discrimination Committee. Accessible at www.aaadc.org.

McCabe, Kristen. 2012. *Foreign-Born Health Care Workers in the United States*. (June). Accessible at www.migrationinformation.org/USfocus/display.cfm?id=898.

McCauley, Mary Beth. 2015. Why Religion Still Matters. *Christian Science Monitor* (October 12): 26–32.

McCormick, John. 2015. Bloomberg Politics Poll, December 9. Accessible at www.bloomberg.com.

McGurn, William. 2009. New Jersey's "Italian" Problem. *Wall Street Journal* (July 28): A15.

McIntosh, Peggy. 1988. *White Privilege: Unpacking the Invisible Knapsack*. Wellesley, MA: Wellesley College Center for Research on Women.

McKinney, Karyn D. 2003. I Feel "Whiteness" When I Hear People Blaming Whites: Whiteness as Cultural Victimization. *Race and Society*, 6: 39–55.

Meagher, Timothy J. 2005. *The Columbia Guide to Irish American History*. New York: Columbia University Press.

Melia, Michael. 2017. White Privilege Essay Contest Stirs Passions in Upscale Town. January 31. Associated Press. Accessible at www.staging.hosted.ap.org.

Merton, Robert K. 1949. Discrimination and the American Creed. Pp. 99–126 in *Discrimination and National Welfare*, Robert M. MacIver, ed. New York: Harper & Row.

Michigan Civil Rights Commission. 2017. *The Flint Water Crisis: Systemic Racism Through the Lens of Flint*. February 17. Lansing, MI: Michigan Department of Civil Rights.

Miller, David L. 2014. *Introduction to Collective Behavior and Collective Action*, 3rd. ed. Long Grove, IL: Waveland Press.

Mocha, Frank, ed. 1998. *American "Polonia" and Poland*. New York: Columbia University Press.

Monkman, Karen, Margaret Ronald, and Florence Délimon Théraméne. 2005. Social and Cultural Capital in an Urban Latino School Community. *Urban Education* 40 (January): 4–33.

Montagu, Ashley. 1972. *Statement on Race*. New York: Oxford University Press.

Mora, G. Cristina. 2014. Cross-Field Effects and Ethnic Classification: The Institutionalization of Hispanic Panethnicity, 1965 to 1990. *American Sociological Review*, 79 (2): 183–210.

Morris, Edward W. 2005. From "Middle Class" to "Trailer Trash": Teachers' Perceptions of White Students in a Predominantly Minority School. *Sociology of Education*, 78 (April): 99–121.

Mossaad, Nadwa. 2016. *Refugees and Asylees: 2015*. November. Washington, DC: Department of Homeland Security. Accessible at www.dhs.gov.

Moulder, Frances V. 1996. Teaching About Race and Ethnicity: A Message of Despair or a Message of Hope? Paper presented at annual meeting of the American Sociological Association, New York.

Mueller, Jennifer C. 2017. Producing Colorblindness: Everyday Mechanisms of White Ignorance. *Social Problems*, 64: 219–236.

Mujcic, Redzo, and Paul Frijters. 2013. Still Not Allowed on the Bus: It Matters If You're Black or White! March. Working paper (The Institute for the Study of Labor in Bonn, Germany). Accessible at ftp.iza.org.

Myers, Dowell, John Pitkin, and Julie Park. 2004. *California's Immigrants Turn the Corner*. Urban Initiative Policy.

Nahm, H. Y. 2012. *23 Big Milestones in Asian American History*. Accessible at goldsea.com/AAD/Milestones/milestones.html.

Naimark, Norman M. 2004. Ethnic Cleaning, History of. Pp. 4799–4802 in *International Encyclopedia of Social and Behavioral Sciences*, N. J. Smelser and P. B. Baltes, eds. New York: Elsevier.

Nash, Manning. 1962. Race and the Ideology of Race. *Current Anthropology* (June), 3: 285–288.

National Asian Pacific American Legal Consortium. 2002. *Backlash: When America Turned on Its Own*. Washington, DC: NAPALC.

National CAPACD. 2012. *Data Points: Asian American and Pacific Islander Poverty*. (May 1, 2012). Accessible at www.nationalcapacd.org/.

National Center for Education Statistics. 2013. *Digest of Education Statistics*. Accessible at nces.ed.gov/programs/digest/2012menu_tables.asp.

National Center for Health Statistics. 2017. *Health, United States, 2016. With Chartbook in Long-Term Trends in Health*. March 2017. Accessible at www.cdc.gov.

National Conference of State Legislatures. 2017. Voter Identification Requirements/Voter ID Laws. June 5. Accessible at www.ncsl.org.

National Italian American Foundation. 2006. Stop Ethnic Bashing. *New York Times* (January). Accessible at www.niaf.org/news/index.asp?id=422.

National Park Service. 2009. *Chinatown and Little Italy Historic District*. Accessible at www.nps.gov.

Navarro-Rivera, Juhem, Marry A. Kosmin, and Ariela Keysar. 2010. *U.S. Latino Religious Identification 1990–2008 Growth, Diversity & Transformation*. Hartford, CT: American Religious Identification Project, Trinity College. Accessible at www.americanreligionsurvey-aris.org/latinos2008.pdf.

Nawa, Fariba. 2011. Struggling to Stay Bilingual. *Christian Science Monitor* (October 17): 38–39.

Nelsen, Frank C. 1973. The German-American Immigrants Struggle. *International Review of History and Political Science*, 10 (2): 37–49.

New America Media. 2007. *Deep Divisions, Shared Destiny*. San Francisco: New America Media.

Newman, William M. 1973. *American Pluralism: A Study of Minority Groups and Social Theory*. New York: Harper & Row.

Newport, Frank. 2016. Most Americans Still Believe in God. June 29. Accessible at www.gallup.com.

———. 2017. About Half of Americans Say Trump Moving Too Fast. February 2. Accessible on www.gallup.com.

New York Times. 1991. For Two, an Answer to Years of Doubt on Use of Peyote in Religious Rite (July 9): A14.

———. 2005. Warnings Raised About Exodus of Philippine Doctors and Nurses (November 27): 13.

Niebuhr, Gustav. 1998. Southern Baptists Declare Wife Should "Submit" to Her Husband. *New York Times*.

Norton, Michael I., and Samuel R. Sommers. 2011. Whites See Racism as a Zero-Sum Game That They Are Now Losing. *Perspectives on Psychological Science*, 6 (3): 215.

Norwood, Kimberly Jade. 2014. *Color Matters: Skin Tone Bias and the Myth of a Post-Racial America*. New York: Routledge.

Nudd, Tim. 2013. It's 2013, and People Are Still Getting Worked Up About Interracial Couples in Ads. *Adweek* (May 30). Accessible at www.adweek.com.

Obama, Barack. 2017. Remarks by the President in Final Press Conference. January 18. Accessible at www.whitehouse.gov/thepressoffice.

Office of Immigration Statistics. 2009. *Yearbook of Immigration Statistics: 2008*. Accessible at www.dhs.gov.

———. 2016. *Yearbook of Immigration Statistics 2015 and Data Tables*. Accessible at www.dhs.gov.

Ogbu, John U. 2004. Collective Identity and the Burden of "Acting White" in Black History, Community, and Education. *Urban Review* (March), 36: 1–35.

Ohnuma, Keiko. 1991. Study Finds Asians Unhappy at CSU. *AsianWeek* (August 8), 12: 5.

Omi, Michael, and Howard Winant. 2015. *Racial Formation in the United States*, 3rd ed. New York: Routledge.

O'Neill, Maggie. 2008. Authoritarian Personality. Pp. 119–121 in vol. 1, *Encyclopedia of Race, Ethnicity, and Society*, Richard T. Schaefer, ed. Thousand Oaks, CA: Sage.

Orfield, Gary, and Erica Frankenberg. 2014. *Brown at 60: Great Progress, a Long Retreat, and an Uncertain Future*. May 15. Accessible at www.civilrightsproject.ucla.edu.

Orsagh, Matt. 2016. The Current Status of Women on Boards in 2016: A Roundup. *Market Integrity Insights* (October 7). Accessible at blogs.cfainstitute.org.

Pager, Devah. 2003. The Mark of a Criminal. *American Journal of Sociology*, 108: 937–975.

Pager, Devah, and Bruce Western. 2012. Identifying Discrimination at Work: The Use of Field Experiments. *Journal of Social Issues*, 68 (2): 221–237.

Pager, Devah, Bruce Western, and Bart Bonikowski. 2009. Discrimination in a Low-Wage Labor Market: A Field Experiment. *American Sociological Review*, 74 (October): 777–799.

Pais, Jeremy, Kyle Crowder, and Liam Downey. 2014. Unequal Trajectories: Racial and Class Differences in Residential Exposure to Industrial Hazard. *Social Forces* (March): 1189–1215.

Pariser, Eli. 2011a. *The Filter Bubble: What the Internet Is Hiding from You*. New York: Penguin Press.

———. 2011b. In Our Own Little Internet Bubbles. *The Guardian Weekly* (June 24): 32–33.

Park, Robert E. 1928. Human Migration and the Marginal Man. *American Journal of Sociology* (May), 33: 881–893.

———. 1950. *Race and Culture: Essays in the Sociology of Contemporary Man*. New York: Free Press.

Park, Robert E., and Ernest W. Burgess. 1921. *Introduction to the Science of Sociology*. Chicago: University of Chicago Press.

Parks, Sarah J., and Hyung Choi Yoo. 2016. Does Endorsement of the Model Minority Myth Relate to Anti-Asian Sentiments Among White College Students? The Role of a Color-Blind Racial Attitude. *Asian American Journal of Psychology*, 7 (4): 287–294.

Parrillo, Vincent. 2008. Italian Americans. Pp. 766–771 in vol. 2, *Encyclopedia of Race, Ethnicity, and Society*, Richard T. Schaefer, ed. Thousand Oakes, CA: Sage.

Passel, Jeffrey S., and D'Vera Cohn. 2009. *A Portrait of Unauthorized Immigrants in the United States*. Washington, DC: Pew Hispanic Center.

Pattillo, Mary E. 2013. *Black Picket Fences: Privilege and Peril Among the Black Middle Class*. 2nd ed. Chicago: University of Chicago Press.

Paul, Annie Murphy. 2011. The Roar of the Tiger Mother. *Time* (January 31): 34–40.

Peri, Giovanni. 2014. Does Immigration Hurt the Poor? *Pathways* (Summer): 15–18.

Perlmann, Joel. 2005. *Italians Then, Mexicans Now: Immigrant Origins and Second-Generation Progress, 1890–2000*. New York: Russell Sage Foundation.

Perry, Barbara, ed. 2003. *Hate and Bias Crime: A Reader*. New York: Routledge.

Pew Forum on Religion and Public Life. 2008a. *U.S. Religious Landscape Survey.* Washington, DC: Pew Forum. Accessible at religions.pewforum.org/pdf/report2-religious-landscape-study-full.pdf.

———. 2008b. *U.S. Religious Landscape Survey: Religious Beliefs and Practices: Diverse and Politically Relevant.* Washington, DC: Pew Forum on Religion and Public Life.

———. 2011b. *Unauthorized Immigrants: Length of Residency, Patterns of Parenthood.* (December 1). Washington, DC: Pew Hispanic Center.

Pew Research Center. 2015. *Multiracial in America: Proud, Diverse, and Growing in Numbers.* June 11. Accessible at www.pewresearch.org.

———. 2015a. *U.S. Public Becoming Less Religious.* November 3. Accessible at www.pewresearch.org.

———. 2016. *On Views of Race and Inequality, Blacks and Whites Are Worlds Apart.* June 27. Accessible at www.pewresearchcenter.org.

Pew Research Center for the People and the Press. 2013. *Big Racial Divide over Zimmerman Verdict.* July 22. Accessible at www.people-press.org.

Pincus, Fred L. 2003. *Reverse Discrimination: Dismantling the Myth.* Boulder, CO: Lynne Rienner.

———. 2008. *Reverse Discrimination.* Pp. 1159–1161 in vol. 3, *Encyclopedia of Race, Ethnicity, and Society*, Richard T. Schaefer, ed. Thousand Oaks, CA: Sage.

Pitt, Nicola Ann. 2013. *The Cultural and Political Significance of Tiger Mothering.* Doctorate. Monash University.

Polzin, Theresita. 1973. *The Polish Americans: Whence and Whither.* Pulaski, WI: Franciscan Publishers.

Porter, Eduardo. 2015. For Immigrants, America Is Still More Welcoming Than Europe. *New York Times* (December 8). Accessible at www.nytimes.com.

Portes, Alejandro 1998. Social Capital: Its Origins and Applications in Modern Society. *Annual Review of Sociology* 24 (1): 1–24.

———. 2006. Paths of Assimilation in the Second Generation. *Sociological Forum* (September), 21: 499–503.

Portes, Alejandro, and Rubén G. Rumbaut. 2006. *Immigrant America*, 3rd ed. Berkeley: University of California Press.

Potok, Mark. 2016. The Year in Hate and Extremism. *Intelligence Report* (Spring): 35–42.

Powell-Hopson, Darlene, and Derek Hopson. 1988. Implications of Doll Color Preferences Among Black Preschool Children and White Preschool Children. *Journal of Black Psychology* (February): 14: 57–63.

Preston, Julia. 2007. Polls Surveys Ethnic Views Among Chief Minorities. *New York Times* (December 13).

Proctor, Bernadette D., Jessica L. Semega, and Melissa A. Kollar. 2016. *Income and Poverty in the United States: 2015. Current Population Reports* P60-256(RV). Accessible at www.census.gov.

Quillian, Lincoln. 2006. New Approaches to Understanding Racial Prejudice and Discrimination. Pp. 299–328 in *Annual Reviews of Sociology 2006*, Karen S. Cook, ed. Palo Alto, CA: Annual Reviews Inc.

Reardon, Sean F., Lindsay Fox, and Joseph Townsend. 2015. Neighborhood Income Composition by Household Race and Income, 1990–2009. *Annals of the American Academy of Political and Social Sciences*, 660 (1): 78–97.

Regan, Pamela C., Saloni Lakhanpal, and Carlos Anguiano. 2012. Relationship Outcomes in Indian-American Love-Based and Arranged Marriages. *Psychological Reports*, 110 (3): 915–924.

Reskin, Barbara F. 2012. The Race Discrimination System. *Annual Review of Sociology*: 38.

Rhee, Nissa. Segregation Nation. 2016. *Christian Science Monitor* (September 17): 25–32.

Rich, Motoko. 2013. Creationists on Texas Panel for Biology Textbooks. *New York Times* (September 29): 16, 20.

Richey, Warren. 2016. A Florist Caught Between Faith and Discrimination. *Christian Science Monitor* (August 15): 26–32.

Richmond, Anthony H. 2002. Globalization: Implications for Immigrants and Refugees. *Ethnic and Racial Studies* (September), 25: 707–727.

Roberts, Sam. 2011. Little Italy, Littler by the Year. *New York Times* (February 22): A19.

Robnett, Belinda, and Cynthia Feliciano. 2011. Patterns of Racial-Ethnic Exclusion by Internet Daters. *Social Forces*, 80 (No. 3, March): 807, 828.

Roediger, David R. 1994. *Towards the Abolition of Whiteness: Essays on Race, Politics, and Working Class History (Haymarket).* New York: Verso Books.

———. 2006. Whiteness and Its Complications. *Chronicle of Higher Education* (July 14), 52: B6–B8.

———. 2009. To Be Continued? The "Problem of the Color-Line" in the Twenty-First Century. Pp 281–286 in *Twenty-First Century Color Lines*, Andrew Grant-Thomas and Gary Orfield, eds. Philadelphia: Temple University Press.

Roof, Wade Clark. 2007. Introduction. *The Annals* (July), 612: 6–12.

Rose, Arnold. 1951. *The Roots of Prejudice.* Paris: UNESCO.

Roth, Wendy D., and Nadia Y. Kim. 2013. Relocating Prejudice: A Transnational Approach to Understanding Immigrants' Racial Attitudes. *International Migration Review* 47 (Summer): 330–373.

Rugh, Jacob S., Len Albright, and Douglas S. Massey. 2015. Race, Space, and Cumulative Disadvantage: A Case Study of the Subprime Lending Collapse. *Social Problems*, 62: 186–218.

Rugh, Jacob S., and Douglas S. Massey. 2014. Segregation in Post–Civil Rights America: Stalled Integration or End of the Segregated Century? *DuBois Review*, 11 (2): 205–232.

Russell, Jan Jarboe. 2015. *The Train to Crystal City.* New York: Scribner.

Russell, Stephen T., Lisa J. Crockett, and Ruth K. Chao. 2010. Asian American Parenting and Parent-Adolescent Relationships. *Journal of Youth and Adolescence*, 40: 245–247.

Ryan, Camile. 2013. Language Use in the United States: 2011. *American Community Survey Report* (August 2013). Accessible at www.census.gov.

Ryan, Patrick. 2016. Streaming, Cable Networks' Diversity Record Is … Diverse. *USA Today* (November 2): 3D.

Ryan, William. 1976. *Blaming the Victim,* rev. ed. New York: Random House.

Saad, Lydia. 2006. Anti-Muslim Sentiments Fairly Commonplace. *The Gallup Poll* (August 10).

Saperstein, Aliya, and Andrew M. Penner. 2012. Racial Fluidity and Inequality in the United States. *American Journal of Sociology*, 118 (3): 676–727.

Sassler, Sharon L. 2006. School Participation Among Immigrant Youths: The Case of Segmented Assimilation in the Early 20th Century. *Sociology of Education*, 79 (January): 1–24.

Saulny, Susan. 2011. Black? White? Asian? More Young Americans Choose All of the Above. *New York Times* (January 29): A1, A17–A18.

Schachter, Ariela. 2016. From "Different" to "Similar": An Experimental Approach to Understanding Assimilation. *American Sociological Review*, 81 (5): 981–1013.

Schaefer, Richard T. 1976. *The Extent and Content of Racial Prejudice in Great Britain.* San Francisco: R&E Research Associates.

———. 1986. Racial Prejudice in a Capitalist State: What Has Happened to the American Creed? *Phylon,* 47 (September): 192–198.

———. 1992. People of Color: The "Kaleidoscope" May Be a Better Way to Describe America Than "the Melting Pot." *Peoria Journal Star* (January 19): A7.

———. 1996. Education and Prejudice: Unraveling the Relationship. *Sociological Quarterly* (January), 37: 1–16.

———. 2008b. Nativism. Pp. 611–612 in vol. 1, *Encyclopedia of Social Problems,* Vincent N. Parrillo, ed. Thousand Oaks, CA: Sage.

Schaefer, Richard T., and William Zellner. 2015. *Extraordinary Groups,* 9th ed. Long Grove, IL: Waveland Press.

Scott, Mark, and Melissa Eddy. 2016. Hate Speech Laws Test Facebook. *New York Times* (November 29): B1, B3.

Scully, Marc. 2012. Whose Day Is It Anyway? St. Patrick's Day as a Contested Performance of National and Diasporic Irishness. *Studies in Ethnicity and Nationalism,* 12 (1): 118–135.

Semple, Kirk. 2016. U.S., Shifting Policy, Will Step Up Deportations of Haitians. *New York Times* (September 23): A4.

Shah, Priyank G. 2012. Asian Americans' Achievement Advantage: When and Why Does It Emerge? Dissertation. The Ohio State University.

Shanklin, Eugenia. 1994. *Anthropology and Race.* Belmont, CA: Wadsworth.

Sharkey, Patrick. 2014. Spatial Segmentation and the Black Middle Class. *American Journal of Sociology,* 119 (January): 903–954.

Shin, Hyon B., and Robert A. Kominski. 2010. Language Use in the United States 2007. *Census Brief ACS-12.* Washington, DC: U.S. Government Printing Office.

Sigelman, Lee, and Steven A. Tuch. 1997. Metastereotypes: Blacks' Perception of Whites' Stereotypes of Blacks. *Public Opinion Quarterly,* 61 (Spring): 87–101.

Simon Wiesenthal Center. 2008. *iReport: Online Terror + Hate: The First Decade.* Los Angeles: Simon Wiesenthal Center.

Simpson, Jacqueline C. 1995. Pluralism: The Evolution of a Nebulous Concept. *American Behavioral Scientist,* 38 (January): 459–477.

Skrentny, John D. 2008. Culture and Race/Ethnicity: Bolder, Deeper, and Broader. *Annals* 619 (September): 59–77.

Slavin, Robert E., and Alan Cheung. 2003. *Effective Reading Programs for English Language Learners.* Baltimore: Johns Hopkins University, Center for Research on the Education of Students Placed at Risk.

Smith, Bryan. 2015. Spike Lee Sounds Off on Chi-Raq, Gun Violence, and Rahm. *Chicago* (October 22).

Smith, Stacy L., Marc Choueiti, and Katherine Pieper. 2016. *Media, Diversity, and Social Change Intuitive.* Los Angeles: USC Annenberg School for Communication and Journalism.

Smith, Tom W. 2006. *Taking America's Pulse III. Intergroup Relations in Contemporary America.* Chicago: National Opinion Research Center, University of Chicago.

Snipp, C. Matthew. 1989. *American Indians: The First of This Land.* New York: Sage.

Society for Human Resource Management. 2010. *Workplace Diversity Practices: How Has Diversity and Inclusion Changed over Time?* Alexandria, VA: SHRM.

———. 2011. *SHRM Survey Findings: An Examination of Organizational Commitment to Diversity and Inclusion.* Alexandria, VA: SHRM.

Soltas, Evan, and Seth Stephens-Davidowitz. 2015. Are All Muslims Terrorists? *New York Times* (December 13), sect. WK, 1, 6.

Soltero, Sonia White. 2008. Bilingual Education. Pp. 142–146 in vol. 1, *Encyclopedia of Race, Ethnicity, and Society,* Richard T. Schaefer, ed. Thousand Oaks, CA: Sage.

Song, Tae-Hyon. 1991. Social Contact and Ethnic Distance Between Koreans and the U.S. Whites in the United States. M.A. thesis, Western Illinois University, Macomb.

Sorkin, Andrew Ross. 2017. Frantic Phoning Among CEOs: How to Address Trump Ban? *New York Times* (January 31): 1, 2.

Southern Poverty Law Center. 2010. *Ten Ways to Fight Hate: A Community Response Guide.* Montgomery, AL: SPLC.

———. 2015, 2017. *Speak Up: Responding to Everyday Bigotry.* January 25. Accessible at www.splcenter.org under Publications.

Stark, Rodney, and Charles Glock. 1968. *American Piety: The Nature of Religious Commitment.* Berkeley, CA: University of California Press.

Steinberg, Stephen. 2007. *Race Relations: A Critique.* Stanford, CA: Stanford University Press.

Steinhardt Social Research Institute. 2016. American Jewish Population Project. Accessible at ajpp.brandeis.edu/publications.php#section3.

Stone, Emily. 2006. Hearing the Call—In Polish. *Chicago Tribune* (October 13): 15.

Stonequist, Everett V. 1937. *The Marginal Man: A Study in Personality and Culture Conflict*. New York: Scribner's.

Sue, Derald Wing. 2010. *Microaggressions in Everyday Life: Race, Gender, and Sexual Orientation*. New York: John Wiley.

Swarns, Rachel L. 2015. Long Banned, Mortgage Bias Is Back as Issue. *New York Times* (October 21): A1, A3.

Takaki, Ronald. 1998. *Strangers from a Different Shore: A History of Asian Americans*. Updated and revised. Boston, MA: Little, Brown, Back Bay edition.

Taylor, Paul (ed.). 2013. *The Rise of Asian Americans*, updated edition. Accessible at www.pewresearch.com.

Taylor, Stuart, Jr. 1987. High Court Backs Basing Promotion on a Racial Quota. *New York Times* (February 26): 1, 14.

Teranishi, Robert T. 2010. *Asians in the Ivory Tower: Dilemmas of Racial Inequity in American Higher Education*. New York: Teachers College Press.

Thakore, Bhoomi C. 2014. Must-See TV: South Asian Characterizations in American Popular Media. *Sociology Compass*, 8 (2): 149–156.

Thomas, Oliver. 2007. So What Does the Constitution Say About Religion? *USA Today* (October 15): 15A.

Thomas, William Isaac. 1923. *The Unadjusted Girl*. Boston: Little, Brown.

Thomas, William Isaac, and Florian Znaniecki. 1996. *The Polish Peasant in Europe and America* (5 vols.), Eli Zaretsky, ed. Urbana: University of Illinois Press.

Thompson, Ginger, and Sarah Cohen. 2014. More Deportations Follow Minor Crimes, Data Shows. *New York Times* (April 7): A1, A12.

Tomaskovic-Devey, Donald, and Patricia Warren. 2009. Explaining and Eliminating Racial Profiling. *Contexts*, 8 (Spring): 34–39.

Tonelli, Bill. 2004. *Arrivederci, Little Italy*. (September 27). Accessible at nymag.com/nymetro/urban/features/9904/.

Toppo, Greg, and Paul Overberg. 2014. Second Immigration Wave Reshapes Nation. *USA Today* (October 22): 1A, 5A.

Torkelson, Jason and Douglas Hartmann. 2010. White Ethnicity in Twenty-First-Century America: Findings from a New National Survey. *Ethnic and Racial Studies*, 33 (8): 1310–1331.

Townsend, Sarah S. M., Hazel R. Markos, and Hilary Bergsieker. 2009. My Choice, Your Categories: The Denial of Multiracial Identities. *Journal of Social Issues*, 65 (1): 185–204.

Ture, Kwame, and Charles Hamilton. 1992. *Black Power: The Politics of Liberation*. New York: Vintage Books.

Two Bridges. 2017. Two Bridges Neighborhood Council. Accessible at www.twobridges.org.

Tyson, Karolyn. 2011. *Integration Interrupted: Tracking, Black Students, & Acting White After Brown*. New York: Oxford University Press.

United Nations High Commission on Refugees. 2015. Figures at a Glance. Accessible at www.unchr.org.

———. 2016. Indicators of host country capacity and contributions, mid-2015. Accessible at www.unchr.org.

U.S. English. 2017. Official English. Accessible at www.usenglish.org/official-english/.

Victor, Daniel. 2017. "White Privilege" Essay Contest for Students Stirs Up Connecticut Town. *New York Times* (February 4): A18.

Wagley, Charles, and Marvin Harris. 1958. *Minorities in the New World: Six Case Studies*. New York: Columbia University Press.

———. 2015. *The Cross-Border Connection: Immigrants and Their Homelands*. Cambridge, MA: Harvard University Press.

Wall Street Journal. 2011. Tiger Mom's Long-Distance Cub. (December 24).

Wallerstein, Immanuel. 1974. *The Modern World System*. New York: Academic Press.

Wark, Colin, and John F. Galliher. 2007. Emory Bogardus and the Origins of the Social Distance Scale. *American Sociologist*, 38: 383–395.

Warner, W. Lloyd, and Leo Srole. 1945. *The Social Systems of American Ethnic Groups*. New Haven, CT: Yale University.

Waters, Mary. 1990. *Ethnic Options. Choosing Identities in America*. Berkeley: University of California Press.

Waters, Mary C., Philip Kasinitz, and Asad L. Asad. 2014. Immigration and African Americans. *Annual Review of Sociology*, 40: 369–390.

Weber, Max. 1947. *The Theory of Social and Economic Organization* [1913–1922], trans. by Henderson and T. Parsons. New York: Free Press.

The Week. 2016. The Tiger Mom's Children. (February 19): 12.

Weinberg, Daniel H. 2004. Evidence from Census 2000 About Earnings by Detailed Occupation for Men and Women. *CENSR-15*. Washington, DC: U.S. Government Printing Office.

Welch, William M. 2011. More Hawaii Resident Identify as Mixed Race. *USA Today* (February 28).

Williams, Kim M. 2005. Multiculturalism and the Civil Rights Future. *Daedalus*, 134 (1): 53–60.

Willoughby, Brian. 2004. *10 Ways to Fight Hate on Campus*. Montgomery, AL: Southern Poverty Law Center.

Winant, Howard. 1994. *Racial Conditions: Politics, Theory, Comparisons*. Minneapolis: University of Minnesota Press.

———. 2004. *The New Politics of Race: Globalism, Difference, Justice*. Minneapolis: University of Minnesota Press.

Winerip, Michael. 2011. New Influx of Haitians, But Not Who Was Expected. *New York Times* (January 16): 15, 22.

Wines, Michael, and Stephanie Saul. 2015. Supremacists Extend Reach Through Web. *New York Times* (July 6): A1, A3.

Winseman, Albert L. 2004. *U.S. Churches Looking for a Few White Men*. Accessible at www.gallup.com.

Winter, S. Alan. 2008. *Symbolic Ethnicity*. Pp. 1288–1290 in vol. 3, *Encyclopedia of Race, Ethnicity, and Society*, Richard T. Schaefer, ed. Thousand Oaks, CA: Sage.

Witt, Bernard. 2007. What Is a Hate Crime? *Chicago Tribune* (June 10): 1, 18.

Woesthoff, Julia M. 2008. Muslims in Europe. Pp. 925–928 in vol. 2, *Encyclopedia of Race, Ethnicity, and Society*, Richard T. Schaefer, ed. Thousand Oaks, CA: Sage.

Working, Russell. 2007. Illegal Abroad, Hate Web Sites Thrive Here. *Chicago Tribune* (November 13): A1, A15.

World Bank Group. 2016. *Migration and Remittance Factbook 2016*. Third Edition. Washington, DC: World Bank Group.

Wu, Frank M. 2002. *Yellow: Race in America beyond Black and White*. New York: Basic Books.

Wyman, Mark. 1993. *Round-Trip to America. The Immigrants Return to Europe, 1830–1930*. Ithaca, NY: Cornell University Press.

Xu, Jun, and Jennifer C. Lee. 2013. The Marginalized "Model" Minority: An Empirical Examination of the Racial Triangulation of Asian Americans. *Social Forces*, 91 (4): 1363–1397.

Yancey, George. 2003. *Who Is White? Latinos, Asians, and the New Black–Nonblack Divide*. Boulder, CO: Lynne Rienner.

Yemma, John. 2013. Teaching the Freedom to Believe. 2013. *Christian Science Monitor* (June 17): 5.

Young, Jeffrey R. 2003. Researchers Charge Racial Bias on the SAT. *Chronicle of Higher Education* (October 10): A34–A35.

Yosso, Tara J. 2005. Whose Culture Has Capital? A Critical Race Theory Discussion of Community Cultural Wealth. *Race Ethnicity and Education* 8 (March): 69–91.

Zafar, Sadia, and Erin C. Ross. 2015. Interreligious Contact, Attitudes, and Stereotypes: A Study of Five Religious Groups in Canada. *Canadian Journal of Behavioral Sciences*, 47 (1): 36.

Zeng, Zhen, and Yu Xie. 2004. Asian-Americans' Earnings Disadvantage Reexamined: The Role of Place of Education. *American Journal of Sociology* (March), 109: 1075–1108.

Zimmerman, Seth. 2008. *Immigration and Economic Mobility*. Washington, DC: Economic Mobility Project.

Zittrain, Jonathan. 2008. *The Future of the Internet and How to Stop It. With a New Forward by Lawrence Lessig and New Preface by the Author*. New Haven: Yale University Press.

Zogby, James. 2010. *National Survey: American Teen-Agers and Stereotyping*. Submitted to the National Italian American Foundation by Zogby International. Acceessible at www.niaf.org/research/report_zogby-asp?print=1&.

Index

A

abolitionists, 140
abortion, 158
absolute deprivation, 70
Academy Awards, 58
acting White, 174–5
affirmative action, 85–90, 171
African Americans
  acting White/Black, 174–5
  calls for secession, 25
  Du Bois on double consciousness, 15–6
  economic impact of immigration on, 113
  hate crimes against, 72
  higher education, 168
  life expectancy, 168
  median income comparisons, 77–8, 168
  middle class, 176–8
  population demographics, 3–4
  poverty rates among, 168
  racial profiling of, 49–50
  religion, 152–3
  segregation index for metro U.S., 25–6
  state comparisons, 179
  views on state of race relations, 52–3, 55
  wealth gap (1977-2013), 82–3
African National Congress (ANC), 27
Afrocentric perspective, 32–3
Age Discrimination Act (1975), 31
Airbnb, 81
Alaskan Natives, population demographics, 3–4
Alba, Richard, 134
alcoholism, myth of ethnic relationship to, 141
Ali, Muhammad, Jr., 115
Alien Act (1798), 100
Alito, Samuel, 146
all-weather bigot (Merton), 41–3
all-weather liberal (Merton), 41–3
amalgamation, 28
American Apartheid (Massey and Denton), 25
American Colonization Society, 25
American Indians. *See* Native Americans
American Revolution (1765–1783), 139
Amish, 8, 159
amnesty. *See* naturalization
Ancient Order of Hibernians, 140
Anderson, Elijah, 20
annexation, 22
Anti-Defamation League (ADL), 72
anti-Semitism. *See also* Holocaust
  against Jewish Americans, 45, 181
  against Polish Americans, 148
  in U.S., 45
  use of social media and, 181
apartheid, in South Africa, 25, 27
apologies and reparations, 24, 103
Arab Americans. *See also* Muslim Americans
  blended identity, 107
  Islamophobia, 8, 49, 72–3
  population demographics, 4
Armenia, 25
arranged marriage, 119
Asante, Molefi Kete, 32–3
Asia, history of emigration to U.S. from, 104, 105
Asian Americans. *See* Asian Pacific Americans
Asian Indian Americans
  arranged marriage, 119
  population demographics, 4
Asian Pacific Americans (APAs). *See also specific groups*
  education, 168, 171
  family life, 168–9
  hate crimes against, 172
  median income comparisons, 77–8, 173
  model minority myth, 167–73
  population demographics, 3–4
  poverty rates among, 168, 173
  segregation index for metro U.S., 25–6
  state comparisons, 179
  views on state of race relations, 52–3, 55
assimilation
  among Latino/Hispanic Americans, 145
  defined, 29–30
  ethnic paradox and, 133, 136
  on intergroup spectrum, 23
  segmented assimilation, 30
  subordinate-group status and, 23, 29–30
asylees, 121–2
Australia
  apologies to Aboriginal population, 24
  foreign-born population of, 98
The Authoritarian Personality (Adorno), 46
authoritarian personality theory, 46, 47
aversive racism, 50–1
Awad, Nihad, 72–3

B

Badgett, M.V. Lee, 89
bamboo ceiling, 173
Battle Hymn of the Tiger Mother (Chua), 169, 170
Bean, Frank, 134
Becker, Howard, 19
Bell, Derrick, 93
The Bell Curve (Herrnstein and Murray), 11–2
Bellah, Robert, 153
Bhutan, forced encampment of Hindus in, 24
Bhutanese Americans, 2, 24
bias crimes. *See* hate crimes
bilingual education, 112
bilingualism, 112–3, 178
biological race, myth of, 10–2
biracial identity, 13–6
bisexuals. *See* LGBT community
Black Americans. *See* African Americans
Black Lives Matter (BLM), 32, 35, 49
Black Picket Fences (Pattillo), 176–7
blaming the victim, 19, 167
Blanchard, Fletcher, 178, 180
Blauner, Robert, 180
blended identity, 107

204

Bogardus, Emory, 59
Bogardus scale, 59
Bourdieu, Pierre, 175
brain drain, 106–8
Brazil, colorism in, 7
Brewer, Linda, 177
Brewster, David, 165
Brokaw, Tom, 170
Brown v. Board of Education (1954), 53, 79
Buddhists, 8, 150, 152
Burgess, Ernest, 59

C

California
  foreign-born population, 99
  population demographics, 6
Canada
  foreign-born population of, 98
  history of emigration to U.S. from, 99, 105
Capone, Al, 144
Carmichael, Stokely, 74
Castile, Philando, 2, 32
Catalyst, 92
Catholics. *See* Roman Catholics
Central Pacific Railroad, 101
chain immigration, 98
Chicanos. *See* Mexican Americans
Chinese Americans
  early immigration, 101–3, 116, 128
  family life, 168–9
  parenting techniques, 169, 170
  persistence of racism toward, 172
  population demographics, 4
  racial profiling of, 172
Chinese Exclusion Act (1882), 102–3, 116
Chiricahua Apache tribe, 65
Chobani, 2
Christianity, membership demographics, 151. *See also specific denominations*
Chua, Amy, 169, 170
Church of Jesus Christ of Latter-day Saints (Mormons), 8
Church of Scientology, 153
Church of the Transfiguration, New York City, 128
Cisneros v. Corpus Christi Independent School District (1970), 112
citizenship. *See* naturalization
civil religion, 153–4, 156
Civil Rights Act (1964), 79–81
civil rights movement, 27, 56–7
Clark, Kenneth, 53

Clark, Mamie, 53
class
  Protestant denominations and, 156–7
  stratification by, 16–7
Collins, Patricia Hill, 33
Colombian Americans, 4
colonialism, 22–3
color-blind racism, 50–1, 173, 181
colorism, 7
Confederacy insignia and monuments, 51, 73
conflict theory
  on brain drain, 108
  defined, 18–9
  on deprivation, 70
  on gang formation, 54
  on model-minority myth, 173
  on pollution and minority communities, 84
  on racial/ethnic hostility, 46
  on treatment of Chinese immigrants, 102
Confucius, 170
contact hypothesis, 59–60
corporate diversity training, 61–5
Cose, Ellis, 90
Council on American-Islamic Relations (CAIR), 73
Cox, Oliver, 46
creationists, 160
criminal justice system. *See also* law enforcement
  demands for reform of, 33
  penalties for hate crimes, 73
  surveys on expectations of fair treatment, 49
Cuban Americans, 4
Culian, Grigore, 161
cultural capital, 175–6

D

Darwin, Charles, 160
definition of the situation (Thomas), 20
Democratic Party, religious affiliations of members, 154
denomination, 151
Denton, Nancy, 25
deportation of immigrants, 110–1, 115, 122
disabilities, people with, hate crimes against, 71
discrimination, 68–77. *See also* hate crimes; prejudice; *specific groups*
  affirmative action and, 85–90

  as cause of dysfunctions, 18
  distinguished from prejudice, 41–3
  economic factors and, 76–9
  elimination of, 79–81
  environmental justice and, 83–5
  institutional, 73–6, 83–4, 86–7, 172, 176
  relative vs. absolute deprivation, 70
  reverse discrimination, 89–90
  sharing economy and, 81–2
  wealth inequality due to, 76–9, 82–3
  in workplace, 69, 90–2
District of Columbia, population demographics, 6
diversity, in U.S., 2–6, 58, 61–5. *See also* race and ethnicity, introduction; *specific groups*
DNA studies, 11
domestic terrorism, 72–3
dominant–subordinate relations. *See also* hate crimes; minority groups; subordinate-group status; White privilege
  comparison of views on, 52
  resistance and change, 31–3
Dominican Americans, 4
DREAM Act: Development, Relief, and Education for Alien Minors, proposed, 109
Dred Scott decision (1857), 79
Du Bois, W.E.B., 8, 9, 15–6, 34, 51–2
  The Souls of Black Folks, 93
dual citizenship, 118
dysfunctions, 18

E

education. *See also* higher education; public schools
  Asian Pacific Americans and, 168, 171
  bilingual programs, 112
  median income comparisons and, 78–9
  reduction of prejudice via, 57
Edwards v. Aguillard (1987) (Louisiana), 160
Ellis Island, New York, 104
Ellison, Jeremiah, 2
Ellison, Keith, 2
Ellison, Ralph, 35
emigration, defined, 21
employment and workplace issues
  contact hypothesis and, 59–60

employment and workplace issues (*Continued*)
  corporate diversity training, 61–5
  discrimination and, 69, 90–2
  for early immigrants, 145, 147
  economic impact of immigration on, 113–4
  foreign-born workers (2015), 64
  glass ceiling, 90–2
  humor in workplace, 63
  illegal immigrants, 116
  median income comparisons, 77–8
Engel v. Vitale (1962), 158
environmental justice, 83–5
environmental refugees, 123
Equal Employment Opportunity Commission (EEOC), 79–80
Equal Opportunity Commission, 74
equal-status contact, 59–60
Estonia, 25
ethnic cleansing, 24
ethnic groups. *See also* race and ethnicity, introduction; *specific groups*
  as minority groups, 7–8
  in U.S., 2–4
ethnic paradox, 133, 136
ethnic slurs, 41
ethnocentrism, 40
ethnophaulisms, 41
eugenics, 10–1
Eurocentrism, 33
Europe, history of emigration to U.S. from, 99–101, 105, 129–30
European Union (EU). *See also specific countries*
  freedom of movement policy, 25
  Poland as member, and U.S. returnees, 149
Evangelical Christians, 152
evolution, 160
exploitation theory, 46–7
expulsion
  on intergroup spectrum, 23
  of minority groups, 24–5
extermination, on intergroup spectrum, 23–4. *See also* genocide; Holocaust

F
Facebook
  data collection and searches, 61, 82
  discriminatory advertising and, 82
  Germany demands monitoring of hate speech on, 42

familism, 169
family life, intergroup comparisons, 168–9
felony records
  hiring practices and, 69, 74
  voting eligibility and, 74–5
Ferraro, Geraldine, 146
Filipino Americans, 4, 173
The Filter Bubble (Pariser), 61
First Amendment, 56, 157–60
Fisher v. University of Texas at Austin (2016), 87, 171
Fitzgerald, David, 135
Flint, Michigan and environmental justice, 83–4
Florida, foreign-born population, 99
foreign-born population
  country comparisons, 98
  state comparisons, 99–100, 179
  in U.S. workplace, 64, 107
France, expulsion of Roma (Gypsies), 25
functionalist perspective
  on civil religion, 154
  defined, 17–8
  on hiring of illegal immigrants, 116
funeral services, 31
fusion
  defined, 28–9
  on intergroup spectrum, 23

G
gangs, 54
Gans, Herbert, 135
Gates, Bill, 3
gays. *See* LGBT community
gender groups, as minority groups, 9–10. *See also* women in U.S., as oppressed majority
gender identity, 71
genocide, 23–4. *See also* Holocaust
German Americans, 136–9
German-American National Alliance, 138
Germany. *See also* Holocaust
  censorship of hate speech, 42
Giving Pledge, 3
glass ceiling, 90–2
Glass Ceiling Commission, 91–2
glass escalator, 92
glass walls, 92
globalization, 22, 120–1
Glock, Charles, 155
Goering, John, 133

Goodyear Tire Rubber, 80–1
Google, as cultural invisible bubble, 61
Gordon, Milton, 136
Great Recession (2008), 45, 80, 114, 115
Guatemalan Americans, 4
Guerrero, Diane, 110–1

H
Haiti, emigration to U.S. from, 122, 123
Hamilton, Charles, 74
Handlin, Oscar, 132
Hansen, Marcus, 133
Hart-Cellar Act. *See* Immigration and Nationality Act (1965)
Hartmann, Heidi, 89
Hate Crime Statistics Act (1990), 70–1
hate crimes, 144
  against Arab and Muslim Americans, 72–3
  against Asian Pacific Americans, 172
  defined, 71–2
  FBI report on distribution of, 71
  intergroup hostility and, 54
  penalties for, 32, 73
  against Roman Catholics, 140
hate groups. *See also* anti-Semitism
  rise of, 40
  use of social media by, 72, 181
Hawaiian Americans, 6
Heritage language programs, 133
Herrnstein, Richard J., 11
higher education
  affirmative action, 171
  African Americans and, 168
  among Latino/Hispanic Americans, 168
  for Native Americans, 65
Hindus, 24, 150
Hitler, Adolf, 45. *See also* Holocaust
Holocaust
  advocacy of eugenics during, 11
  emigration due to, 148
  extermination of Jews during, 23–4
homophobia, 48
homosexuals. *See* LGBT community
H-1B visa program, 107–8
Hoover, Herbert, 144
Hudson City Savings Bank, 80
Human Genome Project, 11

Huntington, Samuel P., 101
Hurricane Katrina, impact on Hispanics, 166

I

Ignatiev, Noel, 130
illegal immigration, 109, 115–7, 145
Immigrant Legal Resource Center, 109
immigration, 96–126. *See also* assimilation; *specific groups*
  anti-Chinese movement, 101–3
  based on region of last residence (1820-2015), 105
  benefits and concerns, 106
  brain drain and, 106–8
  chain immigration, 98
  defined, 21
  economic impact of, 113–4
  foreign-born population by state, 99–100
  global economy and, 120–1
  illegal, 109, 115–7, 145
  increase in restrictionist sentiment, 103–6
  language barriers, 109, 111–3, 145
  marginality and, 16
  mixed-status families, 109
  national origin system, 103–4, 116, 144
  naturalization process, 100, 102–3, 117–9
  policies under Trump administration, 49, 82, 108
  population growth due to, 108
  refugee policies, 121–4
  to U.S., history of, 98–103, 128, 134–5, 136–49
Immigration and Nationality Act (1965), 104–6, 116
Immigration Reform and Control Act (IRCA) (1986), 115–6
incarceration rates, 2. *See also* felony records
income
  defined, 76
  median income comparisons, 77–8, 168, 173
India, British partition of, 25
inequality. *See* wealth inequality
in-group, 6
institutional discrimination, 73–6, 83–4, 86–7, 172, 176
intelligence quotient (IQ), 11–2
intelligent design (ID), 160

intergroup communication
  face-to-face, 178, 180–1
  online communication, 181–2
intergroup contact, impact on prejudice, 59–61
intergroup hostility, 54–5
intergroup relations spectrum. *See* Spectrum of Intergroup Relations
intermarriage. *See* marriage patterns
Internet. *See also* social media
  dating sites, 60
  hate group Web sites, 72
  online/virtual prejudice, 42, 60–1, 72, 81–2
  sharing economy and discrimination, 81–2
internment
  of German Americans, in U.S., 137–8
  of Italian Americans, in U.S., 144
  of Japanese Americans, in U.S., 103, 138
intersectionality, 33–4
Ireland
  antislavery tradition, 140
  Great Famine (1845–1852), 135, 139
Irish Americans
  advocacy for compulsory inclusion of potato famine in schools, 135
  early immigration to U.S., 137, 139–42
Islam, history of in U.S., 150–1, 152. *See also* Muslim Americans
Islamic terrorists, 49, 50
Islamophobia, 8, 49, 72–3
Israel, secession and statehood, 25
Italian Americans, early immigration to U.S., 128, 137

J

Japanese Americans
  population demographics, 4
  wartime evacuation and internment of, 103, 138
Jehovah's Witnesses, 8, 151, 152
Jewish Americans
  anti-Semitism and, 45, 181
  coming-of-age ceremonies, 153
  early immigration to U.S. and, 148
  as ethnic group, 8–9
  population demographics, 4
  scapegoating of, 45
Jews, Nazi extermination of. *See* Holocaust
Jiménez, Tomás, 134–5
John Paul II, Pope, 148

Johnson, Lyndon B., 104
Judaism, among Jewish Americans, 151

K

kaleidoscope, use of term, 165–6. *See also* United States, as multiracial/ethnic kaleidoscope
Kallen, Horace, 138
Kennedy, John F., 85–6, 138
kinfolk, 120, 132, 147, 172, 176
King, Martin Luther, Jr., 73
Kitzmiller v. Dove Area School District (2005) (Pennsylvania), 160
Korean Americans, 4
Kosciuszko, Thaddeus, 147
Kristallnacht (Night of Broken Glass), Berlin (1938), 24

L

La Guardia, Fiorello, 144
labeling theory, 19–21, 48
laissez-faire racism, 50–1
language barriers, for immigrants, 109, 111–3, 145
language use
  ethnic paradox and, 133
  Heritage language programs, 133
  non-English use at home, 31, 134, 179
  Spanish language use, 134
Latin America, history of emigration to U.S. from, 104, 105
Latino/Hispanic Americans. *See also specific groups*
  as ethnic group, 7–8
  family life, 169
  higher education, 168
  interracial marriage, 29
  life expectancy, 168
  median income comparisons, 168
  panethnicity and, 15
  population demographics, 3–4
  poverty rates among, 168
  racial profiling of, 49–50
  religion, 152–3, 155
  segregation index for metro U.S., 25–6
  state comparisons, 179
  views on state of race relations, 52–3, 55
  wealth gap (1977-2013), 82–3
Latvia, 25
law enforcement. *See also* criminal justice system
  racial profiling by, 48–9

law enforcement (*Continued*)
  sanctuary cities and, 116
  stop and frisk, 49–50
  use of force against drivers, 49–50
Ledbetter, Lilly, 80–1
Ledbetter v. Goodyear Tire and Rubber Co. (2007), 80–1
Lee, Spike, 35
Lee, Wen Ho, 172
Lee v. Weisman (1992), 158–9
lesbians. *See* LGBT community
LGBT community
  contact hypothesis and, 60
  as target of hate groups, 40
  in television broadcast programs, 58
Lilly, Terri, 178, 180
Lilly Ledbetter Fair Pay Act (2009), 81
Lithuania, 25
Louisiana Purchase (1803), 22
Lutherans, 151, 153
Lyft, 81–2
lynchings, 32

M

majority-minority trend, 4–5, 6, 39–40, 175
Mandela, Nelson, 27
marginality, 15–6
marriage patterns
  arranged marriage, 119
  increase of racial intermarriage, 28–9
  religion and, 28
  resistance to fusion and, 28–9
Martin, Trayvon, 32, 49
Marx, Karl, 46, 70, 130
mass media
  portrayal of religion, 154
  reduction of prejudice via, 57–9
  stereotypical images, 66
Massey, Douglas, 25, 33, 134
matrix of domination (Collins), 33, 34
McIntosh, Peggy, 44
melting pot myth, 28, 165
The Melting Pot (Zangwill), 165
Merkel, Angela, 138
Merton, Robert, 41–3
Mexican Americans
  education gap, 145
  history of school segregation, 112
  population demographics, 4
microaggressions, 41, 44
middle class, African Americans as, 176–8
migration, 21–2

minority groups. *See also* subordinate-group status; *specific groups*
  characteristics of, 5–6
  defined, 5
  ethnic groups, 7–8
  gender groups, 9–10
  as numerical majority in specific counties, 6
  population growth by U.S. county (2000-2010), 39
  racial groups, 7
  religious groups, 8–9
  self-fulfilling prophecy and, 20–1, 48
Mitchell v. Wisconsin (1993), 73
mixed-status, in families, 109
model minority, 167–73
Modi, Narendra, 138
Morris, Anna, 177
multiculturalism. *See* pluralism
multiracial identity, 13–6, 179
Murray, Charles, 11
Muslim Americans. *See also* Islam
  blended identity, 107
  intergroup contact and, 60
  Islamophobia and, 8, 49, 72–3
  racial profiling of, 48–9, 50
  religion, 150–1, 152
Myrdal, Gunnar, 124

N

Nation of Islam, 25
National Association for the Advancement of Colored People (NAACP), 8
National Collegiate Athletic Association (NCAA), 65
National Day of Prayer, 129
National Gay and Lesbian Task Force, 72
National Institute Against Prejudice and Violence, 72
national origin system, 103–4, 116, 144
Native Americans. *See also specific tribes*
  expulsion from tribal lands, 24
  genocide of, 24
  population demographics, 3–4
  reservation system, 13, 27, 31, 32, 84
  segregation of, 27
  sports team stereotypical insignia, 19, 65
  state comparisons, 179
  tribal identity, 15, 31
  USSC ruling on religious freedom, 159
  views on state of race relations, 55

nativism, 101, 140
naturalization, 100, 102–3, 117–9
Nazism. *See* Holocaust
Nee, Victor, 134
neo-Nazis, in U.S., 72, 73
New Jersey, foreign-born population, 99
New Mexico, population demographics, 6
New York
  Ellis Island, 104
  foreign-born population, 99
  racial profiling by police, 50
9/11 attacks. *See* September 11, 2001 terrorist attacks, aftermath of
normative approach, to prejudice, 47
Norton, Michael, 131
nurses, foreign-born, 107

O

Obama, Barack
  biracial identity of, 13, 28, 142
  executive order on "Dreamers," 109
  as first Black president, 3, 35
  religious background of, 151
  on united Europe, 138
Obamacare. *See* Patient Protection and Affordable Care Act (ACA) (2010)
Old Order Amish, 159
Omi, Michael, 13
one-drop rule, 13
online/virtual prejudice, 42, 60–1, 72, 81–2
oral contraceptives, 158
Oregon, USSC ruling on religious freedom of Native Americans, 159
organized crime, 144
#OscarsSoWhite movement, 58
out-group, 6

P

Pacific Islanders, 4. *See also* Hawaiian Americans
Pager, Devah, 69
Pakistan, British partition of, 25
panethnicity, 15
pardrone system, 142–3
parenting techniques, among Chinese Americans, 169, 170
Pariser, Eli, 61
Park, Robert, 59, 131
Patient Protection and Affordable Care Act (ACA) (2010), 158

Pattillo, Mary, 176–7
Pentecostals, 151–3
people of color, use of term, 165
Perlmann, Joel, 145
peyote, religious use of, 159
philanthropy, 3
physicians, foreign-born, 107
Pledge of Allegiance, 153–4
pluralism, 23, 30–1, 120–1, 138, 150
Polish Americans, early immigration to U.S., 137, 140, 146–9
The Polish Peasant in Europe and America (Thomas and Znaniecki), 147
Population and Development Review (Rumbaut, Massey, and Bean), 134
population demographics, of U.S. *See also specific groups*
 foreign-born population by state, 99–100, 179
 foreign-born workers (2015), 64
 growth due to immigrants, 108
 minority groups as numerical majority by county, 6
 minority population growth by county (2000-2010), 39
 projected growth in minority school population, 166
 racial and ethnic groups, 2–4
 segregation index for metro U.S., 25–6
 spoken languages and, 111
 U.S. Census race categories, 14–5
postracialism, 50–1
poverty, intergroup comparisons, 168, 173
praising the victim. *See* model minority
prejudice, 38–67. *See also* discrimination
 authoritarian personality theory, 46, 47
 as cause of dysfunctions, 18
 color-blind racism, 50–1, 173, 181
 corporate diversity training, 61–5
 defined, 41
 distinguished from discrimination, 41–3
 exploitation theory, 46
 intergroup hostility, 54–5
 Merton's typology, 41–3
 microaggressions, 41, 44
 normative approach, 47
 online/virtual prejudice, 42, 60–1, 81–2
 reduction of, 56–65
 scapegoating theory, 45–6
 stereotypes and, 47–50
 subordinate-group response to, 51–5
 White privilege and, 43–4
Presbyterians, 151, 153
principle of third-generation interest (Hansen), 133
Protestants. *See also specific denominations*
 as anti-Catholic, 139–40
 as dominant group, 8
 early immigration to U.S. and, 99–100, 134, 139–40
 four theological camps, 155–6
 racial and ethnic groups as, 152
 social class and denominations, 156–7
 public displays, with religious symbols, 160
public schools
 mandated moment of silence, 158–9
 minority students, 166
 segregation in, 27, 79, 112
Puerto Ricans, population demographics, 4
Pulaski, Casimir, 147
pull factors, in emigration, 22, 98
pure race, myth of, 10–1
push factors, in emigration, 21–2, 98

R

race and ethnicity, introduction, 1–37. *See also specific groups and theories*
 blended identity, 107
 conflict theory, 18–9
 ethnic paradox, 133
 FBI report, hate crimes based on, 71
 functionalist perspective, 17–8
 intersectionality, 33–4
 labeling theory, 19–21
 minority groups, 5, 7–8
 resistance and change, 31–3
 social construction of race, 10–6
 sociological study of, 16–21
 studying Whiteness, 129–31
 subordinate-group status, 21–31
 summary conclusion, 34–6
 symbolic ethnicity, 133, 135–6, 141, 146
 third-generation interest, 133
race relations today, views on, 52–3, 55
racial formation, 13
racial groups
 designation of, 7
 in U.S., 2–4
racial intermarriage. *See* marriage patterns
racial profiling, 48–50, 172
racism. *See also* discrimination; prejudice
 color-blind type of, 50–1, 173, 181
 defined, 12
 as dysfunctional to society, 18
 institutional discrimination as, 73–6
 online communication and, 181–2
 Smith College study on, 178, 180
 study on minority viewpoints on, 180–1
Reagan, Ronald, 138, 154
reality tv shows, 58–9
redlining, 80, 84
refugees, 121–4
Regents of the University of California v. Bakke (1978), 87, 88
relative deprivation, 70
religion. *See also specific religions and groups*
 court rulings on, 157–60
 customization of funeral services and, 31
 defined, 150
 FBI report, hate crimes based on, 71
 marriage patterns and, 28
 National Day of Prayer, 129
 political party affiliations and, 154
 religious pluralism, 150–7
Religious Freedom Restoration Act (1993), 159
religious groups, as minority groups, 8–9
reluctant liberal (Merton), 41–3
remittances, 114, 120
reparations. *See* apologies and reparations
Republican Party, religious affiliations of members, 154
resegregation, 27
Reskin, Barbara, 87, 89
respectable bigotry, 144, 157
reverse discrimination, 89–90
Ricci v. DeStefano (2009), 90
ritual animal sacrifice, 159
Roma (Gypsies), 25
Roman Catholics, 8
 diversity among, 154–5
 early immigration to U.S. and, 134, 139–41, 143, 148
 hate crimes against, 140

Roman Catholics (*Continued*)
  racial and ethnic groups as, 152
  size of U.S. denomination, 150
Romney, Mitt, 153
Roosevelt, Franklin D., 144
Rousseau, Jean-Jacques, 153
Rumbaut, Rubén, 134
Rwanda, genocide in, 24
Ryan, William, 19

S

salad bowl, use of term, 165
Salvadoran Americans, 4
sanctuary cities, 116
Santeria religion, 159
Scalia, Antonin, 146
scapegoating theory, 45–6, 47
school prayer, 158–9
school segregation, 27, 112
Scopes, John, 160
search engine filters, 61
secession
  defined, 25
  on intergroup spectrum, 23
secessionist minorities, 159
segmented assimilation, 30
segregation
  court decisions on, 79
  defined, 25–7
  on intergroup spectrum, 23
  in schools, 27, 79, 112
  segregation index for metro U.S., 25–6
self-esteem, studies on, 53–4
self-fulfilling prophecy, 20–1, 48
September 11, 2001 terrorist attacks, aftermath of, 8, 50, 115, 116–7, 172
sexism, 48. *See also* women in U.S., as oppressed majority
sexual identity, 71. *See also* LGBT community
sexual orientation. *See* LGBT community
sharing economy, 81–2
Shater, Walied, 47–8
sinophobes, 102
skin color, 7, 8, 9
skinheads. *See* neo-Nazis, in U.S.
Small Business Administration, 2
Smith College, study on racism, 178, 180
social capital, 176–8
social class. *See* class
social construction of race. *See also specific groups*
  biological meaning, 10–2
biracial identity, 13–6
multiracial identity, 13–6
social meaning, 12–3
social distance, 59–61
social media. *See also* Facebook; Twitter; YouTube, racial and ethnic groups on
  avoidance of intergroup contact on, 60–1
  hate groups and, 72, 181
  as platforms for resistance and change, 32
  sharing economy and discrimination, 81–2
sociology. *See also specific theories*
  defined, 16
  study of race and ethnicity, 16–21
Sommers, Samuel, 131
The Souls of Black Folks (Du Bois), 93
South African apartheid, 25, 27
Southern Baptist Convention, 157
Southern Poverty Law Center
  active hate groups (1999-2016), 40
  Speak Up: Responding to Everyday Bigotry, 61–3
  Ten Ways to Fight Prejudice, 56
Spanish language use, 134
Speak Up: Responding to Everyday Bigotry (Southern Poverty Law Center), 61–3
Spectrum of Intergroup Relations
  defined, 23
  discrimination and, 92
  ethnicity, whiteness, and religion, 161
  immigration and, 124
  racism and, 182
Srole, Leo, 132
Stark, Rodney, 155
step dancing, 142
stereotypes. *See also* hate crimes
  labeling theory and, 19–21
  model minority, 167–73
  prejudice and, 47–50
  in racial profiling, 48–50
stratification
  by class, 16–7
  by gender, 17
subordinate-group status, 21–31
  annexation, 22
  assimilation, 23, 29–30
  colonialism, 22–3
  expulsion, 23, 24–5
  extermination, 23–4
  fusion, 23, 28–9
  migration, 21–2
pluralism, 23, 30–1
secession, 23, 25
segregation, 23, 25–7
Sumner, William Graham, 6
symbolic ethnicity, 133, 135–6, 141, 146

T

Telemundo (tv channel), 35
television
  diversity in broadcast programs, 58
  reactions to biracial family in commercials, 42
Texas, population demographics, 6
Thomas, William I., 20, 147
tiger mother, 169, 170
timid bigot (Merton), 41–3
toxic waste dumps, 32, 84–5
transgender persons. *See* LGBT community
transnationals, 120–1
transsexuals. *See* LGBT community
Treaty of Guadalupe Hidalgo (1848), 22
Trump, Donald, immigration policies, 49, 82, 108
Twitter
  anti-Semitic statements on, 181
  #BlackLives Matter, 32, 35, 49
  #OscarsSoWhite, 58

U

Uber, 81–2
Ulukaya, Hamdi, 2–3
undocumented immigration. *See* illegal immigration
Union Pacific, 101
United Kingdom (UK), partition of India/Pakistan, 25
United Nations (UN), refugee policies, 121, 123
United States, as multiracial/ethnic kaleidoscope, 164–85
  acting White/Black, 174–5
  economic status, 171–3
  education, 169, 171
  family life, 168–9
  intergroup communication, 178–82
  model minority image and, 167–73
  persistence of inequality, 175–8
  progress of ethnic minorities, 167, 168

United States (U.S.). *See also* population demographics, of U.S.; *specific federal agencies; specific states*
  dominance of assimilation, 23, 29–30
  melting pot myth, 28, 165
  refugee policies, 121–4
  sanctuary cities/states, 116
  voter ID requirements by state, 74–5
University of North Dakota, 65
The Uprooted (Handlin), 132
U.S. Bureau of the Census, race categories, 14–5. *See also* population demographics, of U.S.
U.S. Congress, official apologies by, 103
U.S. Declaration of Independence, 100
U.S. Defense Department, use of stereotypical names for operations, 65
U.S. Environmental Protection Agency (EPA), 32, 84
U.S. Justice Department
  hate/bias crime statistics, 70
  racial profiling, 48–9
U.S. Social Security Administration, 113
U.S. Supreme Court (USSC). *See also specific cases*
  on affirmative action, 87–8, 171
  on asylum policies, 122
  on Confederacy insignia, 51
  on hate crimes, 73
  on minority rights, 80
  on racial profiling, 50
  on reverse discrimination, 90
  rulings affecting Native Americans, 159
  rulings on religion, 157–60
  on school segregation, 79, 112
  on slavery, 79

V

vandalism, as hate crime, 71, 72–3
Vaughn, Leigh Ann, 178, 180
Vietnamese Americans, 4
voluntary associations, 79
voter ID laws, as discriminatory, 74–5
Voting Rights Act (1965), 113

W

Walesa, Lech, 148
Wallerstein, Immanuel, 23
Warner, W. Lloyd, 132
wartime evacuation. *See* internment
Washington, Booker T., 34
Waters, Mary, 133
wealth, defined, 76
wealth inequality
  cultural capital and, 175–6
  due to discrimination, 76–9, 82–3
  social capital and, 176–8
Web sites. *See* Internet; social media
Weber, Max, 16, 91–2
White Americans
  as dominant group, 5
  higher education, 168
  life expectancy, 168
  median income comparisons, 77–8, 168
  numerical decline of, 4–5, 6, 39–40, 175
  population demographics, 3–4
  poverty rates among, 168
  state comparisons, 179
  views on state of race relations, 55
  wealth gap (1977-2013), 82–3

White privilege
  advantages of, 44
  defined, 43–4, 130–1
  prejudice and, 43–4
  studies on, 44
White supremacy, 72, 73
Whiteness, study of, 129–31
whiting of European Americans, 7
Whren v. United States (1996), 50
Wiccans, 159
Wickham, De Wayne, 90
Winant, Howard, 13
Wojtyla, Karol Józef, 148
women in U.S., as oppressed majority
  glass ceiling, 90–2
  median income comparisons, 77–8
  as social minority, 10
  stratification by gender, 17
  in television and film, 58
woodwork racism, 74
workplace issues. *See* employment and workplace issues
world systems theory, 23, 98

X

xenophobia, 101, 102

Y

Yanez, Jeronimo, 2
Yankee City (Warner and Srole), 132
yellow peril, 172
YouTube, racial and ethnic groups on, 42

Z

Zangwill, Israel, 165
Zimmerman, George, 32, 49
Znaniecki, Florian, 147